The Mindful

Practice of Falun Gong

The Mindful

Practice of Falun Gong

Meditation for Health, Wellness, & Beyond

Dr. Margaret Trey

TURQUOISE
PUBLISHING

Turquoise Publishing, Inc.
For special book promotions and premiums, contact us at info@deitywellness.com.

Cover design by Kate Vereshka
Interior design & formatting by Liam Hutchison
Cover photography by Daniel Ulrich
Editors: Damian Robin & editorial team

Library of Congress Catalog Number: 2016901262
ISBN: 978-0-9972281-0-6

The Mindful Practice of Falun Gong: Meditation for Health, Wellness, & Beyond / Dr. Margaret Trey.
1. Counseling 2. Falun Gong 3. Health 4. Meditation 5. Mind-body practice 6. Spirituality 7. Wellness

Printed in the United States of America.

For my mother

&

Late father

Contents

Foreword

by Dr. H. Mattner

Writing this opening has been a renaissance of pleasure for me as Margaret's supervisor for her research. Seeing any work of this caliber completed is always significantly satisfying, and seeing it achieve publication is extremely gratifying because it was such well-conducted and credible research.

Without repeating John Court's excellent exposé of the dynamics of the research, I will confirm that *The Mindful Practice of Falun Gong* now provides many people with the opportunity to become acquainted with Falun Gong in a 'socially factual' manner—surpassing the innuendo and superstition that has plagued so many mind-body practices.

My own research has included the first study on anxiety and stress reduction in a randomized comparative trial of yoga and relaxation. Yoga has long suffered the indictments of cynicism, refutation, and trivialization. Now the ever-increasing evidence shows the diversity and strength of its effectiveness and it is regarded with respect and credible fervor as it should be and so hereto, Falun Gong takes greater deserved recognition.

The Australian survey provides striking evidence of the significance of core values for humans in health and well-being; those intrinsic yet profound elements that enable individuals to attain and sustain meaningful lives. Similarly, the impact of spiritual contexts and the worth of belief for humans cannot be understated as we strive everyday to get something out of a life that increasingly alienates people from each other and from themselves.

Margaret's research shows how Falun Gong provides a broad and deep opportunity for enriching personal life, enabling individuals to take charge of their physiological, psychological, social, emotional, and spiritual health—linking their minds and bodies rather than fragmenting them. Her study indicates that Falun Gong brings important benefits for many individuals suffering illnesses, compromised mental health, and chronicity, in safe, sound, and satisfying ways that defy medication and typical curative processes.

The powers of stillness (non-action or *wuwei* in Falun Gong expression), meditation and mind-awareness, peace and contentment, are underestimated and this research provides invaluable illumination of their consequence for individuals through Falun Gong.

This book presents substantiation of Falun Gong without bias or prejudice allowing readers to see and understand for themselves what the practice can offer them.

Barbara, a participant in the Australian survey and its longitudinal follow-up who features prominently in this book, states that Falun Gong offers her insight on how to be compassionate and considerate of others. This corollary of Falun Gong is a goal we could all aspire to and would be a remarkable achievement as its simplicity and simultaneous power embody all that we could offer for a changed world.

Heather Mattner, PhD
Health Psychologist, Adjunct Associate Professor
The University of Adelaide, South Australia

Foreword II

by Dr. J. H. Court

My interest in this book started when I became the supervisor to assist in developing a credible piece of work according to scientific standards.

As an observer of Falun Gong and not a practitioner, I saw real challenges in attempting to assess a transpersonal approach to health management, which by virtue of being a psychophysical/spiritual model, does not fit readily into conventional scientific criteria. After a good deal of consultation, the outcome was a study that focuses on personal and interpersonal behaviors open to some degree of measurement, following well-defined strategies outlined by the researcher.

The Australian study is greatly strengthened by the care taken to create a non-practicing control group, where clear advantages for the Falun Gong group are demonstrated across a range of health indices. We should not be too surprised that strong benefits are reported, since the processes involved in practice are similar in many ways to other transpersonal and behavioral approaches, and strengthened by some careful advantages (regular practice, variety of strategies, emphasis on personal empowerment and moral improvement).

As the individual is the practitioner, and there is no financial disincentive to maintenance, the practitioner is able to undertake regular sustained involvement, not commonly seen in counseling clients (though having parallels with various religious groups, such as monks and mystics). This survey relies on those who claim to faithful commitment to the recommended practices, and the outcomes are impressive. Considering how recently Falun Gong has developed, the unfolding story is one of substantial growth in a short period, even in the face of strong opposition in China.

Identifying underlying values, such as "knowledge, love, meaning, peace, hope, transcendence, connectedness, compassion, wellness, and wholeness" as goals for practitioners emphasizes qualities that are congruent with healthy human adjustment, and widely espoused in all spiritual traditions. Hence, it would appear to be possible to practice Falun Gong and benefit from it, without invoking a strictly religious framework.

In the later chapters, it is made clear that there are implicit beliefs drawn from Buddhism and Taoism. This makes Falun Gong readily acceptable to those from Eastern religious traditions. Practice can give congruence between behavior, thinking, beliefs, and interpersonal relationships that can strengthen the commitment to daily journeying.

This coherently developed position also means that there are limitations to those who may benefit. A number of these are helpfully identified in the text, relating particularly to serious psychological ill health.

As an observer from the Western religious tradition, I see significant differences in the way many of these concepts are addressed. Those who are 'People of the Book' and believers of other spiritual practices would endorse the general personal and interpersonal goals pursued here, while concurrently seeking meaning in a personal relationship with the creator. This is apparent in the description of the practice of Falun Gong, which is inner-directed. Western religious practices are other-directed seeking to strengthen the vertical relationship with God as well as improving the horizontal relationship or connection with fellow human beings and significant others. The well-established healing principle of forgiveness in counseling and spiritual direction is not directly addressed here, but may be subsumed in Falun Gong's clear emphasis on selflessness and compassion.

However, such differences do not stand as a defining critical issue. Rather, they are a reminder that underlying values and beliefs invariably exist behind successful changes in human behavior. Most of the English language literature dealing with psycho-spiritual influences has reported findings from the traditional Western religious groups. Yet, the last twenty years have seen a surge of interest in transpersonal approaches that embrace aspects of Eastern practices.

This carefully documented study stands in that emerging tradition, and shows that scientific measurement, while not easy to achieve, can be undertaken and it can explore the features that make a helpful difference. The author's introduction makes clear that this book started out as a research report, and necessarily makes for heavy going as scientific data are interpreted.

Finally, this book is a service to those who may use this source as a springboard for further work. At the same time, the more human face of lived experiences is woven through the text to provide striking illustrations of the kind of beneficial changes that can occur with Falun Gong practitioners.

John H. Court, PhD
Adelaide, South Australia

Introduction

The *Mindful Practice of Falun Gong* is the fruit of more than 13 years of commitment. The book heralds the *Hearts Uplifted* project that marries the facts from on-going research with writing. This project aims to explore the health-wellness effects of Falun Gong and to use story telling as a means to bring to life the lived experiences of individuals whose lives have been profoundly touched and transformed by Falun Gong.

The main purpose of this book is to present the findings from the Australian survey that investigates the health and wellness effects of Falun Gong, as perceived by those who practice this spiritual meditation and cultivation system. As you weave through the book and find yourself at times enveloped in intellectual matter like dense clouds descending on you, please remember that this book is, after all, a dissertation-to-book endeavor. Nevertheless, this book also includes material extrapolated from the follow-up longitudinal study (the *Hearts Uplifted* project) that explores the beneficial healing effects of Falun Gong through the lived experiences of practitioners.

What distinguishes *The Mindful Practice of Falun Gong* from the doctoral dissertation for the Australian survey is that interwoven with the presentation of the findings is the story of one practitioner's journey to wellness with Falun Gong. She is Respondent 289 from the Australian survey and whom I happened to meet at the Los Angeles Tom Bradley International Airport in 2009. While it is stated that there are no role models in Falun Gong cultivation practice, reading about another individual's story will, nonetheless, help to inspire us in our own journey to mind, body, and spiritual wellness. And it is with this intention that *The Mindful Practice of Falun Gong* opens with her story.

My own introduction to Falun Gong began in 1997. At the time, I was receiving training in Vipassanna meditation from a Burmese monk and I had been practicing yoga for nearly two decades. As a counselor and a natural health consultant following a macrobiotic and holistic lifestyle, I was naturally curious about Falun Gong when my brother introduced me to the practice. I found Falun Gong highly beneficial for my overall mind, body, and spiritual improvement. More importantly, it embodies all of what I was looking for.

Four years later in 2001, I began integrating the practice and its teachings into my professional counseling work. This came about naturally due to my interest in integrating spirituality and meditation with counseling. I had just resumed mainstream counseling practices, working as a counselor at two medical centers in two different country towns in South Australia. The medical centers offered free counseling services; my job was to provide counseling support for those clients referred by the medical doctors. This post was ideal for the integrative work. Whenever appropriate and with the clients' consent, I would introduce Falun Gong exercises, sitting meditation, and/or aspects of the teachings during counseling sessions. What caught my attention was that the integrative practice was especially beneficial for a few challenging cases. Following the termination of the integrative counseling sessions, and to ensure that these clients had on-going support, I would encourage them to join one of the four local group practice sites that I had set up in community centers in several country towns.

Two noteworthy events inspired me to embark on the research journey to explore the health-wellness effects of Falun Gong. The first sprang from the decision to apply for a local community grant. With the help of Falun Gong practitioners in Adelaide, I received a community grant to coordinate a mind-body health and wellness project offering Falun Gong classes to local residents at a community center in a suburb of the City of Adelaide. The project well received. Today, there is still a practice site at the same community center.

The second event was that my hereditary eye problems were rectified after practicing Falun Gong. I suffered from an eye condition that afflicted four generations of my family. By the time I was completing my undergraduate studies at The University of Toronto, Canada, my vision had deteriorated to only about 10 percent in both eyes. At the time, my Canadian ophthalmologist was reluctant to perform surgery since I was still able to live a 'normal' life and achieve an above average grade in English and dramatic literature studies. Upon graduation, I had to have my right eye operated on so that I could find work. Later I had surgery done on my left eye and another two on my right eye. After four surgeries on my eyes, the vision in one eye dropped to the point where I could not longer read with that eye. Two ophthalmologists, my mother's and my Australian ophthalmologist, who had performed three of the four surgeries informed me that my situation would gradually worsen if I did nothing about it. As such, living with poor vision, eyestrain, and uncertainty about my eyesight was an inseparable part of my life—until Falun Gong came into my life. Since then, my eye condition has improved and remained stable.

Coupled with the success in my integrative practice, I became interested to study the health-wellness effects of Falun Gong. In 2003, a window of opportunity came when The University of South Australia School of Psychology, Social Work, and Social Policy opened its doors for the first time to offer the Doctor of Counseling degree. I applied and was accepted into the program. In July of 2003, I embarked on my Falun Gong research journey with much enthusiasm. However, I soon realized that it was not only problematic to find a supervisor to guide me through the labyrinth of research on my chosen topic; conducting a literature review was equally daunting. There were hardly any studies investigating the health-wellness effects of Falun Gong despite its popularity and appeal to millions of individuals. During this time, I came across the field studies completed by Canadian Professor David Ownby, whose research inspired and steered me in my research path.

By the end of 2006, after three years without a supervisor, Dr. John Court, Program Director for the Doctor of Counseling course, benevolently took upon the main supervisor role. Dr. Court, who was already in his seventies, helped to kick-start my research. Soon after Dr. Heather Mattner, who shares a keen interest in yoga and meditation, became my secondary supervisor. When Dr. Court retired in 2008, Dr. Mattner took over the reins as the main supervisor. Thanks to these two special individuals, their extraordinary vision and motivation, my research took shape and reached its completion in 2010.

The Mindful Practice of Falun Gong opens with the story of Barbara Schafer who was Respondent 289 (R289) from the Australian survey. The book's aim is to present the key findings from the Australian Health and Wellness Survey (Lau, 2010a, 2010b), a pioneering study completed outside of China at the doctoral level and under the auspices of a Western academic institution. Dubbed the Australian survey, it seeks to find out whether people who practice Falun Gong experience better health and wellness than those who do not. It also depicts the demographic profile of Falun Gong practitioners outside of China. The term 'practitioners' throughout this book refers to those who practice Falun Gong, instead of its usual meaning of one who conducts a counseling, medical, or other professional practice.

This book contains three parts; the first consists of Barbara's story, what *is* Falun Gong, and the Chinese Communist Party's persecution of Falun Gong. After much reflection, I decided to place the persecution account in a separate chapter—Chapter Four. On the surface China's inhumane persecution of Falun Gong may seem irrelevant to the focus of this book that explores the health-wellness effects of Falun Gong and how the practice can be integrated with counseling. Yet, I believe in the importance of keeping readers informed. Similarly, it has been my counseling protocol to mention this topic briefly to my clients during the informed consent procedure when seeking their agreement and support for an integrated approach.

The second part of the book covers a brief literature review on Falun Gong research and related topics, the research design, and a presentation of the findings from the Australian survey—respondents' health-wellness reports, written responses, and how they compare with non-Falun Gong respondents. The third and final section of the book contains a discussion chapter, recommendations, case scenarios on how the author-researcher-counselor integrated Falun Gong with counseling, and a concluding chapter with material gleaned from the on-going follow-up study.

It is hoped that this book will serve as a springboard for future researchers aspiring to investigate the health-wellness effects of Falun Gong. For counseling and health professionals who have already been blending Eastern meditation techniques with Western approaches in their professional practices, the book can offer some interesting insight. If you are new to Falun Gong and wonder about the practice and its benefits, then reading this book may shed some light on this extraordinary practice. This book will help you to understand Falun Gong as a mind-body spiritual cultivation discipline in its cultural and health-wellness contexts. If you are facing a crisis, a turning point in your life, have been seeing a counselor, considering self-help approaches, searching for meaning in your life, or perhaps just plain curious about Falun Gong, I hope reading this book will assist you in your life's journey.

The author wishes to mention that while there are numerous remarkable and miraculous healing experiences (McCoy & Zhang, n.d.), we are reminded not be attached to seeking role models in Falun Gong cultivation. This is because true cultivation depends on ourselves (H. Li, 2001d), etching our own path. Yet, many practitioners' experiences and their commitment to Falun Gong have been inspirational and unshakable. Since 1999, tens of thousands of Falun Gong practitioners in China have been incarcerated and tortured for their beliefs. Allegations have emerged that the Chinese Communist Party (CCP) has been harvesting and selling the body organs of Falun Gong practitioners for profit (Cheung, 2016; Fernandez, Magnason, & Gnaizda, 2012; Gutmann, 2014; Matas & Kilgour, 2006, 2007, 2009; Matas & Trey, 2012; Reynolds, 2015). Despite 17 years of brutal persecution from the Chinese regime, millions of Falun Gong practitioners in China and around the world persevere in their beliefs, walking the path to mind-body and spiritual wellness. As you are reading this book, still others will be embarking on their journey with Falun Gong. Just what motivates many individuals like Barbara to embark and persevere in their practice? Perhaps the contents of this book could throw a glimmer of light, even hope, while offering valuable insights into this very question.

Throughout the book, I will cite mainly from *Zhuan Falun*, which contains the core teachings of the practice, with occasional citations from supplementary books, articles, and lecture teachings from Master Li Hongzhi, the revered founder and teacher of Falun Gong. Since I had previously used the Fair Winds 2001 publication (H. Li, 2001d), I shall continue referencing from this particular edition. Except for a few words and phrases, this version is almost identical to the more widely circulated Universe Publishing edition (H. Li, 2000). You can buy books on the teachings of Falun Gong from Tianti Books, the official Falun Dafa bookstore in Manhattan, New York, or online from www.tiantibooks.org, or Amazon.com, and major bookstores around the world. However, all books, videos, and other writings are also available for free download from the official Falun Gong website: www.falundafa.org. Due to the dynamic nature of the Internet, certain web links in *The Mindful Practice of Falun Gong* may not be valid or may have changed since publication.

Readers, if you read the book from the beginning to the end in a linear manner, you might notice some repeated points. Note that the chapters are designed this way for non-linear readers who prefer to dip into different chapters of the book. Also, keep in mind that *The Mindful Practice of Falun Gong* is a dissertation-to-book endeavor. The numerous references, though distracting and perhaps interfering with your reading of the contents, are there for aspiring future researchers. There is no premeditated intention to analyze the Falun Gong teachings and if there was any endeavor to explain certain concepts, it was merely to clarify a point and done with references to the teachings of the practice. Any oversight is unintentional. Please bear in mind that the discussions stem from the author-researcher's level of understanding and experience. Naturally, as a counselor who has integrated Falun Gong with counseling, the author wishes to share her experience and offer recommendations for those who might be interested in integrative counseling practices, and you will find this specifically in Chapter 13.

Finally, take this book as a humble exploration of the health-wellness effects of Falun Gong and a stepping-stone to what is beyond. Greater knowledge and deeper insight can only be gleaned and experienced from your own reading of *Zhuan Falun,* the book that presents the core and complete teachings of Falun Gong. I therefore invite you to embark on this journey yourself—walk your own path and invoke a different way of looking at things in order to reach new insights.

Margaret Trey
Doctor of Counseling
University of South Australia
Adelaide, South Australia

CHAPTER 1

The Crossing

We must close our eyes and invoke a new manner of
seeing ... A wakefulness that is the birthright of us all,
though few put it to use. – Plotinus

Los Angeles, 2009

It was early morning on June 3rd. My Qantas flight landed at Tom
Bradley International Airport in Los Angeles after an extended delay
at Melbourne Tullamarine Airport. I stood in the immigration line
waiting my turn with hundreds of passengers from my flight, along
with passengers from a second Qantas flight. Hastily I glanced at my
watch again—barely minutes to board my connection to New York.
I passed through immigration, dashed to the conveyor belt, grabbed
my luggage, raced through customs, and made it to the checking point
to drop off my luggage for New York, with scores of other passengers
from the two Australian flights. Too late: The announcement came.
Our Qantas flights were airborne, en-route to New York, leaving
many and me stranded—perspiring and bewildered—at Tom Bradley.

My first meeting with Barbara Schafer could not have been better
orchestrated. Our paths converged while gripping the airport-ticketing

counter, both of us trying to secure the next seat to New York. Destiny and adversity brought us together. We had arrived from Melbourne on separate Qantas flights that morning. Due to considerable delay back at Melbourne Tullamarine Airport, our flights landed at Tom Bradley later than usual and almost back-to-back. The sea of irate passengers swarmed around us, demanding to know when they could get their connecting flight. The ticketing counter became our fleeting lifesaver. I clung to the counter as though *it* could take me to New York faster. People jostled around amidst the pandemonium; everyone was talking at the same time. Through a swarm of outstretched hands, I looked up and saw the solitary ground staff member behind the counter. She tried to stay composed, facing a tidal wave of loud requests from stranded passengers. Before I knew it, I was shoulder to shoulder with a shorthaired blonde woman who spoke in a clear voice and with a familiar accent. "Excuse me, when is the next available flight? I have to go to New York." "Me, too, I'm also heading for New York," I heard myself singing out to the flustered woman who could barely keep up with dozens of simultaneous requests.

Barbara and I started our first conversation holding tightly to our lifesaver, waiting for our turn. Yes, she was going to the same conference in New York as I was. She had flown in from Melbourne and I from Adelaide, on different Qantas flights. Never mind flying in from different aircraft, the airport staff member said, we could fly to New York together. But there were no vacant seats to New York that day, unless we wanted to arrive at JFK in the middle of the night and on separate flights! My mind was buzzing, my heart torn between traveling alone or with my new companion. "Do you want to take this offer or not?" the loud voice brought me back to the counter. "What else have you got? We want to fly together," one of us responded. "Well, we can put you on the same flight for tomorrow." Working like a pair of chopsticks, we both jumped on the offer before she changed her mind. I waited patiently for the woman behind the counter to sort out the paperwork and re-schedule our itinerary to the following day. Little was I prepared for what was to unfold that evening.

That night Barbara and I stayed at the same hotel. We decided to meet and dine together at the hotel café. During the meal, she found out that I was the researcher of the Australian survey on the health and wellness effects of Falun Gong—a Chinese meditation and spiritual cultivation practice. The online survey, with a total sample size of 590 respondents, was conducted under the auspices of The University of South Australia for the partial fulfillment of the Doctor of Counseling degree in the School of Psychology (Lau, 2010a, 2010b). Barbara smiled cheerfully and said that she completed the survey. I nodded and smiled back graciously thanking her for the contribution. Dinner conversation was social chatter until I asked Barbara the researcher's magic question, "So, how did you start practicing Falun Gong?" She began describing her medical conditions, triggering my memory of written comments from Respondent 289 (R289) in the Australian survey.

R289 was the Falun Gong respondent who reported fully recovering from a multitude of serious and complicated medical problems. She had stated in her written response that she was in a coma for eight days, had multiple injuries—a fractured skull, spinal fluid leakage, compound fractures in her cheekbones, nose, jawbone, wrists, and right knee, and a host of other health problems. I had always wondered about R289. As the Australian survey was an anonymous online questionnaire, it was not possible to identify R289. Hence, it was surreal to find myself face-to-face with a radiant and smiling R289. I was lost for words for the first few seconds. Out of the hundreds of passengers who missed their flight that day, from different itineraries, R289 and I ended up rubbing shoulders with each other at the airport-ticketing counter. My first thought was, "She could not possibly have suffered and survived those multiple injuries." I stared at her, looking for some physical signs of her most unfortunate experience. Instead, Barbara

t me, looking a picture of serene health and inner peace. I
_.ut resist jokingly asking Barbara if she was actually R289's
twin sister. Yet having benefited from Falun Gong myself and hearing
countless reports of unusual recovery from various debilitating medical
conditions, in my heart, I knew everything is possible.

My mind sprinted. The researcher instinct kicked in. The scrumptious
pasta on my plate was forgotten. Bursting with curiosity, I asked
Barbara if she could share her story with me. As I twirled with the
noodle strains, I sprung on Barbara an avalanche of questions, which
she patiently answered in between jovial and nostalgic moments as
she retold her story. "How did you get all those injuries? How did
you find Falun Gong or how did Falun Gong lead you to health and
wellness"? As we talked, more questions popped into my head. We
sat sipping countless cups of hot tea with lemon into the early hours
of the morning, spending nearly six hours together in the hotel café.
The sounds of voices, cutlery clatter, and clinking of glasses faded
into the background as I glued my eyes on her, hanging on to every
word she uttered. Her story mesmerized me and changed my outlook
as a Falun Gong health and wellness researcher. Thankfully, the café
was open 24 hours.

Barbara was 50, basking in the joys of her artistic career when the
accident changed her life completely. Born and bred in Poland she
studied fine arts there for seven years and eventually left her communist
motherland to settle in Australia. That was more than three decades
ago. The Polish-born Australian artist worked as an art conservator
for more than two decades. Like many immigrant Australian families,
Barbara's professional career—fulfilling and challenging at the same
time—was a fusion of love and arduous dedication. Her passion was
restoring and preserving historic buildings. Often she worked alone,
spending long, solitary hours on scaffoldings suspended in mid-air
working on the meticulous details of restoring murals and paintings
on ceilings and walls of old and archaic buildings. Some of her most

memorable projects included restoring the former ANZ (Australia New Zealand Banking Group) building, or the 19th Century English, Scottish, & Australian Bank building in Melbourne's busy Collins Street, the Melbourne Parliament House library, and the 120-year-old Bendigo Town Hall that she had started restoring two years before her fall. With her experience and artistic techniques, Barbara revived these historic landmark buildings to their former splendors.

Thirteen years ago, on November 11, 2003, Barbara was working alone in a Macedonian Orthodox Church, restoring a painting on the high ceiling. She had only just resumed work after a short lunch break and decided to climb up on a chair placed on the scaffolding. Thinking, "Oh, it'll be just for a minute," she did not fasten the safety bars. As she stretched her hand just another inch, Barbara lost her balance and plunged head first 23 feet (seven meters) to the ground. "I stretched out my hands to break my fall. The last thing I heard was the cracking sound as my head hit the concrete," said Barbara. The rest was oblivion. She had no idea for exactly how long she was lying unconscious on the cold church floor, in front of the painting of Mother Mary. "I must have been lying there for a few hours," she added, because the fall happened shortly after she resumed work at one o'clock. It was past five o'clock when an entire medical team attended to her at the hospital.

Barbara said she woke up in a puddle of blood. She realized she had to seek help immediately and the nearest telephone was in the church office. Somehow, she managed to get up and stumbled 22 yards (20 meters) to call the ambulance herself. When asked how she managed, Barbara shook her head and said, "I don't know. I just knew I had to get help." She continued, "My right knee was bending backward, forward, and in all directions. I could only walk very slowly, one step at a time." I could not refrain from asking, "Did you not feel any pain?" Barbara shook her head and added, "I didn't feel scared either. My mind was calm, like one who survived a near-death experience.

I just focused on one task—getting to the office to call for help." Once inside the office, Barbara said she knocked the telephone receiver off its cradle and managed with one stiff finger to dial for an ambulance. "It wasn't easy. I could feel something moving inside my head," she said. "Later I found out that my skull was cracked in several places. My nose and sinuses were crushed. My upper jaw was completely broken off in three places. My hands were shattered and the bones were sticking out." As she was describing her multiple injuries, the skeptic in me was thinking how it was possible for her to get up and walk that far to call the ambulance herself.

My mind suffered, reeling with tidal waves of questions and thoughts, as if struck by miniature tsunamis. I endeavored to rationalize and piece the information together. "All things are possible," I told myself. "Haven't we heard of the power of the mind and the concept of mind over matter? Or the story of the frantic mother who, upon witnessing her child being run over by a car, dashed over and displayed the superhuman feat of lifting the car to pull out her child." Barbara's voice jolted me back to the sleepy café. By this time, the hum of voices intermingled with the sounds of people eating had abated. I could hear Barbara saying she knew she had to get help. Wordlessly I glued my eyes on her sea-green eyes and what I saw melted away any doubts in my mind. I heard her say emphatically that she was destined to live in order to make this crossing—walk the Falun Gong path. When the ambulance arrived, she even attempted to walk to the ambulance herself—shocking the paramedics, who persuaded her to lie on the stretcher bed. "They asked me if I needed pain-killers and I said 'no,' but they gave me an injection anyway that knocked me out." Barbara laughed and said that she must have looked a mess. "Doctors at The Royal Melbourne Hospital refused to grant my wish for a mirror to look at myself before the surgery."

Lost in our world and oblivious of our surroundings, the sounds of clinking glasses again brought us back to the café. It was almost empty except for a solitary waiter who said we could stay for as long as we wanted. But, it was past midnight and we had our flight to catch to New York the next morning. Yet, a part of me yearned to hear her entire story—her full recovery and healing experience with Falun Gong—to which Barbara graciously consented to continue. I had done many Falun Gong interviews and this one—unplanned and impromptu—was different. "Falun Gong literally took away everything that was hurting or bothering me—all my post surgery pain, complications—and facilitated my complete recovery," said Barbara. There was not a trace of skepticism from her during our interviews. She has remained steadfast in her belief and commitment to the practice that has totally transformed her life and has given her body-mind and spiritual wellness.

In the background, the waiter hovered, making sure we felt his unobtrusive presence. As the researcher reflex kicked in once more, question after question poured out. "When did you actually begin the practice? Did you read the book first or do the exercises?" Barbara quenched me with answers that continued to confound me. "I started the exercises first about seven weeks after the surgeries, still covered in bandages like a walking mummy," responded Barbara with her Polish-Australian sense of humor. With a smile, I envisaged Barbara swathed with bandages around her head, face, arms, hands, fingers, and knees. "And what happened then?" I asked. "To my amazement, I felt good. I couldn't believe it," said Barbara her eyes widening as though she still could not believe it. With smiling eyes, both hands lifted and gesturing, she continued emphatically, "Gosh, I wanted more of this Falun Gong." The exercises relieved her chronic pain and encouraged her to keep practicing even though she felt stiff and awkward. At the time, she had no idea how long this good feeling was going to last. Nevertheless, she did not care; it worked and mitigated her pain. Rather than be numbed by painkillers, she diligently 'performed' the exercises to her best ability, despite being hampered by bandages and her lack of mobility.

Just as her artist's brush helped to restore the former grandeur of the old and archaic paintings in those historic buildings she worked on, Barbara's health was restored by a *"magical book"* (Xia, 2014) that facilitated her complete recovery, enlightened her to the true meaning of life, and put her on a new path. Barbara affirmed that the greatest and most miraculous experience with Falun Gong was when she started reading Falun Gong's main book, *Zhuan Falun*. "Two weeks after I started doing the exercises, my friend told me I had to read the book!" At first, she was hesitant. "The accident had adversely affected my vision and I could not understand why it was so important to read the book," said Barbara laughingly. Since the exercises were mitigating her aches and pains, she thought she would just go along with her friend's suggestion. On the first day, she labored over the reading because her eyes were out of focus from the accident and she could not see clearly to read. Nonetheless, she persisted, like the way she got up and walked baby steps to the church office to call the ambulance herself on the day of her accident.

On the second day of reading *Zhuan Falun*, Barbara noticed that her eyesight had improved; she could read a little faster. She finished Lecture One and continued with Lecture Two of the book, finding the contents so fascinating that she could not put the book down. By the end of the third day, something unusual happened. Barbara felt she was getting some energy, like a powerful electric current traveling from her fingers up to her arms. "It took away everything— the pain, the post surgery problems, the spinal fluid leakage, and even the tinnitus, those never-ending strange noises in my head that sounded like heavy machinery in a printing factory, all disappeared and never came back," she exclaimed. She paused and we gazed at each other wordlessly. Then she continued, "At that moment, I knew something miraculous and inexplicable was happening." As she progressed with her reading of the book, Barbara said she found the explanation for her healing experience.

Four months after her accident, Barbara said she was back on the scaffolding doing what she loves. I asked the question that was on the tip of my tongue, which she answered confidently. "No, I wasn't afraid of going back and neither did I have any fear of heights," she said. At the same time, she went on a motorbike rally with her husband and lightheartedly added, "I only needed a bigger helmet." Her recovery was complete. She embarked on the second phase of her daunting project to restore another room in the Bendigo Town Hall. Before her fall, she had spent two years restoring one of the other rooms in the historic building. The restoration work required tedious and laborious hours of work. It was "not a job for the faint-hearted," said Barbara (Turnbull, 2010, p. 100). She had to painstakingly strip off different coatings of the old paints, layer by layer to uncover the original colors and patterns. This complex restorative work took her another two years to complete and much of her time was spent on a scaffold suspended in mid-air. Often she had to stand erect to restore the ornate panels and decorative edgings on the ceiling of the hall.

Photo by David Field/Bendigo Magazine

Barbara Schafer completed the full restoration of the old Council Chambers and its murals inside the Bendigo Town Hall over a period of four years. She was responsible for the intricate gold leafing work in the main hall of the 120-year-old heritage listed building. Bendigo, Victoria, Australia. September 2010.

Photo by David Field/Bendigo Magazine

The artist-cum-conservator fully recovered from her 23 feet fall and was back on the scaffolding—doing what she loves—four months after she started practicing Falun Gong. She spent another two years restoring a second room in the Bendigo Town Hall to its former glory. Bendigo, Victoria, Australia. September 2010.

New York City, May 2013

Following our Los Angeles meeting, Barbara kept in touch and upon the completion and submission of my doctoral dissertation, she agreed to be one of the case studies for the follow-up longitudinal study that explores the health and wellness effects of Falun Gong through the lived experiences of practitioners. We would catch up with each other every six to eight weeks, or as often as necessary. This was done either via emails, video chats, and face-to-face meetings whenever possible, as on May 2013, four years after our first meeting, when Barbara made her annual trip to New York.

Ten years had passed since her complete recovery from the injuries sustained from that 23 feet (seven meters) fall. Sitting on the bench at Dag Hammarskjold Plaza Park on East 47th Street near to the United Nations building, Barbara was glowing with health. She had flown in from Melbourne late the night before and still looked as fresh as a daisy in her yellow Falun Gong T-shirt. Jet-lagged? "No, not a bit," shaking her head and with a beaming smile added, "I got up early to do the exercises before I came here." It was a lovely, sunny spring day. She was at the park, with hundreds of other Falun Gong practitioners from all over the world, to attend a rally to raise awareness of the persecution of Falun Gong practitioners in China by the Chinese Communist Party (CCP). The only telltale sign of her seven-meter fall is a faint line of her fractured skull that remains visible across her forehead.

During this face-to-face interview, Barbara reiterated that her continuing health and wellness is because of Falun Gong. She recollected how the medical profession initially did not give her any hope for complete recovery. "They put all the broken parts together," said Barbara, "but the spinal fluid was dribbling down my nostrils and leaking down the back of my throat after the first surgery. I could taste it in my mouth." She was readmitted for another surgery. But the doctors only stopped the leakage from her nose. She could still taste spinal fluid seeping down the back of her throat. In addition, she was in constant and excruciating pain, having to wake up her husband at night every couple of hours to apply cortisone cream on her back, arms, and hands. The relief was fleeting and the pain would resume with vengeance. There was neither solace nor respite from the heavy machinery noises in her head, she said. Life was wretched and despairing. But, where could she turn for help?

Doctors had told her that she would never fully recover. "They gave me a list of possible health problems that was four pages long," she said. The most challenging was losing her memory. "Once I went to see my doctor and after coming out from of his office, I didn't know if I came by car or public transport. I didn't know my phone number. I couldn't find my keys. After wandering around for half an hour, I found my car. The keys were in the ignition and the motor was still running. The car was almost out of gas." Then she started experiencing similar episodes of memory lapses. "My doctor told me I was not allowed to leave the house without a notebook and to write everything down—my address, phone number, where I was going, what I was going to do, and when I should return. She [the doctor] said that it's going to get worse. That was the most frightening because I realized it was something beyond my control."

Faced with constant pain, the prospect of memory loss, and a four-page list of medical complications, Barbara said she had nothing to lose. "I thought I'd give Falun Gong a try." To her amazement, the effect was immediate. "I didn't know it would be so good until I tried it," she said. As we sat together having our lunch in a small park near Dag Hammarskjold Plaza ten years after her accident and recovery, Barbara said she is eternally grateful for her complete recovery and continuing health and wellness. Smiling she said emphatically, "I haven't had any pain in my head, and I haven't had one headache since taking up Falun Gong."

Make no mistake, Barbara pointed out several times during our conversations that she has been diligent and never misses a single day of exercise and reading the book during the past six years. Whenever she travels, she would always find an empty seat next to hers, she said, so she could sit in full-lotus position to do her meditation, regardless of how full the flight was. "This has happened 14 times," she said with a beaming smile. During successive interviews with Barbara, she shared other experiences from her spiritual practice in her everyday life as an artist, wife, mother, and grandmother. Since she began her journey with Falun Gong, she never looked back, except to marvel at the profundity of the practice. "Falun Gong is the most inconceivable

Barbara and Melbourne practitioners holding the Australian banner during the World Falun Dafa parade. Manhattan, New York, US. May 2013.

Barbara with Australian practitioners, Simon Vereshka and Dean Flynn, while waiting for the Falun Dafa parade to begin. Manhattan, New York, US. May 2013.

Barbara walking in front of the Celestial Marching Band during the Australian Day parade, carrying the Falun Dafa Association sign. Melbourne, Australia. January 26, 2016.

gift I have ever received in my life. It's amazing and special," said Barbara. "And I am grateful to be so well and healthy all the days of my life since I started the practice."

After her recovery, Barbara said she wanted to tell all her friends and relatives to practice Falun Gong. "It took me a while to realize that not everybody has the predestined connection and not everybody was as enthusiastic as I was," laughed Barbara. Then she added, "I have not lost my enthusiasm and I shall continue encouraging others." When the opportunity arises, Barbara said she talks to people about Falun Gong and how the practice has changed her life. She regularly attends Falun Gong activities in Melbourne, other Australian cities, and different regions in the world. "I like to participate in parades—in Australia and the United States—to show people the beauty and the healing benefits of Falun Gong." Whenever she could, the Polish-born Australian would travel back to Poland to join in Falun Gong activities there. "I think it's very important for the public to know how good Falun Gong has been for me. I wish all Chinese people in China could practice as freely as I can." In particular, whenever she could, she partakes in rallies against the CCP's persecution of Falun Gong practitioners in China.

New York has been Barbara's yearly travel destination. Since 2008, for six consecutive years Barbara journeyed to New York City to be with Falun Gong practitioners from all over the world—to participate in the Manhattan Falun Gong parade and to attend the annual experience-sharing conference. Thus, May 2016 will pose another opportunity to have face-to-face meetings with Barbara for the on-going study that explores the health-wellness effects of Falun Gong through the lived experiences of practitioners.

CHAPTER 2

Walking the Path

Millions of individuals from around the world have walked the Falun Gong path to health and wellness. Findings from the Australian survey indicated a similar phenomenon; many Falun Gong respondents reported regaining their health and experiencing a profound mind-body transformation. Falun Gong, also known as Falun Dafa, is an ancient Chinese spiritual system for the overall improvement of body, mind, and spirit. It is a meditative practice rooted in traditional Chinese culture (Falun Dafa Information Center, 2015a). The Chinese terms, 'Fa" means Law; 'lun' means Wheel, and 'gong' refers to energy or movement. 'Dafa' means the Great Law. Hence, the literal meaning of 'Falun Gong' is Law Wheel Practice and Falun Dafa means the Great Law Wheel Practice.

Since its public introduction in 1992, Falun Gong gained tremendous popularity, so much so, that the former Chinese Communist Party (CCP) leader Jiang Zemin banned the practice on July 20, 1999, as a way of political control and started the brutal persecution of Falun Gong practitioners in China. The main teachings of Falun Gong and other works have been translated into 38 languages, according to the Falun Gong website www.falundafa.org. Today, the estimates of people practicing Falun Gong are considered around 70 to 100 million people from all walks of life and from about 100 countries. Due to its nebulous structure, the exact figures of the number of practitioners worldwide is hard to verify, as there is no formal registration of those

Falun Gong practitioners performing the standing meditation prior to the Chinese Communist Party's brutal persecution began on July 20, 1999. Beijing, China.

who practice Falun Gong and this, in a way, has compounded the difficulty for the researcher.

In our modern technological society, health and wellness are important matters for everyone. The Merriam-Webster online dictionary defines "health" as "the condition of being sound in body, mind, or spirit; especially freedom from physical disease or pain" or "the general condition of the body." The Oxford Dictionary defines health as "the state of being free of illness or injury" and "a person's mental or physical condition" (2005, p. 801). These descriptions correspond with the World Health Organization's (WHO) definition that health is not merely being free from illness or injury but also being in an all-inclusive state of physical, mental, and social health (World Health Organization, 2003, 2007). Wellness refers to the optimal state of health and the view of fully realizing one's greatest potential—physically, psychologically, socially, financially, and spiritually. For a group, wellness encompasses fulfilling expectations in the family, community, workplace, and society (B. J. Smith, Tang,

Nearly 6,000 Falun Gong practitioners from around the world gather to practice the five sets of exercises at Liberty Square, in front of the Chiang Kai-shek Memorial Hall. Taipei, Taiwan. November 8, 2014.

& Nutbeam, 2006). Today, wellness has become a widely accepted term. Newspapers, magazines, fitness centers, self-help books, and motivational speakers embrace the wellness concept and lifestyle.

Many counselors recognize that wellness plays a vital role in counseling and consider wellness as a lifestyle for optimum health and well-being (Hattie, Myers, & Sweeney, 2004; Jane E. Myers & Sweeney, 2005; Jane E Myers, Sweeney, & Witmer, 2000). Whichever way it is described, wellness embodies an approach that harmoniously integrates body, mind, and spirit for a fuller lifestyle within a community. Wellness is a spontaneous, dynamic, and developing process. It is a holistic way of life, one that embraces the intertwined relationship of health/wellness with oneself, between individuals and society.

Role of Eastern Meditative Mind-body Practices

More individuals are now seeking health and wellness through Eastern meditative practices and alternative options that go beyond conventional medicine. This trend is catching fire especially in Western countries like Australia, the United States (US), and the European Union (EU) (Bishop & Lewith, 2010; Coulter & Willis, 2004; Frass et al., 2012; Kessler et al., 2001; MacLennan, P Myers, & Taylor, 2006; NCCIH, 2015; Xue, Zhang, Lin, Da Costa, & Story, 2007). Complementary and alternative medicine (CAM) includes complementary, alternative, and integrative approaches. It refers to "interventions neither taught widely in medical schools nor generally available in US hospitals" (Eisenberg et al., 1998, p. 1569; Kessler et al., 2001, p. 262). The US National Center for Complementary and Integrative Health (NCCIH) describes CAM as "a group of diverse medical and health care systems, practices, and products that are not generally considered part of conventional medicine" (NCCIH, 2009b). Cochrane Collaboration, an independent and non-government research organization, describes CAM as a wide variety of health methods, modalities, and practices, used to treat or prevent illness or to promote health and wellness (Mamtani & Cimino, 2002).

CAM practices also include mind-body medicine (MBM) or mind-body therapy (MBT), which are practices that use "a variety of techniques to facilitate the mind's capacity to affect bodily function and symptoms" (Johnson & Kushner, 2001, p. 256; Pelletier, 2002, p. 4). Mind-body medicine is considered a 'new medicine' and a bio-psychosocial spiritual approach to health and total wellness (Johnson & Kushner, 2001). An important characteristic of MBM is its self-care aspect, which inevitably encourages people to take charge of their own health and wellness. Whether we like it or not, people are seeking complementary, alternative, integrative approaches and an increasing number of mainstream health professionals are integrating these meditative practices with conventional health care systems to cater to the needs of these individuals.

MBM falls within the new scientific discipline of psychoneuroimmu-nology (PNI)—a term that most of us hardly ever hear in our everyday conversation. Robert Ader (1980), a psychologist and professor emeritus at the University of Rochester Medical Center at the time, co-founded PNI, which refers to the study of the relationship between the mind (psyche), nervous system (neuro), immune system, and health. There is a mounting body of evidence published on the efficacy in the use of MBM for better health and wellness (Jacobs, 2001; Pelletier, 2002). Goleman and Gurin (1993) classified MBM as a range of modalities, such as meditation and relaxation techniques that utilize the human mind to enhance physical and emotional health and wellness. They supported the integration of MBM within mainstream health care because of MBM's lower costs, lower physical and emotional risks, and higher potential benefits. Jacobs (2001) discerned that the mind plays a vital role in our health and wellness and believed in the concept of mind over matter.

In the United States, over 30 percent of American adults and 12 percent children use CAM or healthcare approaches, not considered as mainstream, conventional medicine (NCCIH, 2008). According to the European Information Centre for Complementary and Alternative Medicine (EICCAM), about 40 percent of EU residents use CAM approaches. Likewise, CAM use in Australia is on the rise. A national survey indicated that Australians made 69.2 million visits to alternative medicine practitioners during a 12-month period (Xue et al., 2007). This figure almost equals the 69.3 million visits to mainstream medical practitioners. Their results revealed that Australians spent over three billion US dollars on CAM therapies during the same period. One study showed that over 52 percent of South Australians used alternative therapies in 2004 (MacLennan et al., 2006). Another South Australian study conducted in Adelaide on patients in four hospitals indicated that CAM use is prevalent even among hospitalized patients. Ninety percent of patients reported CAM use, although most of them did not inform their doctors or nurses (Shorofi & Arbon, 2009).

The results from a US national health survey on trends in CAM use showed that Americans made 629 million visits to alternative medicine practitioners in 1997 (Eisenberg et al., 1998; He, 2011). What is most illuminating is that this figure surpassed the total number of visits to conventional medical doctors. Researchers from Harvard Medical School and other medical establishments reported that Americans spent a whopping $27 billion on CAM therapies back in 1997 (Eisenberg et al., 1998). Ten years later, 83 million adult Americans spent nearly $34 billion on out-of-pocket CAM therapies (NCCIH, 2009b), which included consultations, natural products, classes, and other resources. The national survey also indicated that about 38 percent of Americans had used some form of alternative approaches during that 12-month period.

Self-care expenses comprised the biggest portion of the total CAM expenditure. While Americans spent about 35 percent or nearly $12 billion on CAM consultations, 65 percent went to self-care costs, which included 12 percent, or $4.1 billion spent on Eastern meditative movement practices such as yoga, tai chi, and qigong classes. Rogers, Larkey, and Keller (2009) described these Eastern meditative movement practices as mind-body therapies that combine physical movement or postures with breathing, relaxation, and meditation techniques. These Eastern practices are categorized as mind-body therapies or mind-body medicine (NCCIH, 2008), frequently integrated with other approaches, such as self-improvement, self-care techniques, or self-regulation intervention strategies.

Meditation is among the most widely used mind-body therapies (Mao, Farrar, Xie, Bowman, & Armstrong, 2007; NCCIH, 2008). A report based on the 2012 national survey highlighted prevalent use of mind-body practices; about 18 million adult American practiced meditation (NCCIH, 2015). Meditation broadly refers to the action or practice of being in a state of stillness or in one-pointed concentration on a tranquil activity, such as listening to the breath, music, or chanting a word or mantra repeatedly. It encompasses several aspects—being in a still state, focusing the mind on nothing, or on one thought, an object, or emptying one's thoughts. Meditation can also involve a relaxation response, a changed state of consciousness, or maintaining a state of self-awareness (Perez-De-Albeniz & Holmes, 2000).

Practicing meditation is relatively simple and does not require any expensive equipment. A mat for sitting on the floor or a comfortable chair will suffice. However, there are different forms of meditation; every discipline has a different definition of their practice, while different individuals describe meditation in their own way. A University of Toronto professor, Adam Anderson, who studied the benefits of meditation described meditation as a brain fitness workout. "It's like training any other muscle in your body. You're developing your brain to cope better with the world," said Anderson (cited in Easton, 2005, p. 22). In another scenario, a team of Australian researchers found that even 15 minutes of meditation seated in a chair done in an office setting could have significant stress reduction effect (Melville, Chang, Colagiuri, Marshall, & Cheema, 2012).

Taking Responsibility

While some private insurance providers would marginally cover certain CAM therapies, the national health insurance does not cover the majority of CAM practices. In most countries, people take responsibility and often pay out of their own pockets for CAM expenses. This reflects people's acceptance of CAM, Eastern meditative practices, and their willingness to take responsibility for their health and wellness. Coupled with rising health care costs and societal stresses, promoting and maintaining mind-body wellness has become a major challenge. It demands all health professionals and clients to have better knowledge and insight into the effects of the different mind-body practices offered as CAM therapies. This way people can make informed decisions and take responsibility for their own health and well-being.

Where new learning can be gained, it is important to consider the effects of these Eastern meditative mind-body practices. The results from the Australian survey suggested that Falun Gong presents as one such practice that has positive effects for many individuals. Practicing Falun Gong has led to significant improvement or complete recovery from serious medical conditions in many instances. While Barbara and numerous other Falun Gong practitioners have walked their path to wellness, the effects of the practice remain relatively unknown to the wider community. It was difficult to find information as the Chinese authorities obstruct both internal and foreign investigation of Falun Gong. Although there is much published literature on Falun Gong in the West, very few of these actually focus on the health and wellness effects of the practice. Outside China, reports have focused on brutal and glaring human rights abuses including torture and forced organ harvesting (Fernandez et al., 2012; Gutmann, 2014; L. Li, Director, 2014; Matas & Kilgour, 2009; Stone, 2015). People are generally more familiar with the health effects of yoga, tai chi, qigong, and mindfulness meditation than with Falun Gong, as there are more studies done on these other meditative practices. There is, therefore, a pressing need for researchers to conduct more studies exploring the health-wellness effects of Falun Gong.

Presently, academic studies on the health-wellness effects of Falun Gong are still in their infancy. Apart from the studies conducted by the author (Lau, 2001, 2010a) and the *Hearts Uplifted* project, there are two other recent studies exploring the effects of Falun Gong. The first study was completed in Egypt at the Suez Canal University (Yahiya, 2010), while the second one came from the University of California in Los Angeles (Bendig, 2013). Like the Australian survey, findings from both studies indicated the positive and beneficial effects of Falun Gong.

Linking Religion/Spirituality with Health and Wellness

Since classical times, religion and spirituality have been intrinsically connected with health and wellness. During the Middle Ages, until the 18th century, Western medicine, healthcare, and religion were closely intertwined. Many doctors were affiliated with religious orders that were responsible for training and licensing doctors (Koenig, 2012). Likewise, in traditional Aboriginal, Eastern, and Chinese cultures, mind, body, and spirit are connected and the basis of traditional Chinese medicine evolves around the concept that mind, body, and spirit are inseparable. Good health, healing, and wellness thus require the harmonious balance of the mind, body, and spirit.

It was only during the modern era that religion and health became dichotomized in Western societies. In mental healthcare, psychiatrist Sigmund Freud largely encouraged the split (D'Souza, 2007; Koenig, 2012). Since then, health professionals have viewed religion/spirituality as separated from the counseling and healing process and many

Source: Minghui

Part of a large group practice at Sri Adichunchanagiri Mahasamsthana Math, a rural school with over 2,000 students. Karnataka, India. December 2009.

practitioners hesitate to address religious and spiritual issues in their professional work, in case they were seen as overstepping into the domain of the clergy. Thankfully, there is increasing awareness of, and insight into the positive link between religion/spirituality and health and wellness. A growing number of counselors, health practitioners, and educators realize the importance of integrating religion and spirituality into the helping profession (Canda & Furman, 2009; Cashwell & Watts, 2010; Cashwell & Young, 2011; Court & Court, 2001; D'Souza, 2007; Koenig, 2012; Robertson, 2008). The Association for Spiritual, Ethical, and Religious Values in Counseling (ASERVIC)—a division of the American Counseling Association (ACA)—created the nine spiritual competencies to address spiritual and religious matters in counseling (ASERVIC, 2009; Cashwell & Watts, 2010). Canda and Furman (Canda, 2009; Canda & Furman, 2009) advocated and developed the framework for spiritually sensitive social work that addresses spiritual issues of clients in a holistic and culturally appropriate way. D'Souza (2007) stated that doctors and other health practitioners need to consider and understand how religion and spirituality can beneficially impact clinical interventions.

The Australian survey is based on the premise that there is a link between religion/spirituality and health. It recognizes that religious/ spiritual beliefs and practices have a positive impact on the health and wellness of individuals. Focusing on this link therefore forms the framework for the Australian survey. This is appropriate since Falun Gong fits as a spiritual meditation practice with elements from Buddhist and Taoist teachings.

The link between religion/spirituality and health and wellness existed in Eastern and Western civilizations since time immemorial. Ancient Taoists and Buddhists in the East adopted different cultivation methods for mind-body and spiritual improvement. Many of them were on the quest for good health, longevity, and immortality. In the West, people believe in miracles, prayers, and the importance of religion and

Students and teachers in a Catholic school practice Falun Gong standing exercises. Bangalore, India. August 2008.

spirituality in their life. The Gallup polls have consistently indicated that more than 90 percent of Americans believe in God or a universal spirit (Newport, 2011). Numerous Australian and US studies indicated a positive link between religion/spirituality and health (Coruh, Ayele, Pugh, & Mulligan, 2005; Haynes, Hilbers, Kivikko, & Ratnavuyha, 2007; Hilbers, Haynes, Kivikko, & Ratnavuyha, 2007; Koenig, 1999, 2004a, 2004b, 2007; Koenig & Cohen, 2002; Koenig, E., & Larson, 2001; Peach, 2003; Williams & Sternthal, 2007). Many in the West recognize and support the need to integrate religion/spirituality into counseling, social work, and medical practices (Canda, 2009; Canda & Furman, 2009; Cashwell & Young, 2011; Court & Court, 2001; D'Souza, 2007; Haynes et al., 2007; Hilbers et al., 2007; Koenig, 2004a, 2007, 2012; Robertson, 2008). Court and Court (2001) drew example from the plight of the Australian Aboriginal people, the destruction of their traditional culture, and how the loss of Aboriginal spirituality or Aboriginal Dreamtime has a negative impact on the health and well-being of the Aboriginal people. They addressed the religion/spirituality link with health/wellness as "the forgotten factor" and advocated "reconciliation" (Court & Court, 2001, p. 4). Others like Standard, Sandhu, and Painter (2000) regarded spirituality as the 'fifth force' in the helping profession (Cited in Cormier, Nurius, & Osborn, 2009). A decade later, Garzon (2011) echoed the same theme of religion/spirituality being a prevailing 'fifth force' in counseling and psychotherapy.

The term 'religion' refers to organized beliefs, involving formal practices, rituals, and doctrines that facilitate intimacy with the sacred, God, or a higher power, whereas spirituality does not have a single, widely accepted definition. Spirituality denotes a personal transformation, meaningful experience, or quest for a higher awareness or answers to questions about life that can be devoid from formal religious practices. Hence, the term 'spirituality' conveys a broader meaning and has different connotations for different individuals. Some researchers identified spirituality as "more fluid, eclectic, and individual" than religion (Haynes et al., 2007, p. 2; Hilbers et al., 2007, p. 1). Others like Dr. Harold Koenig (2012), Director of the Center for Spirituality, Theology and Health at Duke University, an expert in the field of religion, spirituality and health, described spirituality as "distinguished from all other things—humanism, values, morals, and mental health—by its connection to that which is sacred, the transcendent" (p. 3). ASERVIC (2015) defines "spirituality as a capacity and tendency that is innate and unique to all persons. This spiritual tendency moves the individual toward knowledge, love, meaning, peace, hope, transcendence, connectedness, compassion, wellness, and wholeness" (p. 1).

Hence, spirituality and religion do not mean the same thing. For instance, one can be both spiritual and religious, or spiritual but not religious, or religious and not spiritual. Koenig (2004a) noted that 90 percent

Over 10,000 Falun Gong practitioners doing the standing exercises in front of the Liaoning Exhibition Hall. Shenyan City, Liaoning Province, China. May, 1998.

Morning practice: Falun Gong practitioners performing a standing meditation in front of the Geology Palace, prior to the Chinese Communist Party's persecution of Falun Gong practitioners on July 20, 1999. Changchun, China.

of patients often described themselves as both spiritual and religious. Researchers noted that there are more studies focusing on religion, assessments of religiosity, rather than on spirituality (Koenig, 2004a, 2004b; Williams & Sternthal, 2007; Yeager et al., 2006). Based on the author's experience with counseling clients, the term 'spirituality' is often more appropriate, acceptable, and inclusive in therapeutic interactions. It neither distinguishes between nor segregates people into different religious groups.

Often the two terms are used synonymously. Some writers chose either to use the two terms interchangeably, or to not differentiate between them, which explains why Falun Gong is often described in the West as a spiritual practice and as a new religion or religious discipline. In fact, before the mid-19th century there was no Chinese word for religion. The Chinese word for religion—*zongjiao*—did not exist in ancient China. In traditional Chinese culture, spiritual philosophies were simply referred to as cultivation or spiritual practices or precepts, as in Confucian, Taoist, or Buddhist teachings. *Zongjiao* originated from the West via Japanese translations in the late 1860s (Ownby, 2005; Penny, 2012). It is a newly crafted term, used to mean religion during the late 19th century by Japanese translating Christian texts (Adler, 2005; Penny, 2012).

Given the absence of the term 'religion' in ancient China and that Falun Gong is rooted in traditional Chinese culture, it is more appropriate to describe the practice as a spiritual discipline. Moreover, Falun Gong does not have churches or temples, memberships, rituals, or the hierarchical structure associated with mainstream religions.

Various studies indicated that having a spiritual or religious belief is beneficial to one's health and wellness. One Australian study conducted at the Sydney Prince of Wales Hospital (POWH) demonstrated that religion/spirituality is important to 74 percent of POWH patients (Haynes et al., 2007; Hilbers et al., 2007). The findings indicated that more than 80 percent of patients reported religious/spiritual beliefs influence their health and become more significant during illness. The patients reported that rituals and religious/spiritual practices offer self-care support, therapy, comfort, meaning, and connection for them during their illness. The POWH study revealed that religion and spirituality play an important role in health care decision-making and can be a resource, coping strategy, or a psychosocial support mechanism for patients (Haynes et al., 2007, p. 1; Hilbers et al., 2007, pp. 27-28). Their results were consistent with other studies that reported a positive link between religious/spiritual involvement and healthy behaviors.

Koenig (2004a) stated that religion/spirituality offers "comfort, hope, and meaning, particularly in coping with a medical illness" (p. 1195). Koenig (2012) reviewed thousands of studies examining the link between religion/spirituality and better physical and mental health. He found that religion/spirituality contributed to better health and wellness states and linked with a string of positive effects, for example, reduced anxiety and depression, and diminished substance abuse (Koenig, 2004a, 2004b, 2012). Other benefits include quicker recovery, lower suicide rates, greater sense of hope and optimism, more purpose and meaning in life, improved social support, greater marital stability and fulfillment, personal empowerment, more positive worldview, and better psychological coping with traumatic life events (Koenig, 2004a, p. 1195, 2004b, p. 78). In other words, religious and spiritual individuals tend to live longer, have healthier lifestyles, possess better coping skills, stronger immune systems, and better protection from serious cardiovascular illness.

Findings from most studies indicated that religion/spirituality play an important role in the health and well-being of many people. They could have a lifestyle-balancing effect. Data from the Australian health-wellness survey (Lau, 2010a) were consistent with these studies, which suggested a positive link between Falun Gong and the health and wellness of Falun Gong practitioners.

Indonesian practitioners performed Falun Gong exercises on a sunny car-free Sunday, conveying the peacefulness of Falun Gong to the busy city. Jakarta, Indonesia. March 16, 2014.

Falun Gong is taught in more than 80 schools in the city of Banglore. Some schools have over 3,000 students doing the exercises in their PE (physical education) classes. Bangalore, India. 2009.

CHAPTER 3

Popular, Uplifting, and Tranquil

"**W**hy has nobody told me earlier that it's this good?" was Barbara's initial thought upon starting the Falun Gong exercises. However, the truth was that she had heard about Falun Gong a few years before her accident. "One of my girlfriends told me about it before, but I told her I never had time for such things" (L. Smith, 2009). During the face-to-face meeting in May 2013 in New York, Barbara laughingly said, "I had to fall on my head to appreciate it." Like many Falun Gong practitioners, she embarked on the Falun Gong journey and found mind-body and spiritual health and wellness.

Falun Gong was "one of China's best-kept secrets in the '90s" (Nania, 2013). Popular, uplifting, and tranquil as Falun Gong was for millions of Chinese people, many in the West did not know about Falun Gong until July 20, 1999, the day the Chinese Communist Party (CCP) launched its brutal persecution of Falun Gong practitioners in China. The CCP targeted foreign media with its anti-Falun Gong propaganda campaigns.

Consequently, "the first and only exposure to Falun Gong" (Nania, 2013, p. 2) for people outside of China at that time was what the Chinese state-run media had fabricated. The foreign media simply portrayed Falun Gong using the CCP's definitions, creating much confusion and misunderstanding about the practice in the eyes of the international community. Today, these misperceptions persist.

What is Falun Gong?

When Falun Gong respondents were asked in the Australian survey to answer this question, the majority (98%, n=351) described Falun Gong as an advanced cultivation practice based on truthfulness, compassion, and forbearance (also translated as tolerance). Only two Falun Gong respondents described the practice, as "a type of qigong," while another two indicated, "Don't know." No respondent identified Falun Gong as a form of religion, a Taoist, or a Buddhist sect, which implied that Falun Gong respondents know what the practice is about and what it is not. While Falun Dafa is more fitting and widely used in Falun Gong literature and among practitioners, Falun Gong remains more popular across different media and search engines. Hence, the author has chosen to use the latter term throughout this book.

So, what *is* Falun Gong? To put it simply, Falun Gong is an ancient spiritual meditation practice made public in 1992 and it teaches exercises and the moral principles of truthfulness, compassion, and tolerance (Pullen, 2000). Rooted in traditional Chinese culture, Falun Gong's most visible characteristic is its distinctive sitting meditation and four simple standing exercises that are gentle and enjoyable to do. However, there is more to Falun Gong than meditating and performing the exercises. Besides, practicing the exercises, Falun Gong practitioners study the teachings of the practice, and endeavor to take the teachings as a guide for daily living.

At the core of the practice are the values of truthfulness, compassion, and forbearance. Falun Gong teaches that these three principles

European practitioners doing the standing meditation in front of the Opera House. Frankfurt, Germany. 2000.

Group practice in front of the Eiffel Tower. Paris, France. June 2014.

Five thousand Falun Gong practitioners in sitting meditation and forming the Chinese characters for Truthfulness, Compassion, and Forbearance. Such large public displays were common before the persecution began on July 20, 1999. Wuhan, China.

comprise the fundamental qualities of the universe and that by embracing them as a way of life, we can experience mind, body, and spiritual health and wellness, as well as boundless wisdom. As individuals from diverse ethnicities and professions take up the practice, many encounter life-changing transformations. They find that forgiveness replaces anger and resentment; tranquility replaces anxiety and stress; frustration gives way to serenity; and depression and hopelessness uplifted and replaced with peace and inner joy. Practitioners seek to be compassionate, selfless, forbearing, aspiring to attain deeper insight and awareness of self and others in different situations—eventually reaching a state of true health and wellness. This is what the Asian tradition refers to as "enlightenment" or "attaining the Dao (Way)."

Benefits

Falun Gong has helped countless individuals like Barbara to regain their health. Most Falun Gong literature describe a list of benefits that includes relieving stress and anxiety, increasing energy and vitality, improving physical and mental health, and promoting spiritual growth and enlightenment. A search on the Falun Gong www.en.minghui.org website for health benefits yield scores of personal accounts and literature about people who have taken up the practice and have experienced tremendous benefits. Likewise, the Australian survey findings showed that the majority of Falun Gong respondents reported better health and wellness after starting the practice. The study suggested that practitioners enjoyed a better quality of life than non-Falun Gong people.

According to the Australian survey, Falun Gong has helped people recover from life-threatening medical conditions, including diabetes, lung, heart, and kidney diseases, various types of cancers, and numerous other medical ailments. The list is long. However, it must be said that those who experienced remarkable recoveries, like Barbara, are fully committed. The practice has inspired many individuals to make the crossing, to give up their old lifestyle of indulgence, for example, addictions to alcohol, crime, drugs, and the desire for fame and personal gain. Falun Gong has helped to calm the frantic minds of many people, uplift their spirits, heal their depression, and help them to maintain positive and righteous thoughts.

While some individuals appreciate not succumbing to the annual rituals of colds, fever, and flu, others re-experience the simple pleasures in life from less anxiety and stress. Every Falun Gong practitioner has his or her own unique situation and a story to tell because everyone's experience is different. Almost all Falun Gong practitioners discover new joys in their life. They experience better health and wellness and healthier relationships with family and friends, as reflected in the results from the Australian survey. Like all laudable endeavors, what practitioners gain from the practice reflects the effort they put into it. For instance, during conflicts Falun Gong practitioners endeavor to examine themselves and to consider other people's interests first, instead of feeling resentful and blaming others. When they are truly able to do this, they feel at peace with any challenging situation. Through this cultivation process, practitioners learn to live in harmony with themselves, the world, and the people around them.

For Barbara, Falun Gong has not only helped her to recover completely from her fall; it continues to offer her answers to many of life's challenges throughout her cultivation path. The practice has helped her and many individuals deepen their understanding of life and offer them a new, enlightened sense of purpose about life and their reason for living. Unlike other practices, Falun Gong does not have churches or temples, membership fees, initiation rituals, donations, or tithing. Practitioners cultivate simply by assimilating and applying the teachings in their own way. With time, constant study, and practice, each practitioner's understanding and experience with Falun Gong continues to evolve. From this perspective, Falun Gong is deeply personal. One is free to practice alone or with a group, or leave at any time.

Falun Gong People

Falun Gong was immensely popular in China in the 1990s; it won the hearts and minds of millions from all walks of life, as well as receiving prizes and official recognition from Chinese authorities (Falun Dafa Information Center, 2015a). At the onset of the persecution in 1999, one in 13 Chinese people was practicing Falun Gong in China (Nania, 2013). Every morning hundreds and thousands of Falun Gong practitioners (as they are referred to by those who practice Falun Gong) would gather in public parks across major cities in China to perform the exercises before going to work. Indeed, it stood out as an ideal practice in our stressful modern-day society.

The results from the Australian survey also reflected the diversity of Falun Gong people outside of China. Many were in the prime of their life and career. They had university education, a profession, an occupation, and came from different social and ethnic backgrounds. They held responsible jobs as artists, musicians, scientists, medical doctors, college professors, information technology experts, senior government officials, business consultants, journalists, as well as university students and both skilled and unskilled workers.

The survey indicated that many Falun Gong people could speak a second or third language fluently. The majority live in the three main regions of the Western world—Oceania, meaning Australia and New Zealand, Europe, and North America, comprising Canada and the United States. By 1999, seven years after its initial introduction to the public, there were 70 to 100 million people practicing Falun Gong in China, according to Chinese authorities' estimate (Authors Unknown, 2002; Kilgour, 2013). As there are no formal registrations or memberships, it is difficult to verify or gage the precise number of Falun Gong people. Perhaps, the sheer numbers are not so important. What touches people's hearts are the inspiring stories of individuals like Barbara's story. Her narrative and other stories spur observers to reflect on their own lives and most important of all, help them to perceive Falun Gong in a different light.

Cultivation

Falun Gong has two key aspects—cultivation and practice. Of the two, cultivation is more important. Cultivation or more specifically, "cultivation of mind" (H. Li, 2001b, p. 89) emphasizes improving one's moral character or cultivating one's heart to become a moral and virtuous person. Cultivation is an Eastern tradition and concept. Ancient people believed that through a disciplined spiritual practice, a human being could eventually transcend this ordinary life and experience bliss and sublime realization. This mind-body transcendence or higher state of being liberates oneself from the pangs of suffering and illusions of this transient world. Since millennia, there have been different cultivation practices in Asia, with their own specific tradition and spiritual path. Different high-level masters passed these traditions to disciples in sheltered or monastic settings. Although Falun Gong is akin to these practices, the student of Falun Gong does not enter a monastery or nunnery. Instead, he or she cultivates in ordinary society with all its complexities and distractions.

The term 'cultivation' has a double connotation in the Chinese language. It consists of two characters—*xiulian*. *Xiu* means "repair" or "fix," while *lian* means "refine," or "polish." Hence, cultivation implies the act or art of refining oneself following the teachings passed down either by ancient Taoist or Buddhist teachings. Self-cultivation means the act of cultivating through one's own efforts. Ancient China is steeped in its tradition of different cultivation practices and Chinese history is full of legends of individuals becoming enlightened to the status of deities, or attaining the Tao through cultivation. The Tale of the Eight Taoist Immortals is one of the most famous cultivation stories from ancient China. More than 2,500 years ago, the Chinese philosopher Laozi wrote the *Dao De Jing* and his teachings became the basis of various Taoist practices. At about the same time in India, Buddha Sakyamuni founded Buddhism, which later spread to China. These two ancient Eastern practices as well as the teachings of Confucius became the foundation for many Chinese bio-spiritual disciplines that include martial arts and qigong practices.

Cultivation is an important aspect of traditional Chinese culture. It is to cultivate oneself—refine and improve one's moral character—and eventually reach enlightenment, after relinquishing all worldly desires and attachments. One follows a spiritual discipline or master and walks a spiritual path aspiring to become an enlightened being. The purpose is to live a virtuous life and cultivate to transcend the ordinary. According to the ancient Taoist way, the master would teach the physical exercises and secret practices to a few chosen disciples, whereas Falun Gong, which involves both mind and physical exercise practice, is open to all who wish to practice cultivation. It emphasizes cultivating *xinxing*, that is, cultivating the heart and improving or developing one's moral character. As such, Falun Gong is a high-level cultivation system for overall mind, body, and spiritual improvement. At the heart of Falun Gong are traditional Chinese values that resonate deeply with China's traditional belief systems, such as Buddhism, Taoism, and Confucianism, as well as with Christianity and other Western religious practices. The practice teaches following a single cultivation discipline until becoming enlightened in that school of practice.

One can say that cultivating the Falun Gong way calls for stepping across the threshold from the 'ordinary world' to the world of cultivation and undertaking to live by the principles of truthfulness, compassion, and forbearance. For 'cultivation of mind', the teachings of Falun Gong serve as a guide. Despite their busy life and facing daily challenges, many Falun Gong practitioners try their best to study the teachings of the practice regularly. Through this they constantly gain new understandings and often these are simple insights relating to day-to-day living, for example, how to be a kinder, more tolerant person and live a morally, upright life. An essential part of the practice involves constantly looking within and examining oneself. Through this process of self-reflection, the practitioner of Falun Gong awakens to new realizations that help him or her to become a better person. Besides moral or *xinxing* cultivation, students of Falun Gong practice the exercises to maintain a strong and healthy physical body. Some prefer to practice at home, while others practice in groups in a park, when the weather permits.

The Exercises

The practice aspect of the Falun Gong involves exercises and meditation. Perhaps, the best things in life are simple. There are only five exercises in Falun Gong: four standing exercises and one sitting meditation. The exercises do not need to be done together, in sequence, or in a special place, or at a particular time of the day and there are no specific breathing techniques. It is therefore convenient for busy people in our modern, fast-paced society. Each exercise has a specific purpose and benefit. The first exercise is called "Buddha Showing a Thousand Hands" or *Fo Zhan Qianshou Fa* in Chinese (H. Li, 2001b, pp. 93, 141-145). Taking about 10 minutes to do, this exercise opens all energy channels in the body. According to traditional Chinese medicine, *qi* or energy flows along pathways or meridians in the body. This first exercise unblocks all energy channels simultaneously and enables the body to absorb energy to correct any disharmony.

The second exercise, called the "Falun Standing Stance" or *Falun Zhuang Fa* in Chinese, is a standing meditation with four wheel-holding arm positions (H. Li, 2001b, pp. 107, 146). The standard practice time is 30 minutes, about seven minutes in each position. This exercise helps to increase strength and boost energy levels in the body. The third exercise, "Penetrating the Two Cosmic Extremes," or *Guantong Liangji Fa* in Chinese (H. Li, 2001b, pp. 113, 147-152), purifies the body through blending the body's energy with the external cosmic energy. This is done with slow upward-downward hand movements, about four to five inches away from the front of the body. Taking about nine minutes to do, this exercise is the shortest. The fourth standing exercise, "Falun Heavenly Circuit," or *Falun Zhoutian Fa* in Chinese (H. Li, 2001b, pp. 120, 153-155), takes about 12 minutes. It improves the overall circulation of energy and helps to harmonize all anomalies in the body.

Small group practice in Victoria Square. Adelaide, Australia. April 28, 2012.

The fifth exercise is a sitting meditation, called "Strengthening Divine Powers," or *Shantung Joachim Fa* in Chinese (H. Li, 2001b, pp. 129, 155-160). It is best to sit in the full-lotus or double cross-legged position. If you are unable to do so, it is fine to sit in a half-lotus or single cross-legged position, on a chair, or a small stool. This meditation calms the mind and body and enhances your energy potency through reaching the state of tranquility, or *ding,* in Chinese. In *Zhuan Falun,* this state is described as when "one sits for a while, one finds that the legs are gone, and cannot think where the legs went; the body is also gone; the arms are also gone; the hands are also gone—only the head is left" (H. Li, 2001d, p. 339). When one meditates beyond this state, "one finds that the head is gone as well, leaving only one's mind, a little thought that one is practicing" (H. Li, 2001d, p. 339). For mind-body and spiritual health, it is necessary to reach this state of tranquility. "When one practices in this state, the body is being fully transformed" (H. Li, 2001d, p. 339). The exercises are performed with

Australian practitioners doing the sitting meditation at the Otisville Veterans Memorial Park. Otisville, NY, US. October 11, 2015.

music instructions available online for free download from the Falun Gong website: http://en.falundafa.org/falun-dafa-video-audio.html.

While doing the exercises regularly is important, cultivating the heart and becoming a morally upright person is more important. True wellness comes from cultivating both the mind and body. In other words, to ensure optimum mind-body and spiritual health and wellness, physical exercises must be combined with cultivation. Falun Gong teaches that moral character cultivation is important for true health and wellness. Hence, the key to mind-body and spiritual health and wellness lies in genuine cultivation coupled with exercise practice.

Describing Falun Gong

Falun Gong, pronounced as *"Fah-loon Gong,"* is an ancient Chinese self-cultivation practice to improve the mind and body. Falun Gong websites, fliers, and information booklets describe the practice as a high-level spiritual meditation system. Also known as Falun Dafa, Falun Gong helps to increase energy and vitality, relieve stress and anxiety, promote health and wellness, and gain spiritual enlightenment. Clearly, one of the reasons for the rapid growth and widespread popularity of Falun Gong was its health and wellness benefits.

Few people know that Falun Gong received numerous official recognition from the Chinese Communist regime in the 1990's before the persecution began in 1999. Mr. Li Hongzhi, the founder of Falun Gong, introduced the practice to the public in 1992. The following year he received the title as the "Most Welcomed Qigong Master" in Beijing (Falun Dafa Information Center, 2015a). That same year a bureaucrat from China's Ministry of Public Security's official newspaper, *The People's Public Security News*, commended Mr. Li for promoting traditional Chinese virtues and upholding social order, security, and morality in society (Falun Dafa Information Center, 2015a). Falun Gong won the 'Star Qigong School' award and was the "most outstanding qigong practice" (H. Li, 2001d, p. 293) at the Beijing state-run Oriental Health Expo. The European Parliament nominated Mr. Li, a five-time Nobel Peace Prize nominee, for the Sakharov Prize for Freedom of Thought. Furthermore, Mr. Li was granted Freedom House's International Religious Freedom Award (Falun Dafa Information Center, 2015a).

While the practice was spreading like wild fire across China in the late 1990s, most people in the West first heard about Falun Gong only when the CCP embarked on a nation-wide persecution campaign against Falun Gong practitioners in China. Before July 1999, there was hardly anything consistently documented about the practice, which compounded the difficulty of explaining Falun Gong, after the persecution began. Many in the West could not come to a consensus on how to describe Falun Gong. Most foreign journalists simply adopted what the state-controlled Chinese media had fabricated. Some chose to remind silent for fear of reprisals and losing their visa to

Over a thousand students do Falun Gong exercises as part of their curriculum at a police officer training college. Delhi, India. April 13, 2009.

work in China. Other writers and researchers scrambled to describe Falun Gong using different terms based on their own perceptions, understanding, or academic orientation.

So, how has Falun Gong been described in Western literature? Various writers and researchers frequently describe Falun Gong as a form of qigong (Burgdoff, 2003; Q. Li, Li, Garcia, Johnson, & Feng, 2005; Lio et al., 2003; Lowe, 2003; Ownby, 2008; D. Palmer, 2007; Parker, 2004; Porter, 2003; Spiegel, 2002). Most agreed that it is a form of spiritual cultivation and meditation discipline, a religion, a Buddhist qigong practice, or a new Chinese spiritual movement (Bruseker, 2000; Burgdoff, 2003; Q. Li et al., 2005; Lio et al., 2003; Lowe, 2003; Ownby, 2000, 2003a, 2005, 2008; D. Palmer, 2007; Parker, 2004; Penny, 2003, 2005, 2012; Porter, 2003; Spiegel, 2002). David Ownby, a history professor at The University of Montreal, Canada, described Falun Gong as "profoundly moral" (Ownby, 2003b, p. 307). The Nova Religio Falun Gong symposium recognized Falun Gong as a new religious movement (Wessinger, 2003) and dedicated eight articles to the practice in its 2003 Journal of Alternative and Emergent Religions.

Irons (2003) and Porter (2005) also described Falun Gong as China's new religious movement.

Yet, others called Falun Gong a cultural movement (Gale & Gorman-Yao, 2003), a New Age spiritual movement (Ackerman, 2005), or a modern Chinese Folk Buddhist practice (Bruseker, 2000). A sociology professor at the University of California, San Diego, Richard Madsen (2000), said Falun Gong is "something one does rather than something one believes" (p. 243). Spiegel, a research consultant for Human Rights Watch, described Falun Gong as a qigong, an ancient Chinese deep-breathing exercise, and meditation system "that enthusiasts claim promotes physical, mental, and spiritual well-being" (2002, p. 8). A researcher from the Faculty of Physical Education at the Suez Canal University in Egypt defined Falun Gong as "a form of ancient Chinese art" that enhances psychological and performance skills in the Japanese martial art of judo (Yahiya, 2010, p. 2394).

Prior to the Communist Party's persecution of Falun Gong practitioners, such large group practice in public parks was common across China. Chengdu, Sichuan Province, China. 1998.

Many writers compared Falun Gong with other Eastern spiritual meditative movement practices. Those familiar with yoga call it "Chinese yoga," while those more accustomed to the slow and gentle movements of tai chi identified Falun Gong with tai chi. Others described Falun Gong as a fusion of many facets. David Matas (2009), a Canadian international human rights lawyer and co-author of *Bloody Harvest*, described Falun Gong as authentically Chinese and "a blend of ancient Chinese spiritual and exercise traditions" (p. 2). Matas stated that Mr. Li has conveyed a belief system that truly reverberates with the Chinese people and the Chinese psyche.

Both David Ownby (2008) and David Palmer (2007) stated that it is necessary to understand Falun Gong within the context of qigong, its emergence, and evolution in China. Interest in qigong for health and wellness maintenance mushroomed in the 1980s. During this 'qigong boom' era, a plethora of qigong masters emerged to introduce various forms of meditative movement practices (Ownby, 2008; D. Palmer, 2007; Xu, 1999). The 1990s, however, marked the tail end of China's qigong boom era. This was when Falun Gong first emerged and spread rapidly by word of mouth across China and later to the rest of world. Mr. Li first introduced Falun Gong as a form of qigong to the public in the City of Changchun in May 1992. He described qigong as an ancient practice with a "newly crafted term that complies with modern people's mindset" (H. Li, 2001d, p. 27), a term first coined in the early 1950s (Xu, 1999). Today, qigong is a generic term referring to different schools and styles of traditional Chinese forms of energy exercises and meditative movement practices.

Between 1992 and 1995, Mr. Li conducted about 56 public lectures and practice sessions in China, all with the help of the state-controlled China Qigong Scientific Research Society. Within a short period, Falun Gong became the most popular qigong practice in China. In 1995, Mr. Li began introducing the practice to the rest of the world, traveling to different countries to give public lectures in Australia,

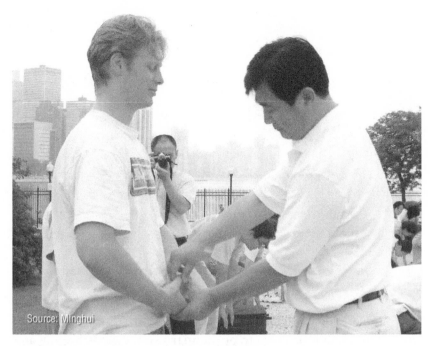

Mr. Li Hongzhi, founder of Falun Gong, adjusting a student's hand position during practice. Chicago, US. July, 1999.

Canada, France, Germany, Singapore, Sweden, Switzerland, Taiwan, and the United States.

While Falun Gong may have emerged from China's qigong boom, Falun Gong is not simply another qigong practice. According to Mr. Li (2001d) Falun Gong is a cultivation system that is "genuinely guiding people to high levels" (p. 1). While most qigong practices focus on qi and keeping fit, Falun Gong emphasizes the cultivation of gong and becoming a morally good person (H. Li, 2001d). There is a notable difference between *qi* and *gong*. *Qi* is explained as a life force or vital energy, whereas *gong* refers to cultivation energy, which is understood as a higher form of energy. In the introductory book, *Falun Gong,* Mr. Li (2001b) described *gong* as a "high-energy substance that manifests in the form of light, and its particles are fine and its density is high"

Falun Gong practitioners doing morning exercises at Buckingham Fountain. Chicago, US. May 6, 2012.

(p. 5). This gong is believed to promote true mind-body healing and spiritual transcendence.

One of the reasons Falun Gong has been frequently described as a religion or a new Chinese religious movement in Western literature is because the teachings of the practice contain words and concepts similar to Taoist and Buddhist terminologies. The practice embodies religious and spiritual elements, such as improving *xinxing* or moral character. However, this is where the similarities end. Falun Gong is not the same as Taoism or Buddhism and Falun Gong people do not describe their practice as a religion. Initially they tried to explain to non-practitioners that Falun Gong *is* not a religion. However, in recent years, Falun Gong practitioners have stopped disputing that their practice is not a religion. They realize that if the term 'religion' helps Westerners to understand the practice better, so be it. If it helps to facilitate an easier communication channel, then it is unnecessary to dispute the description as different individuals and organizations will continue to describe Falun Gong in different ways.

CHAPTER 4

The Persecution
of Falun Gong

The persecution of Falun Gong and the alleged forced organ harvesting of Falun Gong practitioners and other prisoners of conscience in China's labor camps are the most challenging aspects of Falun Gong to research and write about. The Chinese Communist Party's (CCP) persecution of this spiritual practice is relevant to the theme of this book that focuses on the beauty, health, and wellness effects of Falun Gong and its application in integrative counseling. Based on the informed consent protocol for counseling clients, it is equally important and essential for readers to know the truth about the CCP's persecution of Falun Gong.

Background information on the persecution is contained in this separate chapter. Therefore, it is easier for you as a reader to skip or skim through this chapter, and move on if you deem it unnecessary for your immediate needs. For those who thirst for more knowledge, detailed reports are available on the website, www.upholdjustice.org (World Organization to Investigate the Persecution of Falun Gong (WOIPFG), 2004). Others, who prefer independent third party accounts by non-Falun Gong practitioners, should check out the field research conducted by David Kilgour and David Matas (2006; 2007; 2009), as well as Ethan Gutmann (2014). More insight and knowledge on organ harvesting can be gleaned from watching two award-winning documentaries—*Human Harvest* (Lee, 2014) and *Hard to Believe* (Stone, 2015).

Since 1999, Falun Gong practitioners in China have faced the most severe torture and persecution. China under the CCP rule has endured many politically motivated campaigns, such as the 1960s Cultural Revolution and the June 4, 1989 Tiananmen Square massacre. Yet, the most brutal campaign is the on-going persecution of Falun Gong. So why is this popular, uplifting, and peaceful meditation practice persecuted in China? Briefly, three key factors led to the persecution campaign of Falun Gong in China (Falun Dafa Information Center, 2015b).

The first is its popularity, rapid growth, and sheer size, which became a gnawing source of concern for some CCP leaders. The second pertinent factor is the ideological difference. Falun Gong is a meditation practice staunchly rooted in traditional Chinese culture and its guiding principles of truthfulness, compassion, and forbearance were considered ideological threats to a communist party that garnered and sustained power and control through violence and corruption. The third factor was the personal quest of China's former leader, Jiang Zemin.

Jiang Zemin's Role

Besides Falun Gong's persistent popularity, the persecution of Falun Gong began mainly due to one man's jealousy, fears, and insecurity. Many China experts pointed to the then new Party leader Jiang Zemin as being responsible for initiating the persecution of Falun Gong (Falun Dafa Information Center, 2015b; Qi, 2012; The Epoch Times, 2004a, 2004b; Xie & Zhu, 2004; Young, 2012, 2013). Jiang, realizing that he was less popular than his fellow members in the Politburo Standing Committee, asserted his power in the same way that past Party leaders had done through large-scale political campaigns. All he needed was a target and he found the perfect target in Falun Gong (Gutmann, 2009; Xie & Zhu, 2004; Young, 2013).

By 1999, Falun Gong was immensely popular among Chinese people and practically known to every strata of the Chinese society. Everyday, tens of thousands could be seen practicing Falun Gong in public places all throughout China in the early hours of the morning before going to work. A 1998 survey by China's State Sports Commission estimated that there were over 70 million Falun Gong practitioners (Falun Dafa Information Center, 2008). However, it is not possible to determine the exact figures, as Falun Gong does not have any official structure or organization and practitioners are not required to officially register to practice Falun Gong. Matas (2009) noted, "a group of that size no matter what its beliefs, attracts the attention of a repressive government" (p. 2).

Millions were drawn to the practice not only because of its outstanding health-wellness benefits but also because the teachings of Falun Gong—based on Taoist and Buddhist traditions—struck a deep chord in the hearts of Chinese people. Many were disillusioned after the June 4, 1989 massacre. Three years later, along came Falun Gong with its inspiring independent thinking that goes beyond and contrary to the CCP doctrines. Falun Gong offered a glimmer of hope for a better future. Through word of mouth, the practice spread like forest fires across urban and rural China.

Because of the group's popularity, size, and diverse demographics, Jiang perceived Falun Gong as a threat. He was threatened by its ability to attract individuals from all walks of life and its ability to mobilize a huge gathering of people quickly. Perhaps what was frightening for Jiang was that amongst Falun Gong followers were Party members, retired high-ranking government officials, and military officers, including family members of top CCP officials. Even Jiang's wife learned the practice back in 1994 (Qi, 2012).

In addition, Falun Gong's amorphous nature and lack of organizational structure rendered it impossible for the CCP to control the followers or the practice, not that there was any need to exert control as Falun Gong is neither political nor interested in politics. As the group gained popularity and became more visible, tensions with the CCP occurred. In 1996, China's Ministry of Propaganda banned the publication of Falun Gong books after the main text, *Zhuan Falun*, became the best-selling book for three consecutive months. That same year, Falun Gong withdrew from the state-run Qigong Science Research Association of China after it was pressured to charge fees and to set up a CCP division (Falun Dafa Information Center, 2008). By 1998 and early 1999, incidents of police disrupting group practice in parks, and CCP propaganda vilifying Falun Gong escalated.

April 25 Peaceful Demonstration

April 25, 1999 (4-25) marked the turning point in the history of Falun Gong. A large number of practitioners showed up at Zhongnanhai, the CCP's Beijing headquarters, where it is customary for people from all over China to tender their petition about any personal, social injustice, or governmental grievances. About 10,000 to 15,000 Falun Gong practitioners gathered for a silent and peaceful demonstration seeking redress and recognition of their rights to practice their beliefs, after Tianjin police arrested 45 Falun Gong practitioners (Gutmann, 2009, 2014; Qi, 2012). The group was well behaved, unusual for such a huge public gathering. Practitioners came and assembled peacefully, then left the vicinity quietly, leaving no litter behind. They were thoughtful— mindfully living up to their principles and considering others first.

The group dispersed after the then-Premier Zhu Rongji spoke with Falun Gong representatives. Zhu assured them that the Chinese regime was not anti-Falun Gong. He agreed to release the Tianjin practitioners. However, Jiang Zemin had other plans. According to Young (2013), "Falun Gong was very popular, too popular for Jiang's liking" (p.

4) and Jiang seized the opportunity to assert his absolute authority after the 4-25 peaceful demonstration. So obsessed and driven by his insecurities and fears that he wrote a letter to all Politburo members and retired Party leaders demanding an emergency meeting on Falun Gong, accusing Falun Gong of taking away Party members, and falsely claiming that Western anti-China elements were behind the practice (Qi, 2012; Young, 2013). Jiang chose to interpret the peaceful 4-25 incident as a siege of the Central Government compound, and used this as a pretext to launch a nation-wide anti-Falun Gong campaign.

According to sources with access to high-ranking CCP officials, only Jiang wanted to initiate a persecution campaign, while the other six leaders of the Politburo were against Jiang's handling of Falun Gong. Premier Zhu and the then National People's Congress Chairman Qiao Shi had openly supported the Chinese people's right to practice Falun Gong. Jiang ignored them and pushed ahead his own decision to clamp down on the peaceful meditation group. To systematically execute the persecution of Falun Gong, Jiang established a special 'gestapo-like' organization on June 10, 1999, hence earning its name as the '6-10 Office' (World Organization to Investigate the Persecution of Falun Gong (WOIPFG), 2004). A branch of the CCP Political & Judicial Committee, the 6-10 office carried out all directives from the Committee to eradicate Falun Gong (Matas & Cheung, 2012).

Three months after the 4-25 appeal, on July 20, 1999, Jiang launched his nation-wide and global campaign against Falun Gong. He declared he would eradicate Falun Gong within three months. Now in its 17th year, the persecution is showing no sign of ending and the world's governments, foreign media, and international communities have pretty much acquiesced to the CCP's persecution of Falun Gong in favor of favorable economic, trade relations with China. Matas (2009) pointed out that the CCP persecuted Falun Gong practitioners much worse and much more harshly than members of any other spiritual beliefs. Jiang even went as far as to implement three strategies to persecute Falun Gong practitioners, that is, to "ruin their reputation, bankrupt them financially, and destroy them physically" (Qi, 2012; The Epoch Times, 2004b, p. 133; World Organization to Investigate the Persecution of Falun Gong (WOIPFG), 2004). Like Hitler's Gestapo, the notorious 6-10 Office was above the law and oversaw the persecution of Falun Gong under direct orders from Jiang himself (Matas & Cheung, 2012; Qi, 2012; World Organization to Investigate the Persecution of Falun Gong (WOIPFG), 2004). The CCP even gave the 6-10 Office "authority to ignore and violate the law" (Matas & Cheung, 2012, p. 69). This means there was no punishment for police or labor camp officers when Falun Gong practitioners died during cross-examination, torture, or forced feeding while in custody.

Persecution in its 17th Year

Since 1999, hundreds of thousands of Falun Gong practitioners in China have been incarcerated. According to the Falun Gong Information Center, to date, there are over 3,800 confirmed deaths from torture and abuse. This is a conservative number. The real figure is unknown and very likely to be much, much higher. Data collected indicate three common causes of death. The first is death from torture, beatings, and forced-feeding; the second is death from exhaustion, malnutrition, and neglect in forced labor camps, where Falun Gong practitioners are forced to work up to 20 hours a day. The third and the most sinister way of killing of Falun Gong practitioners is the grisly death from forced live organ pillaging and illegal organ removal for profit.

To destroy evidence, police and prison guards often report Falun Gong deaths from torture as suicide and cremate the bodies immediately without proper procedures or identification. Falun Gong practitioners were illegally detained and sent to different forced labor camps across China—like the infamous Masanjia Labor Camp that was dubbed

'Hell on Earth.' It was from this camp that an SOS letter from an incarcerated Falun Gong practitioner found its way into the home of a US citizen in 2013, inside a packet of Halloween decorations. The handwritten note was one of 20 letters written by a Falun Gong practitioner appealing to the recipient of the letter to forward it to an international human rights organization.

Allegations have emerged about the Chinese regime's involvement in live organ harvesting from Falun Gong practitioners and selling the human organs for profit to rich Chinese and unwitting foreigners (Fernandez, 2012; Fernandez et al., 2012; Gutmann, 2014; Matas & Kilgour, 2006, 2007, 2009; Matas & Trey, 2012). Although the numbers are difficult to verify, Ethan Gutmann (2014) indicated in his book *The Slaughter* that the figure could be that over 65,000 prisoners of conscience—mostly Falun Gong practitioners—were killed for their organs from 2000 to 2008.

However, a report by The World Organization to Investigate the Persecution of Falun Gong (WOIPFG) indicated that the numbers of Falun Gong practitioners killed for organs could be staggeringly higher. The WIOPFG report stated that "by September 2014, roughly 176,267 kidney transplants, 40,170 liver transplants, 1,928 heart transplants, and 137,294 corneal transplants were performed" (WOIPFG, 2014, p. 1). Before 2010, there was no voluntary organ donation program and almost no organ donors in China. According to WOIPFG's recent records, 865 hospitals were suspected of forced organ harvesting and by the end of December 2014, 712 of these hospitals that conducted liver and kidney transplants had performed about 400,000 cases of liver and kidney transplants (WOIPFG, 2015).

In response to the persecution and gross human rights violations, Falun Gong practitioners inside and outside of China have employed peaceful means to expose the truth about the Chinese Communist Party's unlawful persecution of innocent people for their beliefs.

Some of these ways have included setting up radio, newspaper, and television network; designing Internet software to break through blockage and censorship; and the publishing of the *"Nine Commentaries of the Chinese Communist Party"* (The Epoch Times, 2004a).

Falun Gong's Popularity

Despite the brutal persecution, Falun Gong practitioners in China and around the world continue to remain steadfast in their beliefs. Practitioners continue to clarify the truth and expose the CCP's crimes against innocent people for practicing Falun Gong and for believing in truthfulness, compassion, and forbearance. Seventeen years too long, but the practice has not lost its appeal. Outside of China, Taiwan has the largest number of practitioners. In 2012, more than 7,000 Falun Gong practitioners gathered in Taiwan for their annual conference to share the good things about the practice (Hedges & Trey, 2012). Annual conferences take place in Asia, Australia, Canada, Europe, UK, and different cities in the US.

For years, New York has been a popular destination for Falun Gong practitioners around the world. In May 2013, over 8,000 Falun Gong practitioners attended the New York conference, held at the indoor Izod Center in the Meadowlands Sports Complex, New Jersey, US. On May 13, 2014, more than 7,000 practitioners from over 50 countries gathered at the Brooklyn Barclays Center for the 18th New York Experience Sharing Conference. It was Mr. Li Hongzhi's birthday and the 22nd anniversary of Falun Gong's introduction to the public. For the first time, the 2014 New York annual sharing conference took place on a weekday so that more people could witness the grandeur and popularity of Falun Gong. Similarly, the English Minghui.org website reported about 8,000 Falun Gong practitioners from 50 countries convened at the Barclays Center in Brooklyn, New York, for the May 2015 conference.

Practitioners from all over the world doing Falun Gong Exercise Two at Union Square. New York, US. May 2014.

For many individuals, the practice's powerful healing potential was what had initially attracted them to Falun Gong—because it works! Due to their personal health and medical conditions, many like Barbara decided to try Falun Gong. These individuals not only recovered from their health conditions but also found their life changed dramatically. A Chinese Falun Gong practitioner at the 2012 Taiwan Falun Dafa experience sharing conference, was quoted saying, "I felt like I had been given new life, my whole body changed; previously my body had been in very bad shape" (Hedges & Trey, 2012). Another conference attendee, a Vietnamese practitioner, talked about how the practice had "changed everything in our attitude, in our thinking, our understanding, and in our relationships as well." Then she continued, "In everything that happens, I always think about others, about their feelings, how I impact others, and I change day by day" (Hedges & Trey, 2012).

The results from the Mainland Chinese surveys conducted before the persecution in 1999 indicated an overwhelming number of people regaining their health and wellness after they began practicing Falun Gong (Authors Unknown, 1999, 2002; Dan et al., 1998; Wang et al., 1998). Various literary sources also attributed the initial appeal of Falun Gong to its healing potential and health-wellness effects (Ackerman, 2005; Kutolowski, 2007; Ownby, 2001, 2008; S. J. Palmer, 2003; Porter, 2003; Pullen, 2000; Wang et al., 1998; Xie & Zhu, 2004; Yang & Nania, 2002; Zhang & Xiao, 1996). Findings from the Australian survey pointed toward similar positive responses. Thirty-one percent of Falun Gong respondents reported that their first attraction to Falun Gong was its physical and mental health benefits (Lau, 2010a).

This was how Barbara began her journey, after sustaining multiple injuries from a 23 feet (seven meters) fall. She had over a 100 stitches on her head and numerous metal screws, plates, and wires placed in her head, face, and hands. "My teeth were loosened and I needed braces to hold them together. My eyes were out of focus and looking in different directions. I lost hearing in my left ear and partial loss of feeling in my left hand," said Barbara. "My backbone was miraculously not broken but the spinal fluid was leaking from inside my head." Her girl friend—the one who had spoken to her about the practice before—once again suggested that she start practicing Falun Gong.

"This time, I said yes I have the time," said Barbara. "I was in a lot of physical pain. To relieve the pain, I had to take painkillers and apply cortisone cream every couple of hours. I was willing to try anything!" Encouraged by her friend, she started the exercises first and felt the immediate effects. "I could feel things moving in my body, strong tingling sensations, as if everything was connecting in my body. It was a warm, pleasant sensation. It was amazing," described Barbara. "I realized then that it was something powerful and special."

Falun Gong's popular appeal lies in its effectiveness. Barbara's remarkable recovery happens to other individuals. The results from the Australian survey indicated similar experiences of Falun Gong practitioners recovering from various illnesses and medical conditions. In our modern Internet age, more people are taking charge of their own health and wellness. They are seeking answers, instead of relying on the doctor for all their health needs. When they have health concerns, they search on the Internet and look for ways to alleviate their condition. The Falun Gong official website, http://en.minghui.org/cc/17/, lists many personal accounts from people who have regained health and wellness after starting the practice. These reports included accounts of individuals recovering from different severe and often untreatable medical conditions, such

Australian practitioners celebrate World Falun Dafa Day with a rally and a parade starting from Hyde Park and ending in Chinatown. Sydney, Australia. May 9, 2015.

as bladder cancer, esophageal cancer, late stage colon cancer, brain tumor, diabetes, and kidney diseases.

Today, despite the persecution, Falun Gong practitioners in China continue to practice and hold onto their beliefs. Once people personally experience the health-wellness effects of Falun Gong, they feel immense gratitude and continue with the practice. As Barbara said, "Falun Gong is magical: It's something you cannot explain with words." Her suggestion for anyone even remotely interested is to try it—because if you don't try, you will never know.

A teacher showing school children how to do Falun Gong Exercise One during an annual summer vacation camp. Benares, India. June 2012.

CHAPTER 5

Related Literature Review

Barbara's 23 feet fall had compelled her to try Falun Gong. Before that and, like the author-researcher, Barbara was practicing yoga. Art was her passion, family her devotion, and yoga a means to establish balance in her busy lifestyle. Not surprisingly, some readers have tried meditation, yoga, mindfulness exercises, or other forms of meditative practices. Yet, it does not matter whether or not we have tried any of these practices, most of us have heard or read about the effects of meditation. This chapter offers an overview of the historical contexts and trends in meditative practices—their role, effects, and relevance to the counseling community, and to show that these practices can play a beneficial role in the health and well-being of individuals.

When speaking of meditation, it can mean various things, including contemplation, relaxation, focusing the mind on nothing or on one thought or an object, or emptying one's thoughts, maintaining awareness, equanimity, or a different state of consciousness. Today, there are many different meditation practices available to the public and a growing number of people are turning to meditation for mind-body and spiritual health and wellness. According to the Merriam-Webster online dictionary, meditation is "the act or process of spending time in quiet thought." It is simple and can be done anywhere. There is no need for any special or expensive equipment; a quiet or natural setting will suffice. For Falun Gong, all that is needed is a mat and maybe a set of earphones for the exercise instruction music, depending on where we choose to do the meditation.

The term 'meditation' includes a range of Eastern "meditative movement" (C. E. Rogers, Larkey, & Keller, 2009, p. 246) practices and Eastern spiritual cultivation disciplines. Also described as mind-body techniques, these practices often combine physical movement or postures with breathing, relaxation, and meditation. Since the 1970s, trends towards wider acceptance of Eastern meditative movement practices and cultivation systems in the counseling context have been evolving. Due to a paucity of research on the health-wellness effects of Falun Gong, the literature review for the Australian survey included the effects of meditation and other Eastern meditative movement practices, such as yoga, tai chi, and qigong.

Historical Contexts, Trends in Meditative Practices

An increasing number of counselors, medical practitioners, and other healthcare professionals recognize the therapeutic potential and benefits of Eastern meditative practices (Atwood & Maltin, 1991; Bogart, 1991; Carpenter, 1977; Easton, 2005; Goleman, 1976; Marlatt & Kristeller, 1999; McCown, 2004; Ospina et al., 2008; Perez-De-Albeniz & Holmes, 2000; Schopen & Freeman, 1992; Shallcross, 2012; Singer, 2006; Walsh, 1989; Walsh & Vaughan, 1993). An article in *Counseling Today*, a publication of the American Counseling Association (ACA), noted that counselors and counseling educators see the beneficial effects of blending Eastern meditative practices with Western counseling techniques (Shallcross, 2012).

Integration practice is not new. During the past four decades, many transpersonal counselors and health professionals explored ways to blend these Eastern meditative practices with Western approaches. Today, this trend is happening in hospitals, clinics, community centers, and even certain businesses like health resorts, spas, and health, fitness, or wellness centers. Many progressive health and wellness service providers are encouraging people to meditate to feel good, cope with stress, manage physical pain, as well as emotional and mental strain associated with different medical conditions.

Gone are the days when meditation is only for a trifling minority of the elite echelon of society or the hippies pursuing unconventional alternative therapies. Most of us would know someone, or have heard, or seen someone practice some form of meditative practice. People are more open to explore new ways of coping, enhance wellness, and seek meaning in life. Various studies have indicated that most people turn to meditation and other mind-body therapies, not because of their dissatisfaction with conventional medicine, but because the philosophies and morals of these practices resonate with their values, beliefs, and attitudes towards a wellness lifestyle (Astin, 1998; Gordon & Edwards, 2005; Wu et al., 2007). While the ancient mystics sought these practices mainly for transcendental cultivation, many individuals today use meditative practices as a self-help, self-regulation strategy for overall mind-body and spiritual improvement. Economic consideration could be another reason for this trend as the bulk of the population is ageing and many meditative practices are either free or less costly than conventional medical care. They are also less invasive and generally have fewer side effects than drugs or conventional medical treatment. Others are attracted to these practices because of their wide-ranging psycho-physiological benefits, which include positive states of mind, such as equanimity, tranquility, joy, and peace that busy individuals with stressful lifestyles are seeking.

Within the counseling and psychotherapy traditions, these meditative practices have been described as "esoteric traditions" (Carpenter, 1977, p. 394), "Eastern psychologies" (Fadiman & Frager, 1994, p. 503), "Asian psychotherapies," "Asian psychologies," or "Asian psychology" (Goleman, 1976, p. 42; Walsh, 1989, p. 547). Meditation became an integral part of transpersonal psychology and counseling as early as the

1970s. Walsh and Vaughan considered meditation as the "royal road to the transpersonal" (1993, p. 47), a technique for transcending, or "going beyond the individual or personal to encompass wider aspects of humankind, life, psyche, and cosmos" (Walsh & Vaughan, 1993, p. 3). These are noteworthy statements about meditation enhancing wellness and taking individuals beyond their being.

Numerous studies explored the efficacy and use of various types of Eastern meditative practices in professional and healthcare settings. One review focusing on studies completed over 25 years showed that meditation is beneficial for older adults (Lindberg, 2005). These simple, low-cost, or free Eastern meditative practices help to provide solace, enhance mind-body health and wellness, and even promote positive ageing that drugs attempt to do with higher costs and often with undesirable side effects. Meditation could help to ease anxiety, lessen despair, offer hope, and enhance self-esteem for older people living in nursing homes (Lindberg, 2005). Another team of researchers recognized that meditation could promote better health and wellness. They reviewed 400 studies across five Eastern meditative practices, namely mantra meditation, mindfulness meditation, yoga, tai chi, and qigong (Ospina et al., 2008). The researchers concluded that future studies on meditation need more rigors in design, implementation, execution, scrutiny, and presentation of findings.

The Role of Meditation in Helping Professions

The role and use of meditation in counseling and psychotherapy pioneered in the 1970s (Marlatt & Kristeller, 1999) focused on using meditation to manage anxiety, physical and psychological distress. Meditation was recommended as a lifestyle change to achieve harmony in our daily life. One author noted that Buddhism, with its emphasis on compassion, inspired the integration of meditation with psychotherapy and counseling practices (Carpenter, 1977). What amplified the momentum for the integration of meditation with counseling and psychotherapy was when the American Psychological Association (APA) recognized the supportive and beneficial role of meditation in the therapeutic process in 1977 (Schopen & Freeman, 1992; Singer, 2006). By the 1980s, meditation was widely used as an adjunct to counseling and psychotherapy in the West (Delmonte, 1985). It began to play an increasing role in the counseling profession. Many writers observed that more counselors, therapists, and other health care professionals began to integrate Eastern meditative approaches with Western practices as they realized the beneficial effects of meditation (Atwood & Maltin, 1991; Bogart, 1991; Carpenter, 1977; Goldberg, 1982; Goleman, 1976; Goleman & Gurin, 1993; Marlatt & Kristeller, 1999; Schopen & Freeman, 1992; Shallcross, 2012; Singer, 2006; Walsh, 1989; Walsh & Bugental, 2005).

While Jungian and psychoanalytic therapists challenged the use of meditation, transpersonal therapists argued in favor of meditation (Bogart, 1991). Transpersonal therapists believe the beneficial effects of meditation far outweigh any perceived notions against its integration with psychotherapy and counseling practices. Walsh and Vaughan (1993) stated that meditation complements and transforms the therapeutic intervention for both the therapist and the client. They explained that meditation could cultivate calmness and equanimity, enhance empathy, offer greater understanding of the mental process and pathological conditions, and hence provide greater insight into the nature of the mind and other transpersonal experiences. Schopen and Freeman (1992) went further to state that meditation could replace counseling "as a healing force or change agent for certain clients" (p. 5). The two described meditation as a 'meta-therapy' that can reduce stress and tension, elicit relaxation, and support insights gained from talk therapy. Hence, meditation can be a useful self-help technique for clients between appointments.

One of the pioneers of mind-body medicine and the first Western-trained medical doctor to blend meditation with medicine is cardiologist Dr. Herbert Benson, founder of the Mind-body Medical Institute at Massachusetts General Hospital in Boston. Benson is the originator of the Relaxation Response, a scientific definition for meditation. His mind-body research focuses on how meditation can play an important role in reducing and managing stress. Other pioneers in the field of mind-body medicine include Dr. Joan Borysenko, author of *Mind the body, mending the mind*, and Dr. Jon Kabat-Zinn, creator of the Mindfulness-based Stress Reduction (MBSR) program (Shapiro, Schwartz, & Bonner, 1998). Kabat-Zinn is the founder of the Stress Reduction Clinic and Center for Mindfulness in Medicine, Health Care, and Society at the University of Massachusetts Medical School. He integrated meditation into his MBSR program—removing its Buddhist context and combined it with yoga breathing techniques.

Similarly, Dr. Russell D'Souza, former director of Clinical Trials and Bipolar Program at the Northern Psychiatry Research Centre of Melbourne pioneers the integration of spirituality in psychiatry and mental health in Australia. D'Souza (2007) highlighted the positive role and application of spirituality in medical practice and offered suggestions on how to approach the topic of spirituality with patients. Another advocate of mind-body meditation is cardiovascular surgeon, author, and television personality Dr. Mehmet Oz. Oz (2003) has integrated meditation with surgical intervention for heart surgery patients, stating that often the best healing intervention dwells in the mind. He referred to a study showing how 15 minutes of meditation twice a day could reduce medical visits over a six-month period—a cost saving of US$200 per person.

Effects of Meditation

Many studies that explore the effects of meditation have indicated the potential benefits of using meditation as a form of mind-body medicine. It has been noted that meditation could help one to attain inner peace and put one on the path to wellness when we feel stressed, anxious, nervous, tense, or worried, and more people today are seeking meditation to manage stress and ease their stress-related health problems. Earlier research shows meditation has physiological, behavioral, and psychological effects and there is evidence that the mind can influence the body and affects one's health (Goleman & Gurin, 1993; Pelletier, 2002; Selhub, 2007). The benefits of meditation include reduced anxiety, reduced substance abuse, hormonal and metabolic changes, lower heart rate and blood pressure, and better muscle relaxation (Delmonte, 1985; Perez-De-Albeniz & Holmes, 2000). A more recent systematic review of over 200 articles reiterated the effectiveness of meditative practices in reducing anxiety (K. W. Chen et al., 2012). Other beneficial effects of meditation included increased positive emotions and positive thoughts (Easton, 2005; Fredrickson, 2000; Lemonick, 2005; Wallis, 2005), higher dopamine levels (Kjaer et al., 2002), changes in brain and immune function (Davidson et al., 2003), and changes in body temperature (Crombie, 2002).

There is increasing research evidence to show that regular meditation can influence brain plasticity, leading to changes in brain structure (Lazar et al., 2005; Ricard, Lutz, & Davidson, 2014) and that neuroplasticity could help to delay ageing. In a follow-up study, one group of researchers was able to prove that meditation produces changes in the brain structure (Holzel et al., 2010; Holzel et al., 2011). They found participants who meditated for 30 minutes daily for eight weeks had measurable changes in gray-matter density in the areas of the brain linked with learning, memory, sense of self, empathy, and stress (Holzel et al., 2010; Holzel et al., 2011; McGreevey, 2012). Magnetic resonance image (MRI) brain scans taken by Holzel's team before and after the eight-week meditation program showed increased density of gray matter in the hippocampus. This is the part of the brain for learning and memory. Findings from a second team of researchers indicated that meditation can rewire and change the human brain circuits to produce beneficial effects for overall mind-body health and wellness (Ricard et al., 2014). This scientific evidence indicates that the adult brain is malleable and can be transformed through a process called neuroplasticity.

Two concepts that support the therapeutic effects of meditation are Benson's relaxation response (Crombie, 2002; Jacobs, 2001) and Wolpe's principle of reciprocal inhibition (Goleman, 1976). According to Benson, meditation produces a beneficial physiological state that he describes as the relaxation response (Crombie, 2002; Jacobs, 2001). This relaxation response elicited by meditation helps to lower and regulate blood pressure, metabolism, breathing, and heart rate (Crombie, 2002). US psychologist Joseph Wolpe (1958) conceived the principle of reciprocal inhibition, which forms the basis of modern behavioral self-regulation techniques. Wolpe postulated that an opposite and positive response could remove or replace a negative response, which means that a healthy and positive response, like meditation, can replace a negative emotion or an unhealthy state of mind (Bogart, 1991; Goleman, 1976; Goleman & Gurin, 1993). Hence, negative and unhealthy mental states, such as anxiety, envy, egoism, selfishness, and worry can be replaced with positive and healthy mental states, like compassion, happiness, insight, joy, mindfulness, modesty, and open-mindedness (Goleman, 1976, pp. 43-44).

Despite its many benefits, meditation may not be ideal for everyone. It may be unsuitable for people with serious mental health issues, acute emotional problems, and challenging obsessive-compulsive behaviors (Goldberg, 1982; Goleman, 1976; Schopen & Freeman, 1992). Likewise, Falun Gong teachings mentioned contraindications and those with serious illnesses should seek medical treatment. The practice is unsuitable for people with psychosis and other mental health problems, such as schizophrenia, bi-polar or manic-depressive disorder. It is not suitable for people prone to delusions, hallucinations, incoherence, and distortions in perceptions of reality. In *Zhuan Falun*, it is stated that a person with mental illness is "like a person who can never take charge of himself" (H. Li, 2001d, p. 219). When a person cannot take charge of himself, the unconscious mind and other environmental factors will disturb him, making it difficult for him to maintain a strong conscious mind or to be mindfully aware that he is cultivating. Practitioners of Falun Gong have to be mindfully aware that they are cultivating because the practice cultivates the conscious mind. This requires the conscious mind to be strong and mindfully aware. However, a person with a serious mental illness tends to have a weak conscious mind and hence is often unable to maintain mindful awareness.

Effects of Other Eastern Meditative Practices

The literature review for the Australian survey included studies on the effects of meditation and other similar Eastern practices, such as yoga, tai chi, and qigong (Lau, 2010a, 2010b). These practices share a common feature in that they include a meditative movement component, with slow and/or rhythmic exercises. Yoga, the Indian mystical way of life, is a mind-body practice (Atkinson & Permuth-Levine, 2009) that consists of three main aspects—postures, stretching and breathing techniques, and meditation. Tai chi and qigong are becoming increasingly popular in the West.

Today, yoga is often used in adjunct to mainstream treatments for different conditions. Many studies indicated the beneficial effects of yoga-based interventions for a variety of health and medical conditions (Atkinson & Permuth-Levine, 2009; Author Unknown, 2009; Carson et al., 2007; K. Chen et al., 2009; Danhauer et al., 2009; Khalsa, 2003, 2004; Singh, 2006; C. Smith, Mattner (Hancock), Blake-Mortimer, & Eckert, 2007). Yoga was found to be beneficial for anxiety disorders, carpal tunnel syndrome, increased self-awareness and enhanced well-being, musculoskeletal problems, pain relief, and stress reduction (Girodo, 1974). Findings from a randomized comparative study of yoga and relaxation demonstrated that yoga was as efficient as relaxation for reducing anxiety and stress, and for enhancing the general health status of respondents (C. Smith et al., 2007). One systematic review of randomized controlled trials (RCT) found no firm conclusion on the efficacy of yoga-based interventions (Ospina et al., 2008). However, a more recent systematic review of RCT studies found evidence supporting the efficacy of yoga for depression, sleep disorders, and other mental health disorders (Balasubramaniam, Telles, & Doraiswamy, 2013). Researchers noted that yoga seemed to attract younger, professional, and more educated white middle-class individuals (Skoro-Kondza, Tai, Gadelrab, Drincevic, & Greenhalgh, 2009).

Various studies indicated that the use of yoga and other mind-body therapies was linked with different socio-demographic factors. These include age (Wu et al., 2007), ethnicity (Barnes, Powell-Griner, McFann, & Nahin, 2004; Wu et al., 2007), higher education level (Astin, 1998; Barnes et al., 2004; Mehta, Phillips, Davis, & McCarthy, 2007; Upchurch et al., 2007; Wu et al., 2007), income, and employment status (Upchurch et al., 2007; Wu et al., 2007). Women were more inclined than men to use mind-body therapies and to partake in yoga and other meditative movement practices (Barnes et al., 2004; Mehta et al., 2007; Upchurch et al., 2007).

Tai chi is a traditional Chinese form of exercise that integrates breathing techniques with rhythmic, continuous, dance-like movements (Sandlund & Norlander, 2000). Legend has it that Zhang Sanfeng, a 12th century Taoist monk, created and developed tai chi as a self-defense form of martial art. Tai chi is often described as a moving meditation or a form of "meditative movement" (C. E. Rogers et al., 2009, p. 246) practice that involves moderate movements with breathing techniques and mental focus (NCCIH, 2009a). It is entrenched in traditional Chinese Taoist philosophy, yin-yang theory, and vital energy flow.

Today, tai chi has been 'diluted' to a form of gentle exercise more popular for older people. Considered a form of qigong, tai chi is popular with older people in China, Asia, and other parts of the world. It is often used as an adjunct to conventional treatment.

Many studies found tai chi therapeutic for older adults (Hogan, 2005; Sandlund & Norlander, 2000). These benefits include muscle relaxation, better balance, fewer falls, decrease in anxiety and fear of falling, greater flexibility, normalized blood pressure, and positive emotions. Findings from a review of 36 RCTs involving nearly 3,800 respondents suggested that both tai chi and qigong practices are beneficial for older adults (C. E. Rogers et al., 2009). However, the spirituality and health-wellness link—a vital aspect of these Eastern meditative practices and one that plays an critical role in positive ageing—is missing from these studies (C. E. Rogers et al., 2009).

Findings also suggested that, given its potential benefits and low-cost, tai chi can improve quality of life, boost resilience, and offer medical cost-saving benefits for the ageing population (F. Li, McAuley, Harmer, Duncan, & Chaumeton, 2001; Voukelatos, Cumming, Lord, & Rissel, 2007). Some researchers found tai chi to be one of the least costly and most cost-effective fall prevention programs for older adults (Frick, Kung, Parrish, & Narrett, 2010). The results from these studies seem to indicate that virtually all seniors could benefit from this low impact traditional Chinese exercise.

Qigong is an ancient Chinese self-healing art that is considered a branch of traditional Chinese medicine. It is a generic term referring to the different schools, styles of traditional Chinese form of energy exercises, and meditative movement practices. In the 1980s escalating interest in qigong as a practice for health and wellness maintenance flourished in China where many qigong masters began to teach a variety of qigong styles in public (Ownby, 2008; D. Palmer, 2007; Xu, 1999).

Studies on qigong suggested the practice has beneficial effects and health-wellness potential (Leung & Singhal, 2004; C. E. Rogers et al., 2009; Sancier, 1996, 1999). There were numerous surveys conducted in China exploring the effects of qigong, but few were empirical studies (Sancier, 1999). Due to translation problems, limited study details, and few suitable journals, very few of these Chinese studies were published (Sancier, 1996). Moreover, these Chinese studies failed to meet Western scientific standards. One researcher elaborated that the conflict lies in applying a Western scientific research model to the study of qigong, a holistic, Eastern meditative movement practice based on the philosophy of the intangible flow of energy that is beyond the realm of empirical science (Ai, 2003). She proposed applying the wellness model to future qigong studies for a more holistic evaluation.

The beneficial effects of qigong include relief from premenstrual syndrome symptoms, anxiety, pain, and general discomfort. Researchers who reviewed RCT studies exploring the effects of qigong for older adults found significant physical health improvement and less conclusive psychological effects (C. E. Rogers et al., 2009). Nonetheless, the cost-saving factor and potential to help reduce individual and public health costs are among the many attractive benefits of qigong. Because of its health benefits and comparatively low-cost, some researchers proposed health workers to recommend qigong as a self-intervention program. On a lighter tone, in one of Oprah Winfrey's 2007 shows, heart surgeon and television personality Dr. Oz said, "If you want to be healthy and live to a hundred, do qigong."

CHAPTER 6

Research on the Effects of Falun Gong

The mini general literature review in the previous chapter provides a smorgasbord of the vast amount of literature on the research done on meditation and other types of Eastern meditative approaches. Numerous studies demonstrated the beneficial effects of these meditative practices. Since there is little empirical research exploring the health-wellness effects of Falun Gong, it was helpful to examine what others have done in similar areas.

Currently, research exploring the health-wellness effects of Falun Gong is still in its infancy. It is inspiring to read Barbara's story and accounts of other people's healing experiences with Falun Gong; and it is also significant to know there are emerging studies showing the positive effects of practicing of Falun Gong. This chapter takes you back and through the labyrinth of research again. However, this time it is to offer an overview of the studies exploring the health-wellness effects of Falun Gong.

Studies on Falun Gong can be broadly classified into three phases. The first phase describes the Chinese health surveys conducted in

China before the onset of persecution. The second phase refers to the studies that mushroomed outside of China after the onset of the Chinese Communist Party's persecution of Falun Gong started in 1999. While this second phase was not focused on the health effects of the practice, most studies indicated that the healing benefits of the practice were an initial attraction. The third or emergent phase of Falun Gong studies included recent university-affiliated health-wellness studies.

Before 1999, when Falun Gong was at the height of its popularity in China, several health surveys were conducted in different regions of China (Author Unknown, 1998; Authors Unknown, 2002; Dan et al., 1998; Porter, 2003; Wang et al., 1998; Zhang & Xiao, 1996). Findings from these health surveys indicated the healing potential of Falun Gong and that practitioners came from all strata of society (Authors Unknown, 2002; Zhang & Xiao, 1996). More than 62 percent of respondents were over 50 years old and there were more female respondents than male (Authors Unknown, 2002).

Data from the Chinese surveys in China are consistent with other reports indicating that more women than men reported using mind-body therapies (Barnes et al., 2004; Lau, 2010a; Upchurch et al., 2007). Women are more receptive to the benefits of integrating mind-body practices with conventional medical treatment and more willing to try something different (Upchurch et al., 2007). Likewise, data from over seven decades of Gallup surveys found women to be more inclined to higher religiosity/spirituality than men (Gallup Jr., 2002; Winseman, 2002a, 2002b, 2003). Women tend to be more religious, more spiritually committed than men (Gallup Jr., 2002; Winseman, 2002a, 2002b, 2003). More women are inclined to use mind-body therapies, practice yoga, and other meditative movement practices (Barnes et al., 2004; Mehta et al., 2007; Upchurch et al., 2007), which suggest the propensity for more female involvement in Falun Gong.

Surveys Conducted in China

Before the persecution started, several large-scale health surveys were conducted in China. Because of Falun Gong's rapid growth rate and its beneficial health-wellness effects, the practice caught the attention and scrutiny from both the medical community and the Chinese Communist Party. In 1998, one year before the persecution began, researchers from several local medical organizations were curious about Falun Gong's health-wellness efficacy. They decided to conduct five separate health surveys in Beijing area, Wuhan, Dalian, and Guangdong province (Authors Unknown, 2002). The results from their studies showed that a whooping 98 percent of respondents from these surveys indicated significant health improvements (Authors Unknown, 2002).

More than 90 percent of the total number of respondents (n=31,000) reported suffering from different illnesses before practicing Falun Gong and over 70 percent experienced "complete or near-complete" recovery from their medical conditions (Authors Unknown, 2002). Researchers were confounded to find that many respondents reported full recovery from various kinds of diseases that medical doctors had diagnosed as serious, difficult to treat, life-threatening, or terminal diseases. Over 82 percent, or more than 28,000 respondents, reported full recovery and general good health-wellness outcomes (Authors Unknown, 2002). And 87 percent of respondents from the Beijing and Guangzhou surveys reported an enhancement in their moral character (Authors Unknown, 2002). Their findings concluded that Falun Gong helped respondents to achieve overall mind-body and spiritual health and wellness.

The Chinese surveys also highlighted the medical/health cost saving potential of Falun Gong. Respondents reported a reduction in medical care spending. This remains a thought-provoking subject as the bulk of the population is ageing and rising medical and healthcare costs have become not only a growing concern for people but also for the country. Falun Gong's healing benefits offered a beacon of hope for many Chinese people, particularly those diagnosed with serious and incurable diseases. Respondents reported remarkable health recovery and savings in health and medical expenses after they started the practice (Dan et al., 1998; Life and Hope Renewed, 2005; Wang et al., 1998; Zhang & Xiao, 1996).

According to the reports from Chinese health surveys, the total medical health care cost savings for Falun Gong respondents was about 70 million Yuan per year, about US$10.6 million, or 2,600 Yuan (US$395) in savings for each Falun Gong respondent (Authors Unknown, 2002, p. 6). (US currency is based on January 2016 exchange rate.) Findings from the Chinese health surveys thus indicated Falun Gong's health cost-saving potential and economic benefits for the individual and the society. However, a lack of uniformity in methodology across these surveys made consolidation of the data difficult.

Studies Outside China

After the onset of persecution on July 20, 1999, it was no longer possible to conduct further research in China. The second phase of Falun Gong research occurred in Canada and the US. In October 1999, a team of Falun Gong practitioners from Canada and the US conducted one of the first known health surveys outside of China, setting a landmark for future health-wellness Falun Gong studies (Authors Unknown, 2003a, 2003c). Their findings provided interesting insights and information on the demographics of the Falun Gong people and the health-wellness effects of the practice. See Table 1 at the end of the chapter for an overview of Falun Gong studies outside China.

These earlier studies showed that Falun Gong practitioners were mainly Chinese, with barely a handful of Westerners. For instance,

Burgdoff's (2003) study indicated that 90 percent of respondents were ethnically Chinese, while Lowe's (2003) Internet survey showed that 98 percent of Falun Gong respondents (n=83) were well-educated Chinese intellectuals. Likewise, Ownby and S. Palmer found that there were 91 percent Chinese and only 9 percent Westerners in their field studies. Falun Gong was described as "unabashedly Chinese" and "overwhelmingly Chinese" (Ownby, 2003b, p. 308). The majority of Falun Gong respondents from these field studies were wealthy, well educated, married Chinese women.

According to Ownby (2008), the typical Falun Gong practitioner is "young, urban, dynamic, a successful recent immigrant largely living the American dream" (p. 138). The average age of these respondents was 40 years old, younger than the respondents in the Chinese studies in China. Ownby (2003b) described Falun Gong in Canada as a "bourgeois movement" and the typical practitioner "lives in the suburbs and drives a Ford Taurus to her job in computers or finance" (p. 312). Likewise, findings from the 1999 survey by North American Falun Gong practitioners indicated that 97 percent of Falun Gong respondents were either Chinese or Asians. They were young, well educated, with the majority working in computer and information technology professions (Authors Unknown, 1999, 2003a). Porter's (2003) field study also showed North American practitioners as younger than mainland Chinese practitioners, with 62 percent under 39 years old.

A relatively unknown Taiwanese study (Lio et al., 2003) found Falun Gong respondents to be physically and mentally healthier than the general Taiwan population. Findings from this study showed that Falun Gong was able to help respondents get rid of unhealthy and addictive lifestyle habits, such as gambling, cigarette smoking, alcohol consumption, and chewing betel nuts—a popular habit in Asian countries. The Taiwanese study also highlighted the medical cost-saving potential of the practice. It indicated a 50 percent reduction in the use of medical health insurance for Falun Gong respondents

Over 7,000 Falun Gong practitioners attend the Taiwan annual Falun Dafa experience sharing conference. Practitioners sat in meditation to create a Falun emblem formation. The emblem has four Taoist yin-yang symbols and five Buddhist swastikas or traditional Chinese symbols of good fortune. Taipei, Taiwan. November 2012.

(Authors Unknown, 2003b). Findings indicated that the beneficial effects of Falun Gong correspond with the number of years of practice. This means that the longer a person practices Falun Gong, the better his or her health is, and the less the person spends on medical care.

There were two other small-scale studies. The first was a phenomenological study on how Falun Gong enabled a US health professional to recover from work-related burnout (Lau, 2001). The second referred to a Russian study involving 12 Falun Gong respondents with different medical conditions, in which medical results for all respondents showed normal blood and urine tests and no signs of the diagnosed conditions. The health improvement rate was 75 percent (Author Unknown, 2003).

All studies exploring the health-wellness effects of Falun Gong share one common characteristic, that is, respondents reported health and wellness improvements after starting the practice. Therefore, what initially attracted many individuals to the practice was its healing potential. For instance, Ownby's (2008) study reported that health benefit was the third most frequent response for respondents' attraction to Falun Gong. Porter's (2003) study indicated that Falun Gong had led to a health improvement for many respondents. Lowe's (2003) Internet survey also showed that one of most common reasons for people to start the practice was its healing benefit.

However, Falun Gong practitioners stated that they later realized the importance of focusing on spiritual cultivation, moral character development, and less on the healing benefits of the practice. This is quite natural and the same for Barbara who went through the same process of later understanding that Falun Gong is not just about healing illness and keeping fit. Practitioners later realized that the health benefit of Falun Gong is an inconsequential outcome of the practice and that the ultimate goal of the practice is not for health and wellness but to achieve overall mind-body and spiritual enlightenment through moral character improvement.

There is one published peer-reviewed article of an evidence-based Falun Gong health study. A team of US medical doctors and researchers investigated the effects of Falun Gong on gene expression and the role of neutrophils in Falun Gong practitioners (Q. Li et al., 2005). They found superior gene expression, improved immunity, and longer lifespan of neutrophils in Falun Gong respondents compared to non-Falun Gong respondents. Their findings indicated that Falun Gong could influence gene expression, enhance immunity, balance metabolic rate, and promote cell regeneration.

University-Affiliated Studies

After the initial wave of studies that flourished outside of China, a new emerging phase developed as an offshoot from the second phase. The third phase of Falun Gong research comprised studies conducted under the auspices of universities—in Australia, Egypt, and the United States. These university-affiliated studies focused on the health effects of Falun Gong. The Australian survey was completed under the auspices of The University of South Australia (Lau, 2010a, 2010b), as a partial fulfillment for the requirements for the degree Doctor of Counseling. It investigated the health-wellness effects of Falun Gong as perceived by those who practice Falun Gong. The survey aimed to ascertain any observed differences or similarities between Falun Gong and non-Falun Gong individuals—whether those who practice Falun Gong experience better health and wellness than those who do not.

Likewise, Benjamin Bendig's (2013) double study was for the partial satisfaction of the requirements for the degree Doctor of Philosophy in psychology at the University of California, Los Angeles. His focus was on the cognitive and physiological effects of Falun Gong. In the first study, Bendig (2013) examined baseline cognitive, physiological, and psychological differences between veteran Falun Gong practitioners and novices. In the second, he assessed the cognitive, physiological, and psychological effects after respondents practiced Falun Gong for 91 minutes. Bendig's (2013) studies showed that Falun Gong was found to boost energy levels and enhance positive mood. His research indicated that regular Falun Gong practice elicits long-term psychological benefits, that the length of practice is linked with psychological effects, while the time spent on studying Falun Gong teachings is linked with improved sleep (Bendig, 2013).

In the Faculty of Physical Education at the Suez Canal University in Egypt, Yahiya (2010) conducted an experimental study exploring the effectiveness of Falun Gong exercises in relation to the Japanese

Children and adult practitioners doing the tranquil sitting meditation at the Manhattan Foley Square during World Falun Dafa Day Celebration. New York, US. May 2013.

martial art of judo. Findings from his study indicated that practicing Falun Gong exercises enhanced the psychological and performance skills for judo competitors (Yahiya, 2010). Both of these studies augment the Australian survey and other existing studies exploring the health-wellness effects of Falun Gong.

Despite few studies exploring the effects of Falun Gong, existing literature indicated that the practice offers beneficial and significant mind-body health-wellness improvements. This review of Falun Gong studies reveals a need for more research on the health-wellness aspects of Falun Gong. To date, the author is immersed in the *Hearts Uplifted* project that focuses on exploring the lived experiences of Falun Gong respondents. The project's aim is to document how Falun Gong people navigate major turning points in their life over a number of years, to gain a better insight into how they cope with their life's challenges, and how they handle these transitions. Hopefully this long-term study will unveil how the practice has helped the Falun Gong people to stay resilient and achieve greater mind-body and spiritual health and wellness.

Table 1
Falun Gong Studies Outside China

Study	Year	Sample	Gender	Ethnicity
Canada, US* (Authors Unknown)	1999-2000	235	M: 42%, 98 F: 58%, 137	Chinese: 97%, 226 Westerners: 3%, 7
Canada & US (Ownby & S. Palmer)	2000-2001	78	M: 44%, 34 F: 56%, 44	Chinese: 91%, 71 Westerners: 9%, 7
Internet Survey (Lowe)	2000	85	Not specified	Chinese[1]: 98%, 83 European: 1%, 1 American: 1%, 1
Adelaide, University of South Australia* (Lau)	2001	1	M: 1	Westerner: 1
Columbus, Ohio US (Burgdoff)	2001	89	Not specified	Chinese: 96%, 85 Westerner: 4%, 4
Moscow, Russia* (Guluoji et al)	2001	12	M: 33%, 4 F: 67%, 8	Not specified
Taiwan* (Lio et al)	2002	1,210	M: 40%, 485 F: 60%, 720	Not specified
Tampa, Florida, Washington DC, US* (Porter)	2003	53	M: 58%, 31 F: 42%, 22	Country of birth: China: 45.3%, 24 Taiwan: 9.4%, 5 US: 34%, 18 Other: 11.3%, 6
Texas, US (Li et al)	2005	12 FG: 6 NFG: 6	M: 50%, 3 F: 50%, 3 for both groups	Asian: 100%, 6 for both groups
Egypt, Suez Canal University (Yahiya)	2010	40	Not specified	Not specified
Adelaide,* University of South Australia (Lau) (The Australian survey)	2010	Total: 590 FG: 360 NFG: 230	M: 42%, 151 F: 57%, 206 Missing: 1%, 3 M: 35%, 81 F: 63%, 146 Missing: 2%, 3	[2]Chinese: 47%, 170 Caucasian: 24%, 88 Australian: 7%, 26 [2]Chinese: 27%, 63 Caucasian: 18%, 42 Australian: 23%, 53
Los Angeles, CA, US* University of California (Bendig)	2012	Study 1 FG: 17 NFG: 14 Study 2 FG: 18 NFG: 10	M: 6; F: 11 M: 10; F: 4 M: 7; F: 11 M: 5; F: 5	Asian: 11, White: 6 Asian: 3, White: 5 Other: 6 Asian: 12, White: 6 Asian: 4, White: 3 Other: 3
New York, NY, US* (Trey)	on-going	7	M: 2; F: 5	Caucasian: 5 Other: 2

M=male, F=female; FG=Falun Gong, NFG=Non-Falun Gong. *Studies exploring health-wellness effects. [1]Chinese from China, Malaysia, & Singapore; [2]Only three most frequently reported groups are included here.

CHAPTER 7

The Australian Survey

The Australian online survey is a pioneering study exploring the health and wellness effects of Falun Gong as perceived by practitioners (Lau, 2010a, 2010b). The study used a descriptive cross-sectional survey, with a mixed methods approach that is often used in counseling psychology and social science research (Hanson, Creswell, Clark, Petska, & Creswell, 2005; Miles & Huberman, 1994; Sandelowski, 2000). Like any descriptive cross-sectional survey, the aim is to describe what is and to collect data during a specified time. The survey method was used to obtain the demographic and health-wellness characteristics of Falun Gong people, their non-Falun Gong friends and family members. Age groups, gender, ethnicity, relationship status, education level, occupations, other demographic details, and their health-wellness reports were captured during a specified data collection period.

Self-reporting forms the basis of the Australian survey. This method of data collection is often used in social sciences and counseling research (Barker, Pistrang, & Elliot, 2005; Heppner, Kivlighan, & Wampold, 1999) to gather information and individual characteristics such as attitudes, behaviors, values, or beliefs of respondents. Self-reporting is practical, time-efficient, and convenient to use online because respondents can complete the survey privately and in their own time. It emphasizes the respondents' perceptions and involves self-assessment. Understandably, there will be concerns about data validity and reliability, arising from the possibility that respondents may not always be honest and truthful, and which could lead to under or over-reporting, distortion of the truth to create a positive or a better impression. More often than not, self-report surveys are designed to elicit honesty and spontaneity because respondents are actually more likely to tell the truth since participation is generally voluntary and anonymous.

Additionally, self-reporting focuses on the respondents' personal views, experiences, and offers meaningful information. It is valuable in counseling research. Just as the client's thoughts and feelings embody the heart of therapeutic interactions, in counseling research the respondents' perceptions of their own health-wellness status form the core of the study. In the Australian survey, self-reporting was used to provide information and understanding about Falun Gong respondents—their beliefs, behaviors, and health-wellness status.

The online survey is convenient to use with a large sample of respondents from different geographical locations. It was deemed the best way to reach out to potential Falun Gong respondents as the Internet is the fastest way to keep abreast with Falun Gong activities and to communicate with practitioners from different regions of the world. Frequently used in social sciences and counseling research, the online survey method helps to maintain "social distance" (Heerwegh, 2009, p. 112) and eliminate, to some extent, the influence of social desirability effects (Heerwegh, 2009; Tourangeau, Couper, & Steiger, 2003; VandenBos, 2007). The latter refers to the tendency for respondents to give answers that create a good impression.

Development Phase

This comprised the first phase in the Australian survey, which included development, data collection, and data processing phases. It included preparing research materials, selecting methodology, designing survey questions, and establishing a pilot study. This initial phase also involved an extensive literature review and the application for ethics approval with the University of South Australia's Human Research Ethics Committee (UniSA HREC).

Care was undertaken to ensure the research procedure adhered to the UniSA HREC's standards and also the *National Statement on Ethical Conduct in Human Research,* as stipulated by the Australian National Health and Medical Research Council to maintain research merit and integrity, justice, beneficence, and respect for research participants (NHMRC, 2007, pp. 12-13). This is because all human communications, including those in human research, carry ethical implications. UniSA HREC also recommended the involvement of Falun Dafa Associations and requested the author-researcher to seek a written letter of approval from the Australian Falun Dafa Associations for their support and permission to place the web links of the online surveys on Falun Gong websites.

During this phase, two research information documents were developed: Research Information Sheet (RIS) and the letter to Falun Gong practitioners, inviting them to participate in the online survey and to invite their non-Falun Gong family members, friends, or colleagues to do the same. The RIS gave an overview of the research, participation criteria, and instructions for respondents. Both documents were posted on Falun Gong websites and emailed to Falun Dafa Association chairpersons, pilot study members, regional Falun Gong contact persons, and coordinators of various Falun Gong projects in different parts of the world.

Two health surveys, one for Falun Gong respondents and the other for non-practitioners, were developed. Both surveys consisted of multiple-choice questions designed by the author-researcher and the SF-36 Health Survey (McHorney, Ware, Lu, & Sherbourne, 1994; Ware Jr., 2008; Ware Jr. & Sherbourne, 1992). The survey for Falun Gong respondents included an extra section with 21 questions about the practice. The versatile SF-36 Health Survey measures eight health-wellness concepts, including physical, mental, emotional, and social health and wellness, respondents' perceptions of their general health-wellness, and their vitality. Several items in the Australian survey had a text box option for written responses, which provided vital and interesting insights about respondents. It was for one of these questions that Respondent 289 (Barbara) wrote in detail about her multiple injuries, making the researcher wonder about her particular case.

A pilot study was done during the developmental phase. Its aim was to facilitate valuable feedback to refine the research tools. Members of the pilot study were veteran Falun Gong individuals from diverse educational and professional backgrounds, some of whom were key members of regional Falun Dafa associations. Geographically, they were from Australia, the United States, and the United Kingdom. What was meaningful was that feedback from the pilot study members were carefully balanced with those from non-Falun Gong people comprising university staff and doctoral counseling candidates.

Data Collection Phase

Data collection for the Australian survey lasted three months, with no maximum limit placed on the number of respondents. Participation was voluntary and open to Falun Gong practitioners who had engaged in regular exercise practice and study of the teachings for at least six months. Due to the Chinese regime's brutal persecution of Falun Gong practitioners in China and for security reasons, practitioners living in China were excluded from the Australian survey.

Although not a requisite for their participation, Falun Gong respondents were asked to invite their non-Falun Gong family members, friends, and colleagues to complete the second survey.

The criteria for non-Falun Gong people was that they must not be practicing any meditation or any other forms of meditative movement practices, such as yoga, tai chi, or qigong, during the six months before completing the survey. The two questionnaires were posted on the Australian Falun Dafa website, www.falunau.org, and their web links included in the Research Information Sheet (RIS) that was disseminated to Falun Gong coordinators in different regions. Potential respondents could visit the Australian website to complete the online survey, which took about 15 to 20 minutes. Total sample size of the Australian survey was 590. Included in the total was a sprinkling of hard copy submissions from Australia and the United States that found their way by mail to the researcher via the university address. Unfortunately, a few arrived after the expiration date and hence had to be excluded from the study.

Data Processing Phase

The final phase of the study included reporting, analysis, interpretation, and the presentation of the findings. Both quantitative and qualitative data were automatically saved in Microsoft Excel documents and manually transferred to the Statistical Package for Social Sciences (SPSS) software program. There were 360 Falun Gong respondents and 230 non-Falun Gong respondents. The unequal ratio between the two groups implied that either 130 Falun Gong respondents did not invite a non-Falun Gong respondent, or the person they had invited did not complete the survey. There could be different reasons for the discrepancy in the ratio. A plausible explanation would be that some Falun Gong respondents might not know any non-practitioners they felt comfortable to invite to participate in the non-Falun Gong survey. Since it was not mandatory to invite a non-Falun Gong respondent, there was no onus for Falun Gong respondents to find someone. Nonetheless, the discrepancy in numbers between the two groups did not influence the survey findings.

During data transfer, random audit checks were systematically conducted. These included horizontal column checks on every 20th respondent and vertical column scans for every 10th variable for both surveys. Data for both groups were further scrutinized using SPSS descriptive frequency audit checks. The quantitative and qualitative data were reported and analyzed separately. A few questions requesting written responses yielded interesting data. These were analyzed and interpreted following a three-level categorizing or clustering procedure used in qualitative content analysis (Miles & Huberman, 1994), and adapted by other researchers (Graneheim & Lundman, 2004; Hanson et al., 2005; Sharif & Masoumi, 2005).

Key findings from the Australian survey were presented at a conference for Australian Aboriginal counselors and health professionals in Cairns, Australia, in 2007. The presentation, *"Meditating to Optimize Health & Well-Being,"* highlighted Falun Gong as an alternative mind-body meditative movement practice. It explained how Falun Gong is relevant to the health and well being of the Australian Aboriginal people and drew the attention of Aboriginal health professionals who expressed keen interest to learn more about integrating Falun Gong with their work.

CHAPTER 8

The Falun Gong People

"Straight after I started practicing, I wanted to take all my friends and teach them Falun Gong—tell them how beautiful and profound it is," said Barbara. Her face lit up like a shining beacon against the calm, cerulean blue skies, as she reminisced her healing transformation with Falun Gong. Barbara's response is like many Falun Gong practitioners who have had a first-hand experience of the health and wellness benefits of the practice. It is natural that many Falun Gong people are more than happy to tell their story. So, who are the Falun Gong people?

According to Falun Gong sources, there were about 100 million people following the practice when the persecution started in 1999. Despite on-going persecution, threats, intimidations, and harassments, Falun Gong practitioners have not let up. In recent years, the Chinese regime has exported their persecution of Falun Gong overseas. This came in the form of interfering with Falun Gong activities in different regions of the world, such as Malaysia, Singapore, Vietnam, South Korea, Australia, and in the United States. For instance, Falun Gong practitioners had been harassed or assaulted while informing the public of the Chinese Communist Party's (CCP) persecution of Falun Gong practitioners in China, and while assisting Chinese people to quit the CCP (Philips, 2013). Attackers tried to disrupt the *tuidang* activities in Flushing Chinatown, New York. *Tuidang* means to quit the CCP or the Party in Chinese. It refers to the act of publicly renouncing the

CCP and its affiliate organizations—the Communist Young Pioneers and the Communist Youth League[1]. The attackers threw eggs, beat, spat, and cursed at Falun Gong practitioners who volunteered to help more Chinese people withdraw from the Party. According to Philips's article, the New York Chinese Consulate General admitted to orchestrating those attacks. Incidents of the CCP's exported persecution of Falun Gong also occurred in Australia, Canada, and other parts of the world. Nonetheless, Falun Gong practitioners outside of China and around the world continue to engage in peaceful activism to explain the truth about Falun Gong. They meditate and practice the exercises in public parks, sit quietly outside Chinese Embassies, or participate in marching bands and parades in major cities around the world.

Findings from the Australian survey painted an interesting profile of Falun Gong respondents outside of China. The typical Falun Gong practitioner is likely to be female—married, highly educated, and from any walk of life. Her occupation could vary from business, computer information technology, arts, media, social sciences, or clerical and administrative service work. The Australian survey indicated that Falun Gong respondents shared many identical characteristics with their non-Falun Gong friends and family members (Lau, 2010a, 2010b). Demographic data indicated that Falun Gong respondents were like their non-Falun Gong counterparts. Many have tertiary education and professional careers. They have families and occupations in society like non-Falun Gong people. However, when it came to their self-reported medical history, general health-wellness status, quality of life, and attitude towards life, there were differences and even sharp contrasts in some instances between the two groups.

Falun Gong respondents were more likely to report excellent health, no or little use of medication, and less medical and health expenses than non-Falun Gong respondents. They were more positive than

1   http://en.tuidang.org/introduction/what-is-tuidang.html

non-Falun Gong respondents about their own health-wellness status. Many of them reported significantly benefitting from the practice. For a spiritual meditation discipline that has attracted millions of followers, there must be convincing reasons for its popularity. Indeed, many Falun Gong respondents reported the promise of health benefits as one of the initial reasons that drew them to the practice.

Portrait of Falun Gong

The overall picture of Falun Gong respondents shows a community of optimistic and healthy individuals with careers or jobs, and who contribute to the wealth of their country of residence. Findings indicated that there were more female than male Falun Gong respondents: 57.2 percent (n=206) women, 42 percent (n=151) men, and three (0.8%) missing data. The average age range of Falun Gong respondents was around late thirties and forties. Those between 30 to 39 years old formed the largest age group, followed by respondents between 40 to 49 years and 50 to 59 years old respectively. The lowest numbers came from the youngest age range—those less than 20 years old. When asked to indicate their relationship status, nearly two-thirds of Falun Gong respondents (61%, n=218) were married. About 24 percent (n=85) were single and never married, while five respondents reported being in a de facto relationship and 11 percent stated they were divorced or separated at the time of the survey.

The demographic data from the Australian survey indicated that Falun Gong people from outside China came from diverse ethnic backgrounds; 37 ethnicities were identified. There were an African, an Albanian, an Australian Aborigine, two Maori, three Native North American Indians, two Turks, three Filipinos, four Jews, as well as Russian, Polish, and Spanish respondents. Others came from the Mediterranean and Scandinavian regions, India, and different parts of Asia, such as Japan, Korea, Malaysia, Indonesia, Singapore, and

Thailand. Some respondents identified themselves as Anglo-Celtic, Chinese-Vietnamese, Chinese-Korean, Eurasian, Hispanic, Papuan New Guinea, and Russian Slav. Chinese practitioners formed the largest group (47%, n=170), followed by Caucasians (24%, n=86). Seven percent or 26 respondents only identified themselves as Australians and hence it was not possible to establish their ethnic origin, that is, whether they were Aboriginal, Caucasian, Chinese, or other Asian residents of Australia.

The country of birth of Falun Gong respondents is as diverse as their ethnicity. Altogether, there were 45 different countries of birth, from seven continents or regions in the world. This consisted of Asia, Australia and New Zealand, China, Europe, Canada and the United States (US), South America, and the United Kingdom (UK). Asia comprised Indonesia, Malaysia, Singapore, Japan, Korea, Philippines, Taiwan, Thailand, and Vietnam. Europe comprised Austria, Belgium, Denmark, France, Germany, Holland, Italy, Spain, and Sweden. 'Others' included Albania, India, Israel, Libya, the Mediterranean, Mauritius, Poland, and Russia. The largest sub-group was those born in China (28%, n=97); followed by those born in Asia (24%, n=86). The third largest sub-group was those born in Australia and New Zealand (19%, n=68) (Lau, 2010a).

Findings indicated that Falun Gong respondents live in different regions around the world. There were 29 countries and regions identified—including Australia and New Zealand, Asia, Europe, North and South America. Despite this diversity, 75 percent of Falun Gong respondents (n=268) actually resided in two main regions of the world. The first region was Australia and New Zealand, the second Canada and the US. When asked to indicate if English was their first language, 35 percent of Falun Gong respondents (n=128) stated English was the language they grew up with as a child. About two-thirds (n=226) reported English was not their first language, while 44 percent (n=164) reported Mandarin or a

Chinese dialect—Cantonese, Foochow, Hakka, or Shanghainese—as their mother tongue.

The variety of languages respondents could speak reflected the ethnic diversity. Most Falun Gong respondents could speak a second or a third language fluently. The diversity of languages included an Australian Aboriginal language, African Igbo language, Marathi language, North American Native Navajo language, as well as Asian and European languages. The Asian languages were Indonesian, Malaysian, Japanese, Korean, Tagalog, Thai, and Vietnamese. European languages included Albanian, Creole, Croatian, Dutch, French, German, Greek, Hebrew, Hungarian, Italian, Lebanese, Norwegian, Polish, Portuguese, Spanish, and Turkish.

Demographic data from the Australian survey showed that most Falun Gong respondents were well educated: 63 percent (n=224) reported having tertiary qualifications. Thirty percent (n=107) had a Master's, Doctor of Philosophy (PhD), or Doctorate degrees (Lau, 2010a). They reported a variety of occupations, ranging from artistic, professional, executive and senior administrative positions, to being skilled or unskilled workers. To categorize the respondents' occupations in a systematic way, the Australian survey adopted the Australian and New Zealand Standard Classification of Occupations (ANZSCO), provided by the Australian Bureau of Statistics and Statistics New Zealand (ABS & SNZ, 2006).

More than 30 percent reported having a professional career. Over 15 percent (n=54) worked in the arts, media, social sciences, and other professional occupations, while another 15 percent (n=54) were business or computer IT professionals (Lau, 2010a). Clerks, salespeople, administrative, and service workers made up 13 percent of Falun Gong respondents (n=43), while another 13 percent (n=43) were retired or performing home duties. Over 8 percent (n=29) Falun Gong respondents were managers, senior administrators, and in the science, building, transport, and engineering industries. Skilled and unskilled laborers and the unemployed formed the smallest categories of Falun Gong respondents, comprising two percent and 2.5 percent respectively (Lau, 2010a).

Respondents were also asked to report their gross annual household income in their local currency. Due to huge gaps and differences in currency exchange rates, standards, and costs of living between different countries, it was not possible to make any useful interpretation or comparison. Nonetheless, their qualifications and occupations, to some extent, were indicative of their socio-economic status in their respective societies.

Their Health Wellness Status

The Australian survey asked respondents to report their medical history, such as the number of visits to the doctor, reasons for these visits, medication intake, and their medical and health expenses. This is because it is a reasonable belief that if one does not have to see a doctor, take prescription or over-the-counter drugs, one must be relatively healthy and well, more so than those on regular prescription drugs or those who visit the doctor frequently. Findings from the survey showed that Falun Gong respondents were healthy individuals, with healthy lifestyle habits. They reported a high quality of life and an optimistic outlook about life and their health and wellness. They did not smoke cigarettes, drink alcohol, use prescription, or recreational drugs, and hardly spend any money on medical and health expenses. About 90 percent of Falun Gong respondents (n= 316) reported they had not visited a doctor during the six months prior to completing the survey. Eight percent or 30 Falun Gong respondents visited a medical practitioner between one to three times; five went between four to six times and only three reported visiting a medical practitioner between seven to nine times during the six months prior to completing the survey. Those who visited a medical practitioner reported going for pregnancy or routine job-related medical check-ups.

The majority of Falun Gong respondents (95%, n=341) did not use any form of medication, over counter drugs, vitamins, and health supplements. Seven respondents reported using prescription drugs and only one took over-the-counter drugs, such as Aspirin and Panadol. One respondent opted for Western herbal remedies and homeopathic remedies, while five reported taking vitamins and health supplements. The majority of Falun Gong respondents (92%, n=330) did not spend much money on medical and health expenses. Only eight percent (n=30) stated they spent money on health and medical expenses. Of those who indicated having health and medical expenses, a few reported health insurance premiums as their only expense, which is unavoidable in Australia where it is mandatory for taxpayers to contribute to the Australian government public healthcare Medicare fund.

Lifestyle habits, such as cigarette smoking, alcohol intake, and recreational drug use are indicative of one's health. Respondents were asked to report on their usage and if they had plans to stop using these substances. Ninety-eight percent of Falun Gong respondents (n=352) reported not smoking any tobacco cigarettes. Of those who smoked tobacco cigarettes (n=68) before the practice, 82 percent (n=56) stated that they quit smoking after starting the practice. Less than 1.4 percent (n=5) reported still smoking cigarettes and two of these of five individuals planned to quit the habit. Similarly, 97 percent of Falun Gong respondents (n=349) reported not drinking any alcohol. Of those who reported consuming alcohol (n=174) before practicing Falun Gong, 97 percent (n=168) stopped alcohol consumption after they started the practice. About two percent (n=8) admitted to drinking alcohol across a range of amounts. Almost all Falun Gong respondents (99%, n=355) reported not taking any recreational drugs.

Quality of Life Reports

Findings from the Australian survey indicated that Falun Gong respondents experience a high quality of life. They perceived themselves as physically, mentally, and emotionally very healthy and well. They reported a positive and optimistic outlook of their health-wellness status. Fifty-four percent of Falun Gong respondents (n=192) indicated having excellent general health status. Nearly 90 percent (n=317) reported having either an excellent or very good general health status. Only one Falun Gong respondent indicated poor general health status. When asked about their general health one year ago, 28 percent (n=101) stated they were "much better" than a year ago, while 29 percent (n=105) reported being "somewhat better." However, one respondent reported being "much worse" in general health than a year ago.

Most Falun Gong respondents were able to engage in a variety of normal daily and social activities, ranging from vigorous, moderate, to light activities. Nearly 75 percent (n= 261) reported being able to perform various kinds of vigorous activities, such as running or lifting heavy objects. Over 90 percent (n=333) reported not being limited by their health to perform moderate activities like moving a small table, using a domestic vacuum cleaner, lifting or carrying groceries, or climbing one flight of stairs. When asked if their health had restricted them from climbing several flights of stairs, 87 percent of Falun Gong respondents (n=314) reported "no." The majority of respondents reported that their health had not limited them from doing other activities, such as bending, kneeling, stooping, and walking several blocks or more than a mile. Over 95 percent (n=342) stated they were able to walk one block, bathe, and dress themselves.

Findings from four items of the SF-36 Health Survey that measures physical health and wellness revealed that most Falun Gong respondents did not experience any physical problems that hindered their work or other daily activities. The majority of Falun Gong respondents (95%, n=342) stated they did not have to reduce time spent on work. Most perceived themselves as healthy and well—unrestricted by poor physical health—to perform their work and daily activities. Nearly 95 percent of Falun Gong respondents (n=341) indicated that they did not have any emotional problems that reduce time spent on work. They were able to perform their tasks with ease and care, and do as much as they liked to do.

Similarly, respondents reported not having any physical and emotional problems that affected normal social activities with family, friends, neighbors, or other groups of individuals. About 83 percent of Falun Gong respondents (n=297) stated they were "not at all" affected. In fact, no Falun Gong respondent reported being "extremely" affected by physical and emotional problems. Over two-thirds of Falun Gong respondents (68%, n=244) reported having no pain, while 24 percent (n=87) reported having "mild" pain. Five respondents reported some severe to very severe pain during the four weeks before completing survey. When asked how much this physical or bodily pain had affected their normal work at home and outside the home, nearly 90 percent of Falun Gong respondents (n=314) reported they were not affected at all. Only one respondent reported being extremely affected by pain.

The results from the SF-36 indicated Falun Gong respondents tend to be happy, calm, peaceful, and full of vitality. Over 80 percent of Falun Gong respondents (n= 293) reported they felt calm and peaceful, either all or most of the time. Eighty-two percent of respondents (n=294) indicated having a lot of energy all or most of the time, while 84 percent (n=303) reported being happy all or most of the time. Less than five Falun Gong respondents reported "none of the time" to these four positive mental states. The majority (86%, n=308) reported they were either not nervous or only nervous "a little of the time." About 73 percent (n=262) indicated they did not feel "down in the dumps" (Lau, 2010a, pp. 111, 132). One respondent indicated feeling blue, worn out or tired "all of the time." This latter case could be because the respondent may not have been doing the recommended daily exercise and Fa-study. Falun Gong practitioners who engage in daily practice and regular Fa-study tend to report better health-wellness status. They were able to deal with the stresses in their daily life.

In a separate question, respondents were asked how much of the time did physical or emotional problems affect them. Eighty-one percent of respondents (n=292) indicated "none of the time," while 13 percent (n=48) reported "a little of the time," and three percent (n=10) rated "some of the time." About one percent of Falun Gong respondents (n=5) reported that physical and emotional problems had interfered with their social activities much of the time. In general, Falun Gong respondents displayed a more optimistic outlook about their own health than non-Falun Gong respondents. Ninety percent (n=324) reported they did not expect their health to get worse, while 87 percent (n=313) stating that it was "definitely false" that they became ill easier than other people.

When asked to rate their health-wellness status in positive terms, nearly two-thirds of Falun Gong respondents (65%, n=234) reported that it was "definitely true" that they are as healthy as any person they know. Whereas 13 respondents (3.6%) indicated that it was "definitely false" that they are only just as healthy as anybody they know. More than three-quarters (76%, n=274) actually perceived their health as excellent and only one Falun Gong respondent did not report that their health is excellent.

CHAPTER 9

The Practice

The Australian survey provided some insight into the way Falun Gong respondents dedicated their time to the practice. Findings showed that they take time to do the exercises and to study the teachings of the practice regularly. This does not mean that they sit for hours in meditation or study the Falun Gong teachings all day. Some practitioners may have time to do that on some days or when there is a need to do intensive reading and exercise practice depending on their individual situations. Most Falun Gong practitioners live a busy life, as implied in the demographic findings of the Australian survey. Many Falun Gong respondents were in the prime of their life, with families, occupations, or a professional career, and different Falun Gong-related projects, besides reading and doing the Falun Gong exercises on a regular basis.

Falun Gong respondents from the Australian survey could be described as experienced practitioners with a good understanding of the cultivation practice. More than half of the respondents (54%, n=194) reported having practiced Falun Gong for six, to more than ten years. Only 10 percent (n=35) stated that they practiced Falun Gong for less than two years. Some researchers noted that a variance in the effects of meditation between experienced meditators, neophytes, and those who do not meditate (Goldberg, 1982; Ricard et al., 2014). They found that experienced and regular meditators tend to reap greater health-wellness and transcendental benefits from meditation. Perhaps this is a plausible explanation why the majority of Falun Gong respondents did not consult medical practitioners, used little or no medication, and reported good to excellent health-wellness status. There are other factors to consider.

Findings from the Australian survey indicated that the majority of Falun Gong respondents reported engaging in daily practice, or at least four to five times a week, and doing daily Fa-study. "*Fa*" means the law, way, or principles. The Chinese-English term "Fa-study" refers to reading or studying Falun Gong teachings by oneself or with other practitioners. Fa-study is considered one of the most fundamental aspects of the practice. Hence, practitioners in different cities and regions of the world organize weekly Fa-study gatherings in their local areas to ensure that everyone has the chance to study the teachings of the practice in a supportive group environment.

Time Spent on Practice and Fa-study

Falun Gong respondents reported practicing the exercises on a regular basis. Sixty percent (n=203) engaged in daily exercise, or at least four to five times a week. Nearly 50 percent of respondents (n=174) spent from one-and-a-half hours to two hours practicing the exercises during each session. The frequency for weekly practice and the length of time spent on practicing the exercises depend on the individual and variable factors such as lifestyle, working hours, or study commitments if they are full-time students.

In a follow-up interview with Barbara (or Respondent 289), she mentioned that she practiced "the five exercises everyday, seven days a week." What encouraged her to practice regularly was that she often noticed that she felt good and much better after the exercises. During the interview, she vividly recalled her initial experience doing the second standing exercise that took about 30 minutes. "It was a wonderful experience and it wasn't painful. The second time I did the exercise, I was able to keep my hands up for seven minutes in each of the four positions. That was quite amazing as I was still covered in bandages," said Barbara. Then she continued, "I stood with my eyes closed and felt the energy moving. I could feel the warm, healing sensation all over my limbs and body and I knew then that I wanted to continue practicing Falun Gong."

It is not surprising that the majority of Falun Gong respondents spent time on the practice. The five exercises promote health, healing, and wellness by opening up the energy channels in the human body, thus increasing the energy flow that will rectify blockages and purify the body of toxins. According to traditional Chinese medicine, there are 12 paired and two single energy meridians or pathways in the human body. Poor health, diseases, and imbalances in the body arise from blockages along these meridians. During cultivation practice, these channels will eventually merge into one energy pathway (H. Li, 2001d). When it happens, the cultivator's body will be pure, "the skin will be fair and delicate" (H. Li, 2001d, p. 336). According to the practice, this process occurs only when one is able to reach the state of *ding* or tranquility during meditation. "When one practices in this state, the body is being fully transformed, and it is the optimum state" (H. Li, 2001d, p. 339). When this happens, true healing can take place, leading to overall mind-body and spiritual health and wellness. However, this transformational process arising from meditation only partially explains the health-wellness benefits of the practice. Of far greater importance is the cultivation aspect that requires Fa-study and improving one's moral character (H. Li, 2001d).

Fa-study

Fa-study or studying the teachings of Falun Gong is an essential aspect of the cultivation practice (H. Li, 2001d, 2011). Fa-study enables one to enlighten to new understandings. Hence, Falun Gong practitioners need to study the Fa consistently during their entire cultivation practice, regardless of whether they are novice or veteran practitioners. Practitioners find that when they study the Fa regularly, they can cope better with the challenges in their daily life. Findings from the Australian survey indicated that Falun Gong respondents dedicated time for regular Fa-study. Nearly all Falun Gong respondents (99%, n=349) reported spending some time each week on Fa-study. "Of course, Fa-study is the most important," said Barbara during a follow-up interview. She spent "between one to two hours" each day on Fa-study. "That's just a guide: Sometimes I study longer when I have time. Other times I read less," said Barbara. "I read *Zhuan Falun* most of the time—sometimes the other teachings too," she added.

Fa-study is one of the three important tasks for Falun Gong practitioners. It holds the key to improving oneself. In *Zhuan Falun* and various short articles, "called 'scriptures' by practitioners" (H. Li, 2001a, p. 44), Mr. Li mentioned the importance of Fa-study (H. Li, 2001a, 2001d, 2002a). He stated, "As long as you read Dafa, you are changing; as long as you read Dafa, you are elevating" (H. Li, 2001a, p. 98). His inscription for practitioners in the City of Changchun, China reads: "Study the Fa, obtain the Fa; Compare how you study, compare how you cultivate; Measure yourself against the Fa in everything; Putting into action, that is cultivation" (H. Li, 2002a, p. i). Whenever Mr. Li attended the US experience-sharing conferences, he would often remind practitioners on the importance of studying the Fa. At the 2011 US Fa Conference in Washington DC, he dedicated an entire Fa lecture to Fa-study: "Dafa Disciples Must Study the Fa" (H. Li, 2011, p. 1). "You really need to study the Fa with utter seriousness ... If you don't study the Fa well, there are many things you will not be able to do well" (H. Li, 2011, p. 1). Mr. Li (2011) emphasized that Fa-study is "the most, most important thing—it is the fundamental guarantee for all that you are to do. If you cannot keep up in Fa-study, then there is no hope" (p. 2). During the 2014 San Francisco experience-sharing conference, Mr. Li once again reminded practitioners to "Study the Fa. Everything is contained in it. All these people here came to understand things by studying the Fa" (H. Li, 2014, p. 16).

While total time spent on Fa-study varies for each respondent, 64 percent of Falun Gong respondents (n=224) reported spending from six to fifteen hours each week on Fa-study. These hours correspond with Barbara's seven to 14 hours of Fa-study each week. For some staunch respondents, the maximum reported hours spent on Fa-study per week was sufficient to finish the entire book of *Zhuan Falun* in seven days. Besides the weekly group Fa-study, sometimes practitioners in different regions would organize a whole-day intensive Fa-study, while others would coordinate a weekly three-lecture Fa-study on the weekend. When asked to indicate the frequency of their Fa-study, nearly three-quarters of Falun Gong respondents (72%, n=253) reported engaging in daily Fa-study. Sixteen percent (n=55) engaged in Fa-study four to five times a week, while 11 percent (n=38) studied Fa two to three times a week. Less than two percent (n=7) reported studying Fa just once a week.

The majority of Falun Gong respondents from the Australian survey understood the importance of Fa-study: 92 percent of Falun Gong respondents (n=329) identified "Study Falun Gong teachings" as the most important aspect of the practice. They realized the link between regular Fa-study and *xinxing* or moral character improvement. Those who merely practice the exercises and meditation, but neglect Fa-study, cannot be genuinely "considered a Falun Dafa disciple" (H. Li, 2001d, p. 93). According to Falun Gong teachings, genuine cultivation directly involves improving one's *xinxing* or moral character. Fa-study holds the key to *xinxing* improvement. When people first crossed the threshold to begin the practice, most of them were unaware of the close link between Fa-study, moral character improvement, and mind-body cultivation practice that leads to overall mind-body and spiritual health and wellness. Barbara recalled that she was initially not enthusiastic about reading the book. Her eyes were out of focus after her accident. Nevertheless, she began reading the book and a phenomenal healing moment occurred.

"The first day it took me a very long time—almost the whole day to read a portion of Lecture One," said Barbara. The next day she found that she could read a little faster: "I completed Lecture One and Lecture Two." Her vision improved even more on the third day. She finished Lecture Three, one of the longer chapters in the book, and started reading Lecture Four, which is about loss and gain, the transformation of karma, and improving *xinxing*. "It was so interesting; I couldn't put the book down," said Barbara. That night she read till 2:30 AM. Reluctantly she put the book down to go to sleep. Shortly afterward, a strong current went through both of her hands, waking her up, she said. "I sat up in bed and held my hands out. It felt like I was getting a strong electric shock sensation traveling from my fingers right up my arms. I quickly woke my husband up," enthused Barbara. "The sensations lasted for several minutes. It was amazing!" said Barbara. "It was the first time since my fall that I slept peacefully through the night." Before the 'electric shock' sensations, Barbara said she had to wake up her husband every couple of hours each night to have him apply cortisone cream on her back and hands. "From that moment, all my pain disappeared and never returned! It was a miracle," she uttered with marvel in her voice, as though she was saying it the first time.

Barbara's experience is not an isolated case. Similar miraculous healing occurrences have happened to other Falun Gong individuals. Many reported recovering completely from their health problems, including serious medical conditions, after starting the practice. Often practitioners share their experiences in small, informal groups or at formal Falun Gong conferences. Many of these healing reports have been documented and posted on the Minghui.org website under the section on health benefits.

For Barbara, Fa-study—reading *Zhuan Falun*—marked the turning point in her path to wellness: "From that moment on, everything in my body started to heal quickly," said Barbara. "My hands felt warm and I was able to actually feel them. Before, three fingers on my left hand were numb: I couldn't move these fingers and I couldn't open my hand." After that night's experience, she noticed that her hand movements returned. "I was able to wash my face," said Barbara.

Ten years had passed since the fall. Yet, the memory remained vivid. As she talked, her face glowed with an indescribable radiance and joy, feeling as though the healing occurrence had just happened yesterday. She was eager to talk about the benefits of the practice: "I felt the miraculous recovery in a short space of time. I asked myself why nobody had told me this earlier. The book answers all the questions that I have never been able to find any answers before." She stated that from that moment on, she started taking her cultivation practice seriously—doing the exercises and reading the book regularly, sharing her story, and rectifying inaccurate notions about Falun Gong, especially those spread by the Chinese Communist Party.

The Five Health-Wellness Domains

Falun Gong respondents in the Australian survey were also asked to answer five questions pertaining to how the practice has impacted their life across five health-wellness domains. These questions focused on changes in their physical, mental and emotional health, stress coping ability, relationship with significant others, and outlook toward life. Data indicated significant improvements for respondents across all five health-wellness domains. Nearly 83 percent of Falun Gong respondents (n=297) reported significant improvement in physical health, while over 90 percent (n=325) stated significant change in mental and emotional health after practicing Falun Gong. Seventy percent of Falun Gong respondents (n=252) disclosed that a positive change in their relationship with their significant others (Lau, 2010a).

The results from the Australian survey showed that the greatest change is reflected in respondents' attitude toward life. Ninety-three percent of Falun Gong respondents (n=335) reported a significant positive shift in their outlook toward life. This is a consistent theme in the follow-up study that explores the lived experiences of Falun Gong respondents. During one of the interviews in 2012, Barbara was asked again to rate her health and wellness status according to these five domains, to which she responded stating that she had been extremely good in all five health-wellness aspects. Her words captured the beneficial effects of the practice: "Falun Gong has given me a second chance in life. I would not have been so well and healthy if I hadn't started the practice in 2003." She spoke about how Falun Gong has helped her maintain health and cope with the pressures of the modern, hectic society. "There are days when I don't feel so good but Falun Gong provides me with the tools to resolve my life's problems." The practice has contributed to her overall health and wellness and equipped her with a loftier coping mechanism to handle the tribulations of everyday life. Through consistent Fa-study, applying the teachings of the practice in her daily life, and assimilating with the three Falun Gong principles of truthfulness, compassion, and forbearance, Barbara said she has maintained mind-body and spiritual health and wellness since starting the practice.

The self-reports of Falun Gong respondents from the Australian survey demonstrated the healing effect of the practice that Barbara spoke about. Many respondents reported significant changes in their physical, mental, and emotional health. The majority (98%, n=346) reported physical health improvement since starting the practice. Only two respondents indicated a worsening of their physical health out of the 360 Falun Gong respondents. When asked to rate any change in mental and emotional health since commencing Falun Gong, 93 percent (n=325) perceived a noticeable improvement. Again, two respondents reported a worsening of their mental and emotional health. As life is often full of challenges, deadlines, and frustrations in our modern world, stress has become a familiar sliver of life. While a small dose of stress can be a good thing, living under constant stress is unhealthy and can undermine the quality of our life.

The conclusion from the Australian survey indicated that Falun Gong offers an effective way of managing stress. More than 90 percent of Falun Gong respondents (n=317) reported improvement in their stress-coping ability after starting the practice. Many Falun Gong respondents are professionals. Faced with the stresses of daily life and work demands, having a mind-body cultivation practice that helps them to manage stress effectively is a welcomed relief.

We can vouch that quality of relationships with significant people in our life makes a good indicator of the quality of our life. The majority (91%, n=325) of Falun Gong respondents reported an improvement in their relationship with their significant others since they began the practice. Only two percent or eight Falun Gong respondents indicated a worsening of their relationship. These figures suggested that after beginning the practice, most Falun Gong respondents enjoyed a happier, more harmonious, and fulfilling relationship with the significant other people in their life. While the findings from the Australian survey cannot furnish an answer for this phenomenon, conversations with respondents from the longitudinal study helped to provide insight into how practitioners change and maintain a better relationship status with their significant others. Falun Gong teaches that conflicts in our relationships and interactions with others occur due to our inability to let go of attachments—the behaviors or traits we are unable to relinquish. For instance, being attached to self, ego, pride, fear, worry, and other undesirable mental and emotional states. Since cultivation focuses on letting go of attachments, improving *xinxing* or moral character, practitioners endeavor to follow the teachings of the practice. This involves being compassionate and considering others first, becoming tolerant toward others, being able to let go of self-interests and selfishness, and improving one's moral character. All these will naturally lead to harmonious relationships with their significant others and therefore improve the quality of their life.

Respondents' change of attitude toward life can be another reliable gauge to the quality of life. Nearly 95 percent of Falun Gong respondents (n=335) reported an improvement in their attitude toward life. They find meaning in life. For instance, Barbara mentioned that walking the path with Falun Gong has given her a sense of purpose and new meaning in life. Like many respondents, her outlook on life has changed dramatically. She has become more optimistic and positive about life in general. Nonetheless, one Falun Gong respondent from the Australian survey indicated, "no difference" in outlook toward life, while two out of the 360 respondents reported experiencing deterioration in their attitude toward life.

Additionally, the findings showed that nearly 60 percent of Falun Gong respondents (n=211) reported their medical conditions had significantly improved. Only five percent (n=19) indicated slight improvement. It is not so surprising to read about the positive health-wellness self-reports from Falun Gong respondents. Moreover, it is a widely accepted in our modern society that regular exercise, positive states of mind (or strong righteous thoughts in Falun Gong expression), and a strong faith and belief in a spiritual practice that teaches people to be good, all contribute toward a healthier wellness lifestyle. These positive aspects—all merged in Falun Gong—become an antidote for overall mind-body and spiritual health and wellness. However, one Falun Gong respondent reported becoming slightly worse and another respondent reported a significantly worsening of her condition across all five health-wellness domains. Despite her worsening situation, this respondent continued to practice.

Adverse Findings

As in all research, it is pertinent to report adverse results. The Australian survey showed that a handful of Falun Gong respondents indicated no difference or even experienced a worsening of their situation across the five health-wellness domains (Lau, 2010a). One Falun Gong respondent reported being significantly worse for each of the five health-wellness dimensions—physical health, mental/emotional health, stress-coping ability, relationship with significant other, and outlook toward life. About 1.4 percent of Falun Gong respondents (n=5) reported no change or improvement in their physical health. Nearly two percent of respondents (n=7) revealed a slightly worsening in their relationship with significant others, while 4.4 percent (n=16) stated no difference in their relationship with significant others in their life (Lau, 2010a).

This low occurrence of adverse findings has several implications. It could imply genuine responses. Other explanations for fewer adverse results included the number of years and frequency of practice, time spent on practicing the exercises and doing Fa-study, as well as respondents' understanding of the teachings of Falun Gong. Additionally, there would be certain individuals who might experience strong body purification effects after they started practicing Falun Gong. Another factor could be because there are immediate or short-term and long-term benefits of meditation and that there *is* a disparity in the effects of meditation between novice and experienced meditators (Goldberg, 1982). While this disparity may exist with other types of meditation, it is not comprehensive in Falun Gong. Many individuals, like Barbara for instance, experienced the positive effects of the practice as soon as she began the practice. On the third day after she started reading *Zhuan Falun*, she felt the miraculous healing benefit of Falun Gong.

From the Falun Gong perspective, a worsening of situations or no difference could be due to one's cultivation state, *xinxing* issue, poor understanding of the Fa, or the person's inability to let go of his attachments and undesirable states of mind and emotion. A cultivator, even one who has been practicing for a number of years, can be 'stuck' due to interfering factors, and hence unable to awaken to a higher understanding on certain matters. Falun Gong teaches "different levels have different Fa" (H. Li, 2001d, p. 8) and that one cannot increase one's cultivation energy "without cultivating one's inner self and one's *xinxing*" (H. Li, 2001d, p. 38). As the Australian research was an anonymous online survey, there was no opportunity to delve deeper into what could have caused a worsening reaction for those particular Falun Gong respondents.

Although this data implies that a few people did not gain contentment and benefit from Falun Gong, for transparency and honest reporting, this negligible discrepancy deserves attention. Data revealed that Respondent 27, or Nancy (not her real name), reported a significant worsening of her medical condition across all five health-wellness domains. Nancy was in her thirties and had been practicing Falun Gong for four to six years. Hence, she is considered a veteran practitioner. Her self-reports indicated that she practiced the exercises two to three times a week and devoted 11 to 15 hours a week for daily Fa-study. This is quite a significant dedication to the cultivation practice. Despite the worsening of her conditions, Nancy continued to practice Falun Gong. She stated it was because of "a predestined relationship," or *yuanfen* in Chinese. Her belief in predestined relationship with Falun Gong and her understanding of Falun Gong teachings had encouraged her to continue with the practice. Answers that throw light on the reasons for her enduring steadfastness can only be obtained through a longitudinal qualitative study.

Goal of Cultivation Practice

While the health-wellness effects of Falun Gong improve the quality of life for practitioners, many realize that Falun Gong is more than just a panacea for healing and fitness. Every veteran Falun Gong practitioner knows that the secret to his or her health and wellness lies in genuine cultivation, truly following the teachings of Falun Gong, and living according to the principles of truthfulness, compassion, and forbearance in one's daily life. Falun Gong teaches that the primary purpose of being a human being is to "return to one's origin and true self" (H. Li, 2001d, p. 5) through cultivation. As such, practitioners realize that the ultimate goal of cultivation practice is to reach consummation: a term used in Falun Gong to refer to spiritual awakening or enlightenment and returning to one's original and true self. For the sake of cultivation and genuine aspiration for consummation, Falun Gong people endeavor to modify their behaviors, improve their moral character, and assimilate the teachings of the practice into their daily life. They endeavor to be "True, Good, and Endure" (H. Li, 2003, pp. 12-13). Health and wellness is only one of the many benefits that result from their individual cultivation state.

Another way of looking at the reported adverse reactions is to consider it from the perspective of complementary and alternative medicine (CAM). In CAM practices, healing and purification reactions, or a reversal process may arise when past health conditions or symptoms reappear before the person ultimately gets better (Wilson, 2008). There exists also a difference between healing and illness symptoms. Healing symptoms are often milder and pass quickly. For example, one may have a sore throat, fever, or flu symptoms without feeling the tiredness usually associated with those conditions. This is often the case with Falun Gong practitioners, as these symptoms do not interfere with their everyday work. Falun Gong practitioners either regard such symptoms as karma elimination or body purification, and respond by maintaining strong positive or righteous thoughts, stepping up on Fa-study, and looking within, or examining one's actions to improve their *xinxing* or heart-mind nature.

About 6,000 Falun Gong practitioners from all over the world gather at Liberty Square, in front of the Chiang Kai-shek Memorial Hall to create a formation that shows a Bodhisattva in the image of a fairy holding the book *Zhuan Falun* and sprinkling heavenly flowers. The eight Chinese characters mean "The Buddha-light shines everywhere, and harmonizes everything." The formation symbolizes the benefits Falun Gong brings to practitioners and the whole of society. Taipei, Taiwan. November 8, 2014.

Close-up of character-image formation: Falun Gong practitioners from Taiwan and all over the world—Europe, Hong Kong, Korea, Japan, North and South America, Singapore, Vietnam, and other countries—sit in the meditation pose to form this magnificent image. Taipei, Taiwan. November 8, 2014.

CHAPTER 10

Written Responses

Since its public introduction in 1992, Falun Gong has spread by word-of-mouth to millions of people across China and throughout the world. Millions of people experienced unique healing and complete recovery upon starting the practice. So, what are they saying about the practice? Findings from the Australian survey indicated that Falun Gong respondents have a lot to say about the practice. Their written responses offered an extra dimension to the survey and provided insight into the health and wellness effects of Falun Gong. This chapter documents their written responses and snippets of conversation from the interviews with Barbara for the on-going study that is part of the *Hearts Uplifted* project.

Data presented here came from five questionnaire items. One of the questions asked respondents to state their medical conditions and their reasons for consulting a medical practitioner. Another question requested Falun Gong respondents to state their medical condition (if any) before they started Falun Gong, while two more questions focused on what first attracted them to Falun Gong. The fifth source of written data came from the question that asked respondents to state how, in their opinion, Falun Gong practice has led to better health and wellness in their life. Instead of using numbers, the author has assigned a pseudonym for some of the respondents.

Healing Occurrences

"I tried it on the off chance that it would help, having tried many other things. I decided that I would give it a shot, and in a month, arguably up to three months, I was 100 percent!" wrote Sebastian, who was Respondent 182. A Caucasian living in Canada, Sebastian was diagnosed with Guillain-Barre Syndrome, a disease that affects the peripheral nervous system leading to gradual paralysis. He wrote in his self-report: "I had problems moving around, double vision, etc. It was suggested to me that it [Falun Gong] could help my condition. Upon watching the Falun Gong video, I suddenly felt better than I had in a long time." Then in his thirties, Sebastian decided to start practicing and found himself completely recovered from the crippling disease within a few months.

"I just began practicing Falun Gong at that time and the problem completely went away with no damage to my heart or health. Doctors were confounded. I have had no further health problems since practicing," wrote a US-born Caucasian practitioner. Harry (or Respondent 297) was in his twenties at the time of data collection. He reported having viral myocarditis—an inflammation of the heart muscle due to a viral infection that can cause heart attacks and damage to the heart tissues.

Like Sebastian and Harry, Barbara (or Respondent 289) also fully recovered from her complex medical and health problems, to the amazement of her doctors. She sustained multiple medical complications that included spinal fluid leakage, fractured skull, damaged sinuses, broken jaw, wrists, and cracked kneecap, deafness in the left ear, distorted vision, noise in her head, back and neck pain, and partial loss of feeling in her left hand. In addition, she reported having "serious digestion problems, allergies, migraines, aches and pains, anxiety, and depression" before her fall. After starting Falun Gong, she fully recovered from everything.

Ten years later, during a follow-up interview in New York, Barbara said that whenever she recalls her first crossing with Falun Gong, she feels as she did then. "It was amazing, a miracle. I could see that the practice was something very powerful and special." Due to her serious head injuries, doctors thought, and told her, that she would never fully recover. They warned her to expect the worst and gave her a four-page list of all the medical problems she would have to live with after the surgeries.

When fully recovered, she still had to visit her doctors every month. "I told them that I don't need the appointments. They checked me and were very surprised," said Barbara. She continued, "They couldn't believe that I had recovered so quickly. One of the doctors asked me what I had been doing; so I gave her the Falun Gong fliers." Her doctors, family, and friends continued to be amazed by her full recovery.

The impact of the 23 feet (seven meters) fall broke her upper jaw into three segments. Doctors had to wire her loosened teeth together. "The orthodontist told me that after everything healed, they would do dental prostheses. He couldn't believe it when he saw that all my teeth had tightened up again without any dental procedure. I didn't lose one tooth," said Barbara. Her dentist had actually told her at the time that her teeth would go black within a couple of years. "Now it has been 10 years. Nothing has happened to my teeth," continued Barbara during our 2013 face-to-face interview. She smiled, showing her gleaming white teeth. It was difficult to envisage her with loosened or blackened teeth as her dentist had warned 10 years ago.

Reasons for Consulting a Medical Practitioner

According to the raw data from the Australian survey, 37 Falun Gong respondents and 156 non-Falun Gong respondents reported their medical conditions and stated their reasons for consulting a medical practitioner (Lau, 2010a). However, 30 percent (n=11) of the responses from these 37 Falun Gong respondents included dental as well as medical visits. Their written responses comprised mostly one word, or two or three listed conditions. This information was analyzed and interpreted using a simple three-level categorizing or clustering procedure adapted from approaches to qualitative content analysis (Graneheim & Lundman, 2004; Hanson et al., 2005; Sharif & Masoumi, 2005).

Findings indicated that about 90 percent of Falun Gong respondents (n=320) did not consult a medical practitioner during the six months before completing the survey. No Falun Gong respondents reported visiting medical practitioners for serious or life threatening medical conditions. More non-Falun Gong respondents consulted medical practitioners than Falun Gong respondents did. Data showed that 68 percent of non-Falun Gong respondents (n=156) reported seeing medical practitioners, compared to just 10 percent of Falun Gong respondents (n=37). Non-Falun Gong respondents reported 47 instances, of either two or multiple listings of medical conditions, compared to just three cases from Falun Gong respondents.

Medical Conditions before Practicing Falun Gong

One of the most interesting written responses from Falun Gong respondents came from one question that asked participants to specify medical condition(s) as diagnosed by medical practitioners before they started Falun Gong practice. Forty-six percent of Falun Gong respondents (n=164) provided written responses for the question that requested Falun Gong respondents to state their medical condition (if any) before they started Falun Gong. What stood out was that many of those Falun Gong respondents who reported pre-existing medical conditions had even more complicated health issues and serious medical problems than non-Falun Gong respondents. Due to the number of entries and complex range of medical conditions, it was simpler to use a three-level categorizing system than to present each respondent's case. All written responses were first recorded as meaning units, and then classified into four broad categories. Four categories were identified: mental health, muscular-skeletal, respiratory, and other medical conditions. When many respondents reported a particular ailment, that condition was sub-categorized. For instance, mental health was sub-categorized into four key themes—anxiety disorder, depression, chronic fatigue, and miscellaneous mental health conditions because the frequency of reports for these four ailments was high. There were 21 reports for anxiety disorder, 17 for depression, 24 for chronic fatigue, and 21 miscellaneous mental health conditions that included nervous breakdown, psychoses or psychotic episodes, insomnia, and mental stress (Lau, 2010a).

Respiratory ailments comprised 25 reports of allergies and hay fever, 18 cases of asthma, and 26 counts of miscellaneous respiratory conditions comprising bronchitis, cold, influenza, and sinusitis. Data showed 28 reports of chronic/life-threatening illnesses that included five cancer cases, 13 reports for heart disease, three for diabetes, five for hypertension, and two for hypotension. The cancers were breast, cervical, and skin cancer. Ethel (Respondent 283) was in her seventies at the time of the data collection. Besides suffering from arthritis, bronchitis, headaches, and urethritis, Ethel reported having multiple surgeries—including mastectomy, gastrectomy, and cholecystostomy (Lau, 2010a).

There was also a sub-category for 12 gynecological reports. These included cysts, endometriosis, dysmenorrhea, irregular period, thrush, yeast infections, menopausal symptoms, such as hot flushes, and one report of a major fibroid operation. This sub-category excluded the breast and cervical cancer, and mastectomy cases, which were already classified in the chronic/life-threatening category. In the other/miscellaneous category, there were 69 instances of different conditions.

This list consisted of headaches, migraines, gastro-intestinal conditions, such as stomach ulcer and irritable bowel syndrome, eye and ear conditions, and other chronic ailments like kidney disease, hepatitis, hyperthyroidism, and hypothyroidism. Miscellaneous muscular-skeletal conditions included arthritis, carpal tunnel syndrome, Guillain-Barre syndrome (GBS), multiple sclerosis, osteoarthritis, repetitive strain injury (RSI), rheumatoid arthritis, and scoliosis. Likewise, back (and neck) pain deserved a separate listing because of its high occurrences (Lau, 2010a).

As noted earlier, asking respondents to state their medical condition produced fascinating results. Written comments indicated that many Falun Gong respondents had serious medical and/or chronic health problems before they started practicing Falun Gong. Besides Barbara, Harry, and Sebastian, there were three other cases with multiple and complex medical conditions that stood out. Eliza (Respondent 89), in her fifties, reported suffering from a host of medical health problems. She stated that she had "incurable chronic conditions due to thyroid, adrenals, and pituitary gland," plus "severe allergies, sleep disorder, chronic fatigue, anxiety, and degenerated discs causing loss of mobility and pain." Mary (Respondent 216), in her sixties, reported having "stomach ulcer, chronic headaches, fatigue, arthritis, incontinence, knee weakness, anxiety, and fear." The third case was Bartholomew (Respondent 219) who was in his seventies. He wrote he had multiple medical conditions: "seasonal attacks of cold-cough-sinus congestion, retina-migraine, grand-mal seizures [sic], indigestion, constipation, and diabetes in the family tree" (Lau, 2010a). All three reported significant remission from theses conditions after taking up Falun Gong practice.

They were two other respondents who were diagnosed with cervical cancer. At the time of data collection, these two Australian respondents reported significant improvement and healing after they started practicing Falun Gong. As the Australian study was an anonymous online survey, it was not possible to contact these respondents to verify their on-going health-wellness status. There was no prospect to track the lived experiences of these respondents, as the researcher could do with Barbara. Apart from Barbara, the other respondents for the on-going study are new cases and independent from the Australian survey.

Data from the Australian survey also indicated that 50 percent of the 164 Falun Gong respondents (n=82), who reported having medical conditions, had either two or more pre-existing medical conditions (Lau, 2010a). Their written responses about their pre-existing medical conditions revealed their poor health and wellness status before they started practicing Falun Gong. Many turned to Falun Gong when there seemed to be no respite or cure using conventional medical approaches. However, findings from the survey indicated a distinguishing characteristic, that is, many Falun Gong respondents' health and wellness improved significantly after they started practicing Falun Gong, with even some reporting complete recovery from serious and life-threatening medical conditions.

Nonetheless, the reported cases from the Australian survey were not isolated occurrences. Across the Falun Gong community around the world and in China, there are numerous stories of the healing benefits of the practice. One case was the story of a well-known traditional Chinese brush artist, Zhang Cuiying. In 1996, Zhang was diagnosed with severe arthritis that afflicted her fingers. Her condition worsened and she found herself unable to hold a paintbrush or lift a rice bowl with her fingers. She consulted both Western-trained and traditional Chinese doctors: "I spend over $10,000 on medicine and treatment" (Chai & Pan, 2002). Compounded by her inability to paint, Zhang felt hopeless: "I was living a life in which I'd rather die." Then her husband saw an advertisement in the local paper about a nine-day seminar on Falun Gong. Zhang attended the seminar. She noticed that her pain and discomfort subsided. This prompted her to start the practice. Within a short time, she not only found herself fully recovered from the debilitating rheumatoid arthritis, she was able to resume her painting. A grateful Zhang said that Falun Gong has given her a second life.

Another Australian case was the story of Rowena (not her real name). Her mother described her as mentally challenged, with a slightly deformed spine and a fused lumbar area. Rowena endured constant pain and could only stand for short periods. She had to use a wheelchair whenever she went out. Within a few days of learning the first standing exercise, Rowena was able to stand up to do all the four standing exercises. Four weeks later, Rowena found herself sitting in the half-lotus position to do the sitting meditation. Soon she started walking—first for 20 minutes each day—and eventually she did not have to use the wheelchair for outings. Her quality of life significantly improved after she started practicing Falun Gong.

The Practice's Appeal

The promise of health benefits from Falun Gong has been the initial attraction for many practitioners. Findings from the Australian survey indicated that 31 percent of Falun Gong respondents (n=111) stated that the practice's appeal is its healing potential (Lau, 2010a). Faced with their debilitating medical conditions, all these individuals, like Barbara, were open to try the practice. They found relief and fully recovered from their medical ailments to the surprise of their family members and even their medical physician, as was Barbara's case.

Just what else is the Falun Gong appeal? The results from the Australian survey indicated that people were drawn to the practice for different reasons. Respondents were invited to choose three examples of what "first attracted them to the practice." The prominent attractions were Falun Gong's teachings and the belief in a predestined relationship with the practice. Fifty-one percent of Falun Gong respondents (n=182) were drawn to the teachings of the practice. Forty-nine percent (n=176) chose "predestined relationship" or *yuanfen* in Chinese, implying that they knew they were meant to practice Falun Gong. Forty-eight percent (n=172) selected searching for meaning in life, while 38 percent (n=136) were attracted to the practice because of "spiritual enlightenment offered by Falun Gong" (Lau, 2010a). Eight percent of respondents (n=27) mentioned that specific and personal factors initially attracted them to the practice.

Seventy percent of these written comments (n=19) contained a phrase or a one-sentence response. Their responses were categorized into different themes, such as curiosity, turning points in life, positive regard for Falun Gong practitioners, free-of-charge teachings, the Chinese regime's persecution of Falun Gong, and unusual encounters with Falun Gong. Miscellaneous comments included the concept of repaying karmic debt or having an enduring affinity with traditional Chinese culture. For instance, an Australian female respondent, born in China wrote, "You can keep your youth and beauty by practicing Falun Gong."

Several respondents expressed curiosity about the practice. A young woman from Taiwan wrote, "I was very curious about why Falun Gong was so popular in China but banned by the Chinese Communist Party (CCP) and would like to find the true story behind [it]." Another respondent, a young New Zealand-born high school student wrote, "I was curious, and after I was told it was a type of cultivation practice, I liked it even better." A female respondent from Singapore wrote, "I was more interested to find out what Falun Gong is about [after] all those news that were broadcast from CCTV" (China Central Television) [sic]. Then there was a US-born American in his twenties who reported that he started the practice because of the CCP's persecution of Falun Gong. "Initially I wanted to learn what the persecution was about. I knew if the [Chinese] regime was trying to cover it up, it [Falun Gong] must be something powerful." Likewise, a retired Australian wrote, "I felt that Falun Dafa (Falun Gong) must be a very powerful spiritual path to be so severely persecuted by elements within the Chinese government!"

Two respondents alluded to significant moments in their life and that their first encounter with Falun Gong coincided with a major turning point in their life. A young Japanese woman in her twenties wrote, "I knew my life had to be changed for [the] better and I felt that Falun Gong is the one to help me through" the crisis in her life. Then there was Cynthia (Respondent 142), an Australian in her fifties, who reminisced the different stages of her life crossings. Cynthia wrote in her report:

> "I ventured into many aspects of alternative or complementary therapies, then into the metaphysical arena. Some years on, I came upon Falun Gong, after having practiced tai chi, and different forms of meditations. Each step of this naturally unfolding journey in [a] way and time [had] led me to the Fa [Falun Gong] and which revealed unexplainable and incredible realizations of my understandings of the cosmos, all of life, and myself."

Another two respondents pointed out that the demeanor of Falun Gong practitioners was what had first attracted them to the practice. A European Falun Gong respondent living in the United States wrote, "The fact that all the practitioners I met were very nice and good people" had drawn him to the practice. Across the Pacific Ocean, a Korean-Chinese respondent living in Japan reported that he wanted to know more about the practice because his friend—a Falun Gong practitioner—"is so different from an everyday person."

Yet, others reported beginning their practice because of their personal encounter with Falun Gong and the fact that it was free for everyone. A Greek Australian respondent stated that he was attracted to Falun Gong because it was free of charge. Then Mervin, or Respondent 16, a British-born Australian, reported, "My wife visited a Falun Gong stall at the Mind-Body-Spirit Festival and was attracted by the energy, and the fact that they weren't selling anything." The couple had seen a CNN news story of the April 25, 1999, peace appeal at Zhongnanhai showing "a Chinese government spokesperson criticizing the behavior of the Falun Gong protestors when the footage clearly showed their behavior as exemplary." Mervin wrote, "We were most impressed with such a silent and orderly 'protest.' We thought that if the CCP was so against Falun Gong, then it was probably very good because we knew a lot about the previous crimes of the CCP."

Findings indicated that the CCP's anti-Falun Gong propaganda had the opposite impact on Mervin, his spouse, and many other individuals. Instead of deterring people, more individuals in the West found out about Falun Gong. Upon reading up about Falun Gong, they found the practice beneficial for mind-body and spiritual improvement and offered a meaningful sense of purpose in their life. Data indicated that nearly 50 percent of Falun Gong respondents from the Australian survey attributed their initial attraction to the practice to the search for meaning in life. Falun Gong instills hope in them and likewise to the millions who take up the practice to cultivate to become morally better individuals, with the aim of reaching enlightenment and returning to their original true self.

Different individuals seem to be attracted to Falun Gong for different reasons. A Caucasian Australian disclosed that she was in a phase of her life when she was attracted to everything about China. And Falun Gong "came from China," she wrote. Another Australian, a retired teacher, attributed her initial attraction to Falun Gong to "having a lifelong affinity with traditional Chinese culture and having learned Mandarin for three years." Others were seeking for answers, like a Korean-Chinese female respondent wondered whether Falun Gong could help her resolve the conflict with her mother, while a Spanish Australian wrote, "I was looking for a way to pay back debt incurred through doing the wrong thing" [sic].

Several respondents mentioned the profundity of Falun Gong teachings. A Mainland Chinese living in the US described "Master's [Li Hongzhi] teachings [as] very powerful and relevant." A Greek Australian in his thirties, Tobias (Respondent 303) alluded to the mind-body balance and the universal principles of truthfulness, compassion, and forbearance as Falun Gong's unique appeal. Cynthia (R142) mentioned earlier that Falun Gong teachings revealed extraordinary realizations for her. Then Rhonda (Respondent 321), an Australian teacher in her forties wrote, "Over time, with continual reading of *Zhuan Falun,* I found an inner wisdom and profound truth that I could not turn my back on."

Others also stated Falun Gong's potential health benefits. Jayson or Respondent 195, a Caucasian from the US, wrote that he was looking for a practice "to build internal energy and none of the martial arts had what I was looking for," while Australian Respondent 211 stated that family members' illnesses had first attracted him to Falun Gong. Two Malaysian-born Australians mentioned they were looking for an exercise practice to enhance their health and wellness. Logan (Respondent 32) said he was "looking for some form of exercise to improve my health and joined Falun Gong exercise by chance—without any knowledge of what it was all about." In his fifties and diagnosed with hepatitis, Logan reported that after starting the practice his medical condition "significantly improved." He stated that exercise practice and regular Fa-study led to his better health and wellness. Molly (Respondent 48), who was in her fifties, wrote: "I was looking for some type of qigong to learn and saw people practicing Falun Gong near my house, and so I joined in." Molly stated that she suffered from asthma and had to take medication before she started practicing Falun Gong. She reported that her condition significantly improved after she started the practice.

Then there was Ben (Respondent 301), a young Caucasian Australian in his twenties, who reported suffering from severe depression. In his written responses, he mentioned having mystical experiences soon after he started the practice. "These, along with the numerous other supernatural experiences I have encountered, gave me so much confidence. I knew well it was an upright teaching," wrote Ben. At the time of the survey, Ben had practiced Falun Gong for nearly four to six years, engaging in regular practice and daily Fa-study. Data from the written responses came from individuals from diverse backgrounds. Their comments provided insight into what first attracted them to the practice. In some instances, these written responses shed light on the determination of some of these individuals who remained steadfast in their cultivation path despite the CCP's brutal persecution of Falun Gong and attempts to spread anti-Falun Gong propaganda overseas.

Better Health and Wellness with Falun Gong

So, what has led to better health and wellness for these millions of Falun Gong people around the world? Falun Gong respondents were asked to choose a maximum of three reasons as to how the practice has led to improved health and wellness. The majority of Falun Gong respondents (91%, n=328) stated that *xinxing* improvement or improving moral character contributed to better health and wellness. Seventy-eight percent (n=280) mentioned regular Fa-study as another reason for better health and wellness. About half of the Falun Gong respondents (n=170) chose Falun Gong exercise routine as the contributing factor, while 44 percent of Falun Gong respondents (n=158) believed that a positive change of attitude toward life had helped them to achieve better health and wellness. Over 14 percent of respondents (n=51) cited an improved stress coping ability as a reason for better health and wellness. About seven percent (n=24) mentioned Falun Gong experience-sharing conferences, while five percent (n=18) referred to being in a community of Falun Gong practitioners.

Nearly 1.4 percent or seven respondents wrote specific remarks. A university student living in the UK wrote that Falun Gong had led to better health and wellness because the practice "gave life a meaning." Then a US-based marketing manager in his twenties stated that Falun Gong helps to improve the overall wellness of society. Both respondents, however, did not elaborate their meaning. Cynthia (R142) wrote that all the factors mentioned above—*xinxing* improvement, regular Fa-study, exercise practice, positive change in attitude toward life, better stress-coping ability, attending conferences, and being with a community of practitioners—play "a pivotal role in my overall health and well-being."

Then there was Sebastian (R182) who fully recovered from Guillain-Barre syndrome after he started practicing Falun Gong. Sebastian described "an incredible change in perspective, namely seeing the bigger picture of situations, as opposed to focusing on [my] own needs." He referred to a shift of inner awareness. "This was not a one-time occurrence but an enlargement of perspective that has been happening regularly since I started to practice," wrote Sebastian. What he had described was his understandings gleaned from regular Fa-study, looking within, letting go of self, and considering others first.

The last written comment came from Lucas (Respondent 196), who identified himself as a European Caucasian from Canada. Lucas wrote, "body purification by Shifu" (a Chinese term for a master or a teacher), as one of the reasons that had led to better health and wellness. Body purification is a process that most practitioners will come to understand upon starting to practice Falun Gong. It refers to the cleansing process that many practitioners will experience after they begin the practice. Body purification may occur quickly for some individuals when they first start the practice. For others, body purification could happen as a gradual process during any stage of their practice, like peeling away the many layers of an onionskin. As body purification remains a keen topic for both neophyte and experienced Falun Gong practitioners, Chapter 12 on 'Mind over Matter' will revisit this concept.

CHAPTER 11

Falun Gong and Non-Falun Gong Respondents

Observing the similarities and differences between Falun Gong and non-Falun Gong respondents provide some insights into the demographic landscape of Falun Gong practitioners, their health and wellness status, and their cultivation practice. Findings from the Australian survey displayed similarities and variances between the two groups. Apart from their spiritual beliefs, the two groups typically shared similar demographics. The non-Falun Gong respondents comprised family members, friends, or colleagues—people who lived or worked together with Falun Gong respondents. Family and friends of Falun Gong may not be the ideal choice for a comparison group. However, despite their similar home or work environment and proximity to each other, one group would emerge as a strong variant in terms of their health and wellness. Like all research, of course, other considerations could influence the results.

Observable differences between the two groups manifested in their medical history, health-wellness self-reports, and perceived state of their health and well-being. While non-Falun Gong respondents were healthy individuals, those who practice Falun Gong reported experiencing even better health-wellness than those who did not practice Falun Gong. Findings from the Australian survey indicated that Falun Gong respondents were more likely to report excellent health, display more optimistic self-perception, and have a more positive regard about their health-wellness status and general life situation. Refer to Table 3 and 4 for a summary of the similarities and differences between the two groups.

One of the similarities between the Falun Gong and non-Falun Gong groups was that both groups had more female respondents. This occurrence was consistent with the results from other Falun Gong studies inside and outside of China. That there were more female respondents within each group suggested that women might be more receptive and spiritually inclined to Falun Gong than men. This phenomenon is hardly surprising as data from over seven decades of Gallup surveys consistently indicated that women were more inclined to higher religiosity and spirituality than men (Gallup Jr., 2002; Winseman, 2002a, 2002b, 2003). Findings from the Gallup polls demonstrated that women tend to be more religious, more spiritually committed, more diligent in their practice, and more proactive in their involvement with the religious community. Some of the reasons given for the gender difference included traditional, social, and cultural roles of women as mothers, caregivers, nurturers of the family, and the multifaceted differences in the female and male consciousness.

Other studies also indicated that women were more inclined to use mind-body therapies, such as meditation and meditative movement practices (Barnes et al., 2004; Mehta et al., 2007; Upchurch et al., 2007). More women than men reported using Complementary and Alternative Medicine (CAM) and more Asian American women with higher education preferred meditation, Eastern meditative practices, and other types of CAM therapies (Mehta et al., 2007). Women were seen as more willing to try something different. They are also more receptive to integrating CAM with conventional medical treatment. In many families, women are "often the managers of health care within the family" (Upchurch et al., 2007, p. 103), a role that befits the traditional social roles of women.

Another parallel between Falun Gong and non-Falun Gong respondents was that the average age range for both groups was about the same. The age range for most respondents from both groups was between the 30 to 39 and 40 to 49 years old—closer towards the forties age group. As respondents were not asked to give their specific age, the age range was only indicative that the average age of both groups of respondents was below 50 years old. This age range was comparable with the average age of Falun Gong respondents in three different North American studies, whereas findings from the five Chinese health surveys showed that over 62 percent of the total sample were over 50 years old. Data indicated that Falun Gong people outside of China are slightly younger compared to those in China. One possible explanation for this younger age phenomenon could be the impact of immigration laws in Australia, New Zealand, Canada, and the United States—the four popular destination countries for emigrating Chinese—where the majority of Falun Gong respondents from the Australian survey identified as their country of residence. These countries generally favor and grant student or permanent resident visas to younger and educated individuals.

Yet, another parallel between the two groups was their education level. Thirty-three percent of the Falun Gong (n=117) and 34 percent of non-Falun Gong respondents (n=79) had at least an undergraduate degree. Both groups indicated completion of high school as the second highest frequency of occurrence: 29 percent for Falun Gong and 32 percent for non-Falun Gong respondents. However, more Falun Gong respondents had post-graduate qualifications. Thirty percent of Falun Gong respondents (n=107) versus 16 percent of non-Falun Gong respondents (n=36) reported having a master's, doctor of philosophy (PhD), or a doctorate degree.

Finally, another affinity between the groups was in certain occupations. For instance, 15 and 16 percent for Falun Gong and non-Falun Gong respondents respectively were business and computer technology professionals. The resemblance in their demographic profile, education, and professional background was not surprising since part of the inclusion criteria was having Falun Gong practitioners invite their family members, friends, and colleagues to complete the non-Falun Gong survey.

Diversity in Ethnicities

An interesting similarity between Falun Gong and non-Falun Gong respondents is the diversity in ethnicities. Thirty-seven and 33 different ethnicities were identified for Falun Gong and non-Falun Gong respondents respectively. This diversity is conveyed in their mother tongue or the language they grew up with. English was not the first language or mother tongue for nearly two-thirds of Falun Gong respondents. Forty-four percent of Falun Gong respondents (n=164) put down Mandarin or a Chinese dialect, such a Cantonese, Hakka, or Foochow as their mother tongue. Many Falun Gong respondents were bi-lingual or multi-lingual. They could speak English, Mandarin, several Chinese dialects, or another language. For instance, Barbara speaks English and Polish and helps with English-Polish translation of Falun Gong-related materials. Many respondents residing in Europe could speak three or more languages. They reported speaking Mandarin and English, plus a third language, such as German, Italian, Portuguese, Russian, Spanish, or Swedish.

Data for countries of birth also reflected this phenomenal diversity. Falun Gong respondents were born in 45 countries, while the non-Falun Gong respondents were born in 37 countries. However, 75 percent of Falun Gong and 81 percent of non-Falun Gong respondents resided predominantly in two main regions of the world. These are Australia and New Zealand in the Southern hemisphere and Canada and the United States in the Northern hemisphere. These four Western countries were preferred destinations for Falun Gong respondents. Many Falun Gong respondents were immigrants, foreign students, or temporary visitors. Due to the brutal persecution in China since July 1999, mainland Chinese Falun Gong practitioners who were foreign students or visitors to these countries could apply for a green card or permanent resident visa to reside in these two regions of the world. Although this is not a formality, those active in Falun Gong human rights activities were able to obtain asylum or protection visas, as returning to China would put their life at risk.

As mentioned earlier, the results from the Australian survey indicated that Chinese formed the largest group among Falun Gong respondents. Chinese comprised 47 percent (n=170) of the 37 ethnicities identified. Among non-Falun Gong respondents, Chinese also comprised the largest group although their figures (27%, n=63) were significantly lower than the Falun Gong group. Studies outside China also reflected a higher distribution of Chinese Falun Gong respondents. (See Table 1 in Chapter Six for an overview of Falun Gong studies completed outside China after the onset of the persecution.) Both the Falun Gong and non-Falun Gong groups had respondents reporting dual ethnicities. For example, a few Falun Gong respondents wrote Anglo-Celtic, Chinese-Vietnamese, Chinese-Korean, while some non-Falun Gong respondents identified themselves as Acadian Cuban, African Indian, or Lebanese-Polynesian. Yet many others simply stated they were Americans or Australians and hence it was not possible to know their ancestral ethnicity.

The profile of Falun Gong and non-Falun Gong respondents from the Australian survey could be described as multi-ethnic and multicultural. For the Falun Gong in Australia, this ethnic diversity manifested in smaller communities where Caucasians, Asians from

Malaysia, Cambodia, Korea, Japan, the Philippines, Vietnam, and other minority ethnic groups sometimes outnumbered born-in-China Chinese practitioners during local group activities. The diversity of ethnicity in the Australian survey suggested that Falun Gong has become popular and spread to people from diverse ethnic and cultural backgrounds. Whereas the earlier studies of Falun Gong outside China reflected the initial development beyond China, the Australian survey conducted in 2007 showed that the Falun Gong community outside China had become more established (Lau, 2010a).

The ethnic diversity for both groups in the Australian study could be due to the fact that the online survey had attracted many Internet-savvy Falun Gong practitioners from around the world. They in turn would have non-Falun Gong friends and family members with access to the Internet to form part of the comparison group. While more Asians or Chinese populate large-scale Falun Gong public activities—such as rallies, parades, peaceful sit-ins outside Chinese consulates, and Falun Gong conferences—the Australian survey reported a higher percentage of Westerners and English-speaking Falun Gong respondents. One reason could be that the online survey was in English and hence more accessible for English-speakers. However, Chinese translations of the survey were also posted online. A few Chinese-speaking respondents actually mailed completed hard copies of the translated survey back to the researcher who organized manual translations and transfer into the database.

Differences between Groups

The differences between the two groups were predominantly in their medical history, lifestyle habits, quality of life, general health-wellness status, attitude towards life, and their perceptions of their health and wellness. While both groups were healthy, findings indicated that Falun Gong respondents consistently reported better health and wellness than non-Falun Gong respondents. Falun Gong respondents hardly ever visited medical practitioners. They took less or no medication or health supplements and spent very little on medical and health expenses. Just over eight percent of Falun Gong respondents (n=30) visited a medical practitioner one to three times, compared to 55 percent of non-Falun Gong respondents (n=127) during the six months before completing the survey. The data showed that when Falun Gong people visited a medical practitioner it was usually for a pregnancy or work-related medical check up or to procure a medical certificate for work purposes.

The second noticeable difference between the two groups was that Falun Gong respondents reported less existing medical conditions than the non-Falun Gong at the time of the survey. Less than three percent of Falun Gong respondents (n=10) reported visiting a medical practitioner for minor health issues, whereas over 30 percent of non-Falun Gong respondents (n=73) stated they visited a medical doctor during the same period. Similarly, less than two percent of Falun Gong respondents (n=6) compared to 12 percent of non-Falun Gong respondents (n=27) reported having chronic or long-term illness. Additionally, no Falun Gong respondents reported suffering from severe non-life threatening or life threatening illness since starting the practice, while more than five percent (n=12) of non-Falun Gong respondents stated they had either severe non-life threatening or life threatening illnesses.

The third and startling difference between the two groups is the use of medication and health supplements. Ninety-five percent of Falun Gong respondents (n=341) reported not taking any medication, homeopathic remedies, multi-vitamins, or health supplements, compared to 35 percent of non-Falun Gong respondents (n=81). Likewise, 92 percent of Falun Gong respondents (n=330) stated that they did not spend money on any medical and health expenses, compared to 33 percent (n=77) from the non-Falun Gong group.

Lifestyle Habits Disparity

The fourth difference between groups concerns lifestyle habits on cigarette smoking, alcohol consumption, and the use of recreational drugs. Nearly all Falun Gong respondents did not smoke cigarettes, drink alcohol, or use recreational drugs. Eight Falun Gong respondents reported consuming alcohol while one disclosed taking recreational drugs. Data indicated that they were novice practitioners. Those who took these substances reported quitting the habits soon after they started the practice. This quick change of behavior and lifestyle habits is common among newcomers to Falun Gong. Many relinquished their addictions to substance use when they realized that these unhealthy lifestyle habits and desires will hinder their cultivation practice, and their overall mind, body, and spiritual health improvement. Falun Gong teaches that a practitioner's body has a certain level of *gong* or cultivation energy. As soon as practitioners realize that smoking and alcohol consumption will undermine this *gong* and the body purification process and hence affect their mind-body cultivation energy level, they stop these habits. For instance, drinking alcohol makes one lose the ability to think rationally. Since Falun Gong cultivates the conscious mind, which in turn affects and transforms the physical body, it is important to retain a pure and rational mind.

For one New York practitioner, Sterling Campbell, snapping out of old habits was fast. Campbell, who started practicing Falun Gong in 1998, said, "Being a musician, my surroundings were not the healthiest." Formerly a drummer with David Bowie, Campbell described his work environment as "being the giant current of bad influence." It got him into plenty of trouble, said Campbell, but he made a clean break within the first month of the practice. When asked how he did it, Campbell replied, "I just snapped out of all those environmental hazards, alcohol, and drugs." Today he is still immersed in his music career and walking the Falun Gong path. With a winning smile that lit up his kind eyes, Campbell said he has not veered back on that old path of unhealthy habits since practicing Falun Gong.

What stood out most about lifestyle habits between Falun Gong and non-Falun Gong respondents was alcohol consumption. Ninety-seven percent of Falun Gong respondents (n=349) reported not drinking any alcohol, compared with 37 percent of non-Falun Gong respondents (n=85). Of those who reported drinking alcohol before Falun Gong practice, 97 percent of them (n=168) stated they stopped the habit when they started the practice. This was not the case for the non-Falun Gong respondents. More than half of those non-Falun Gong respondents who reported consuming alcohol had no plans to stop. Data from the survey indicated that Falun Gong respondents readily changed their lifestyles to follow healthy habits and this is not the case with the non-Falun Gong group.

Quality of Life Disparity

The fifth noticeable difference between the two groups came from the findings from the SF-36 Health Survey, which gages quality of life. Over half of Falun Gong respondents (54%, n=192) reported excellent general health status, compared to just 10 percent of non-Falun Gong respondents (n=24). Falun Gong respondents reported more often that their physical health did not restrict vigorous, moderate, and other daily activities, such as climbing several flights of stairs, bending, kneeling, or stooping, or walking long distances. They also indicated more frequently that physical or emotional issues had not affected their social life. The majority of Falun Gong respondents expressed having positive thoughts and feelings about their life situations. About 81 to 84 percent of Falun Gong respondents (n=293 to 303) reported being full of life, happy, calm, and peaceful, and having lots of energy most of the time. When asked about how things had been for them and whether negative feelings had affected them, most Falun Gong respondents reported "none or a little of the time." Similarly, their self-perceived health-wellness status is more optimistic than the non-Falun Gong group. Table 2 highlights the differences between Falun Gong and non-Falun Gong respondents for some items in the SF-36 Health Survey.

Additionally, Pearson chi-square calculations for the SF-36 Health Survey items indicated that the differences between Falun Gong and non-Falun Gong respondents were all statistically significant at p=<0.001. According to the Pearson chi-square test results that check for the likelihood of the observed data being due to chance, there is one in a thousand probability that the difference in the health-wellness status between the two groups were due to chance alone. This in turn suggested that Falun Gong could be the reason for the perceived differences between the two groups. However, the findings from the Australian survey alone could not establish a causal link between the practice and the health-wellness of Falun Gong respondents.

To establish causality, the researcher has embarked on a follow-up longitudinal study—the *Hearts Uplifted* project—to explore the long-term effects of Falun Gong on the health-wellness of practitioners. This on-going study looks at how practitioners cope with the daily stresses in life and how they handle significant turning points in their life. Nevertheless, the results from the SF-36 Survey suggested that Falun Gong had a positive health-wellness effect on Falun Gong respondents. We shall look at how optimism and having a positive attitude (described as having 'righteous thoughts' among Falun Gong practitioners) plays a vital role in the health and well being of these people.

Table 2

Differences Between Groups for the SF-36 Health Survey

Item	Falun Gong respondents		Non-Falun Gong respondents	
General health status	Excellent:	53%, n=192	Excellent:	10%, n=24
Physical health limits various kinds of daily activities	Not limited at all		Not limited at all	
	Vigorous:	73%, n=261	Vigorous:	41%, n=94
	Moderate:	93%, n=333	Moderate:	68%, n=157
	Climb stairs:	87%, n=314	Climb stairs:	58%, n=133
	Bend/kneel/stoop:	91%, n=328	Bend/kneel/stoop:	65%, n=150
	Walk over a mile:	91%, n=326	Walk over a mile:	68%, n=157
How physical or emotional issues affect social life	Not at all:	83%, n=297	Not at all:	56%, n=128
	Slightly:	14%, n=51	Slightly:	27%, n=62
	Moderately:	1.4%, n=5	Moderately	11%, n=25
Positive feelings & how things had been	All or Most of the time		All or Most of the time	
	Full of life:	81%, n=293	Full of life:	55%, n=127
	Calm & peaceful:	83%, n=298	Calm & peaceful:	44%, n=102
	A lot of energy:	82%, n=294	A lot of energy:	44%, n=100
	Happy person:	84%, n=303	Happy person:	64%, n=147
Negative feelings & how things had been	None or Little of the time		None or Little of the time	
	Very nervous:	86%, n=308	Very nervous:	71%, n=162
	Down in the dumps:	73%, n=262	Down in the dumps:	49%, n=113
	Downhearted/Blue:	92%, n=330	Downhearted/Blue:	69%, n=159
	Worn-out:	87%, n=312	Worn-out :	43%, n=98
	Tired:	78%, n=279	Tired:	39%, n=89
Time physical & emotional issues affect social life	None of the time:	81%, n=292	None of the time:	51%, n=118
	Fewer FG respondents reported their social life was affected.		More NFG respondents reported their social life was affected.	
Perceptions of their health-wellness status	Definitely False statements:			
	I seem to get sick a little easier than other people:			
	FG: 87%, n=313, NFG: 47%, n=108			
	I expect my health to get worse: FG: 90%, n=324; NFG: 36.5%, n=84			
	Definitely True statements:			
	I'm as healthy as anybody I know: FG: 65%, n=234; NFG: 31%, n=72			
	My health is excellent: FG: 76%, n=274; NFG: 19%, n=44			
Summary	Self-perceived health reports were excellent & more positive than non-Falun Gong respondents.		Self-perceived health reports were NOT as good or as positive as Falun Gong respondents.	

(Lau, 2010a)	FG: Falun Gong respondents	NFG: Non-Falun Gong respondents

A Positive Attitude

It is widely believed that having an optimistic and positive attitude enhances happiness and one's health and wellness. This view forms the crux of positive psychology, an area of study that focuses on positive states, such as happiness and optimism, and strength-based approaches. Psychology Professor Martin Seligman, author of *"The Optimistic Child"* and *"Authentic Happiness,"* popularizes the concept of positive psychology and considers optimism as a health-wellness enhancing quality. Seligman stated that optimism is linked with mind-body health and wellness, longevity, less depression and, "yes, greater happiness" (cited in Wallis, 2005, p. 44). Other writers also noted the powerful effect of positive thoughts and positive emotions on one's health (Fredrickson, 2000; Lemonick, 2005; H. Li, 2001d; Wallis, 2005). In other words, hope, joy, tranquility, optimism, positive and righteous thoughts can enhance health and wellness, whereas anger, anxiety, depression, fear, jealousy, and other negative emotions have an unhealthy effect. Likewise, traditional Chinese medicine recognizes that strong, and particularly negative emotions can affect the human body (Maciocia, 1989), causing imbalances and various illnesses.

Falun Gong promotes cultivating positive qualities, a positive attitude, and a righteous mind. When positive righteous thoughts rein: mind, body, and spiritual health and wellness prevail. The results from the SF-36 Health Survey indicated that Falun Gong respondents were more optimistic about their health-wellness status than non-Falun Gong respondents. The majority (76%, n=274) perceived their health as excellent, whereas only 19 percent of non-Falun Gong respondents (n=44) felt this way. Ninety percent of Falun Gong respondents (n=324) did not expect their health to get worse, whereas only 37 percent of non-Falun Gong respondents (n=84) felt this way. Nearly 90 percent of Falun Gong respondents disagreed that they tend to "get sick a little easier," compared to 47 percent of non-Falun Gong respondents.

The majority of Falun Gong respondents reported being happy, full of energy, and satisfied with their life's situations. Falun Gong respondents did not expect their health to get worse, whereas many non-Falun Gong respondents did. Data also showed that physical, emotional, and mental problems did not seem to bother Falun Gong people or hinder them from their everyday life activities. In general, Falun Gong respondents reported more positive attitude, felt more positive and optimistic about how things had been and will be for them than non-Falun Gong respondents.

Reflecting on Disparities

The disparities between the health-wellness statuses of the two groups remain clear. Falun Gong respondents reported better health and wellness than non-Falun Gong respondents. The interesting point was that the data showed that Falun Gong respondents had more health and medical problems than non-Falun Gong respondents before they started the practice. Forty-six percent of Falun Gong respondents (n=164) reported a variety of medical conditions before they started the practice. Fifty percent of these individuals suffered from two or more medical problems from which they improved significantly or fully recovered from their conditions, baffling medical doctors.

Practicing Falun Gong offers an insight for these disparities between the two groups. In our modern society, people tend to associate health and wellness with having to spend money, or do something, such as eating healthy or organic foods, doing sports and physical workouts, paying fees to attend meditation or yoga classes, using various health products and services, or popping vitamins and herbal supplements. The Falun Gong way is quite the opposite. Instead of spending money on external things, Falun Gong practitioners are encouraged to look within for reasons and solutions for the conflicts and tribulations in their life. They are expected to cultivate their heart and improve their *xinxing* or moral standard. In order to do well, they need to study the teachings of the practice, do righteous thoughts meditation, and do their part to explain the truth about the practice to others. For optimal mind, body, and spiritual improvement, they need to supplement their mindful cultivation with exercise practice.

Except for the purchase of books to cover printing costs, practicing Falun Gong is free of charge. E-books on the teachings of Falun Gong in English, Chinese, and different languages, videos, and exercise music are available free for downloads from the official Falun Gong website. There are no hidden costs involved, no annual membership registration fees, no tuition fees for exercise classes, no fees for conference attendance, and no fees for other Falun Gong activities.

This mind-body and spiritual practice emphasizes improving our moral character, as this holds the key to overall mind, body, and spiritual wellness. To improve our moral character, we must cultivate our heart and inner self. It entails looking inward to examine oneself rather than searching for external help. This is essential to practicing Falun Gong—observing the universal principles of truthfulness, compassion, and forbearance or tolerance in our daily life. It means fulfilling three tasks practitioners are entrusted to do—regular Fa-study, righteous thought meditations, and clarifying the truth about Falun Gong. The latter refers to explaining the true story of Falun Gong to the public and those who have misunderstood the practice due to the Chinese Communist Party's (CCP) anti-Falun Gong propaganda.

The fact that Falun Gong has made a positive difference for millions of people conveys its efficacy. The practice has inspired millions of individuals to approach the challenges in life differently. It teaches them to relinquish the things that hinder their cultivation and to follow the natural flow of things, without pursuit—cultivating the heart and becoming a more compassionate and better person. Embarking on this path involves a transformational process on all levels. It involves

Children and adult practitioners doing the standing Falun Gong Exercise Three inside the Forbidden City, Beijing, China. December 1998.

letting go of psychological and behavioral attachments, desires, and addictions, such as smoking, alcohol consumption, drug use, gambling, and other vices. It means improving our heart and moral character. This calls for us to be true, compassionate, and able to endure. The goal is to cultivate away our attachments—all undesirable habits, vices, and unhealthy states of mind—and follow Falun Gong teachings, while conforming with ordinary human society, "until not one attachment is omitted. When the hardship is over and sweetness arrives, that is true happiness." (H. Li, 2002a Inscription). This way, overall mind-body and spiritual wellness will prevail.

Although the two groups shared many similar characteristics, there is a fundamental difference between them. The Falun Gong way of doing and looking at everything is different from the non-Falun Gong way. When faced with poor health or illness, everyday people would seek a medical practitioner first, without much thought about examining their heart and mind for proper moral conduct or to be true, compassionate, and enduring. Everyday people do not see the intrinsic connection between health and wellness and the improvement of our heart and moral character; whereas Falun Gong teaches practitioners to always look within first to examine their heart for the undesirable or selfish habits and behaviors that they have yet to relinquish. In other words, everyday people focus on the transient state of health and wellness, while the Falun Gong way is sublime and transcendental, aiming at and focusing on moral character improvement and returning to our original true self (H. Li, 2001d, 2002a). With the heart and mind uplifted and content, health and wellness abound.

Oftentimes, the Falun Gong way transcends human logic, like in the stories of full recovery, inexplicable, and miraculous healing experiences of various respondents from the Australian survey. For instance, Barbara, Sebastian who suffered from Guillain-Barre Syndrome, and young Harry who had viral myocarditis. All three recovered from their debilitating conditions. Once people start practicing Falun Gong and study its teachings, they realize that cultivation is not about securing better health and wellness in this lifetime, like the way everyday people expect to keep fit, well, and healthy. They realize that better health and wellness is merely a byproduct of true cultivation.

In a nutshell, the Falun Gong way involves practice, Fa-study, applying the three principles of truth, compassion, and tolerance in daily life, looking inward, and letting go of attachments. As practitioners cultivate, they inevitably have better health and wellness, and make fewer or no visits at all to medical or naturopathic practitioners. They also take less or no medication. If more people have excellent health, use little or no medication, or spend less on medical and health care expenses after practicing Falun Gong, the overall impact on society would be enormous. This phenomenon did happen in China in the late 1990s when Falun Gong was the way of life for millions of Chinese people. Early in the morning, tens of thousands of Chinese people quietly practiced Falun Gong in city parks and public places across China. They gained mind-body health and wellness. Estimates from the 1998 Chinese health surveys placed medical health care savings from Falun Gong respondents at over USD$10 million per year (Authors Unknown, 2002). Falun Gong was the best thing for many Chinese people—until July 20, 1999 when the Chinese communist regime began its nationwide persecution campaign of Falun Gong practitioners. That same year, a Chinese official from China's National Sports Commission stated that Falun Gong could save 1,000 Yuan (US$152) per person in annual medical expenses (Falun Dafa Information Center, 2015a). This would be about 10 percent of the annual income for a Chinese worker in 1999. The article also reported that this Chinese official had publicly said that if 100 million Chinese people were to practice Falun Gong, the savings in medical fees for each year would be 100 billion Yuan (about US$15 billion).

Falun Gong practitioners at the National Cherry Festival Parade in the town of Young. Sydney, Australia. December 5, 2015.

Table 3
Demographic Profile Between Groups

Items	Falun Gong respondents	Non-Falun Gong respondents
Gender	More females than males: F: 57%, n=206; M: 42%, n=151 Missing=3	More females than males: F: 63%, n=146; M: 35%, n=81 Missing=3
Age range	Mode: 30-39 years (26%, n=93) Mean: 3.72; missing=2	Mode: Both 20-29 years & 50-59 years age range (22.2%, n=51) Mean: 3.74; missing=2
Relationship status	Mostly married: 61%, n=218 Never married: 24%, n=85 De facto relationship : 1.4%, n=5 Missing=2	Mostly married: 48%, n=110 Never married: 31%, n=72 De facto relationship: 8.3%, n=19 Missing=2
Ethnicity	37 identified	33 identified
Country of birth	45 countries identified: 1st: China 28%, n=97 2nd: Asia 24%, n=86 3rd: Aust & NZ 19%, n=68 4th: Canada/US 13%, n=46	37 countries identified: 1st: Aust & NZ 40%, n=92 2nd: Asia 21%, n=48 3rd: China 10%, n=23 4th: Canada/US 9.6%, n=22
Country of residence	1st: Aust & NZ 43%, n=154 2nd: Canada/US 32%, n=114 3rd: Asia 14%, n=51	1st: Aust & NZ 66%, n=151 2nd: Canada/US 15%, n=35 3rd: Asia 11.5%, n=26
English as First language	English is 1st Lang: 35%, n=128 English is not: 63%, n=226 Mandarin/Chinese dialects as 1st Lang: 44%, n=164	English as 1st Lang: 57%, n=130 English is not: 41%, n=94 Mandarin/Chinese dialects as 1st Lang: 23%, n=53
Highest education	Mode is undergraduate degree: 33%, n=117, missing=5 High School: 29%, n=105 Master/PhD/Doc: 30%, n=107	Mode is undergraduate degree: 34%, n=79, missing=6 High School: 32%, n=74 Master/PhD/Doc: 15.7%, n=36
Occupation – Top 3 categories	Business/IT: 15%, n=54 Arts/media/social science/misc professionals: 15%, n=54 Clerical, sales, admin: 12%, n=43	Business/IT: 16%, n=36 Clerical, sales, admin & service workers: 4%, n=33 Retired/Home Duties: 14%, n=31
Summary	Mainly Chinese or Asians, with English as their first language. Most live in Australia & New Zealand, or Canada and the US.	More likely to have English as their first language. Most live in Australia & New Zealand, or Canada and the US.
	Both groups comprise mainly females, married, from diverse ethnic backgrounds, with tertiary education qualifications, and a professional career.	

(Lau, 2010a) M=male; F=female
Note: Only salient data are included here: Hence percentages do not add up.

Table 4
Medical History, Health Status Between Groups

Items	Falun Gong (FG) respondents	Non-Falun Gong respondents
Doctor visits[†]	No visits: 88%, n=316, missing=6 1-3 times. 8.3%, n=30	No visits: 28%, n=65, missing=4 1-3 times: 55%, n=127
Reason & number of visits	Had less medical problems: Medical check up: 0.6%, n=2 Minor issues: 2.8%, n=10 Chronic/long-term: 1.7%, n=6 Severe non-life threatening or Life threatening illness: None	Had more medical problems: Medical check up: 11%, n=26 Minor issues: 32%, n=73 Chronic/long-term: 12%, n=27 Severe non-life threatening: 4%, n=9; Life threatening: 1.3%, n=3
Use of medication & supplements	Use no medication: 95%, n=341 Prescription drugs: 1.9%, n=7 Vitamins/supplements: 1.4%, n=5 Over-the-counter drugs: 0.3%, n=1 Homeopathic: 0.3%, n=1 Western herbal: 0.3%, n=1 Chinese herbal: 0%; missing=4	Use no medication: 35%, n=81 Prescription drugs: 32%, n=74 Over-counter drugs: 16.5%, n=38 Vitamins/supplements: 29%, n=66 Western herbal: 3%, n=7 Chinese herbal: 5.6%, n=13 Homeopathic: 4%, n=9, missing=8
Medical health care	Did not spend money: 92%, n=330 Spent money: 8%, n=30	Did not spend money: 33%, n=77 Spent money: 67%, n=153
Cigarette smoking	Did not smoke tobacco cigarette: 98%, n=352, missing=3	Did not smoke tobacco cigarette: 86%, n=198, missing=5
Alcohol consumption	No: 97%, n=349, missing=3 Yes: 2.22%, n=8	No: 37%, n=83, missing=7 Yes: 60%, n=138. Over half of those who drink had no plans to quit.
Recreational drug use	No: 99.7%, n=355, missing=4 Yes: 0.3%, n=1 (The drug is not listed as a recreational drug.)	No: 92%, n=211, missing=11 Yes: 3.5%, n=8 (Four had no plans to stop.)
Summary	Overall, they had very healthy lifestyle habits, experienced better health-wellness than non-FG respondents. Most did not visit medical practitioners, took no medications, and spent very little money on medical/health expenses. Nearly all did not smoke tobacco cigarettes, drink alcohol, or use recreational drugs.	Overall, they were healthy with moderate lifestyle habits. They visited medical doctors more often, took more medication, remedies, and supplements, spent more on medical expenses and health supplements than FG respondents. About half of those who consumed alcohol or used recreational drugs reported no plans to stop.

(Lau, 2010a)
[†]Six months before completing the Australian survey.

Local Falun Gong practitioners participate in the annual Norwood Christmas pageant. Adelaide, Australia. December 2010.

Practitioners in the capital city of South Australia celebrate the 16th World Falun Dafa Day in Victoria Square—doing exercises, handing out information fliers, and collecting signatures to raise awareness about the Chinese Communist Party's persecution of Falun Gong practitioners in China. Adelaide, Australia. May 10, 2015.

CHAPTER 12

Mind Over Matter

"There is no illness of the body apart from the mind."
– Socrates

The idea that we can think ourselves well or worry ourselves sick is not avant-garde. Today, there is plenty of scientific evidence to indicate that our mind—thoughts, beliefs, and attitudes—can positively or negatively affect our health and well-being (Rankin, 2013). In other words, our body responds to the way we think or what is in our mind or thoughts. Staying positive or having strong positive thoughts plays a vital role in our health and wellness. Dubbed the mind-body link, Rankin (2013) uses modern scientific inquiries and research to explain how we can choose to be well and healthy or to be sick—just by how our minds think.

Falun Gong, a mind-body cultivation system, highlights this mind-body link and the idea that the mind can rule over matter. According to Falun Gong teachings, "It's known that what actually causes people to become ill is seventy percent psychological and thirty percent physiological" (H. Li, 2001d, p. 218). In Lecture One of *Zhuan Falun*,

Mr. Li (2001d) stated, "that matter and mind are one thing" (p. 28). This indicates that our thoughts are powerful; they could affect us and influence our health and wellness—making us either ill or well. For instance, a disease will manifest first as a negative thought or disharmony in the mind. "If you always believe that you are ill, you will probably make yourself sick as a result" (H. Li, 2001d, p. 218). Mr. Li (2001d) stated, "As a practitioner, if you always think that it is an illness, you are actually asking for it. If you ask for an illness, it will come inside your body" (p. 218). Hence, we should not be overly concerned or "always worry that it is an illness, for this fear of illness is an attachment and it can bring you trouble just the same" (H. Li, 2001d, p. 218).

It must be emphasized here that greater knowledge of and insight into Falun Gong can only be gleaned by reading the teachings of the practice. The discussions here are based on the understanding of the author-researcher in connection with the findings from the Australian survey. The results of the online survey indicated the health and wellness effects of Falun Gong as reported by practitioners outside of China. After reading the written comments from respondents who had experienced complete recovery, unusual healing experiences, and/or dramatic improvement from presenting health and medical problems, how the practice has helped countless individuals to regain health and wellness remains in question. Often these inexplicable healing experiences are referred to as 'miracles.' It is therefore of interest and relevance to briefly mention a few cultivation concepts, such as karma, body purification, righteous thoughts, virtue, looking within, and *xinxing* improvement, that is, character or moral improvement.

The Concept of Karma

Let us go to the root of the matter and begin with the topic of karma. The online Merriam-Webster Dictionary defines karma as "the force created by a person's actions that is believed in Hinduism and Buddhism to determine what that person's next life will be like." Karma is a Sanskrit term, meaning actions, work, or deeds carried out intentionally or knowingly. Karma is therefore connected to the concept of reincarnation or rebirth—the belief that one's soul exists beyond death, and that it incarnates or goes through countless life cycles. In this way, the effect of one's good or bad actions in one lifetime is passed from one life cycle to the next. It is important, however, to point out that Christians do not believe in reincarnation.

Everyday people often differentiate good karma from bad karma. In Falun Gong usage, karma carries only a negative connotation, whereas virtue is used to describe goodness or good deeds. This means that no karma is good because karma typically arises from wrongdoing. Falun Gong teaches that there are two types of karma (H. Li, 2001d). When people commit wrongdoing in their different lifetimes, they create karma: "Therefore, there will be birth, old age, illness, and death. These are ordinary karma" (H. Li, 2001d, p. 244).

A second type of karma, described as "thought karma" (H. Li, 2001d, p. 244), occurs when people develop impure thoughts for fame, material gain, lust, anger, and other negative emotions. This thought karma accumulates from many different lifetimes and could have a serious impact. An inscription for Falun Gong practitioners in the City of Changchun stated, "it is not that the path of cultivation is agonizing; it is the karma from lifetime after lifetime" (H. Li, 2002a) that hinders our cultivation. In other words, past wrongdoings or wrong thinking create karma leading to our present life situations.

Falun Gong teaches that there is a link between karma and sickness. "The fundamental cause of one's being ill and all of one's misfortune is karma and the black substance's karmic field" (H. Li, 2001d, p. 291). Karma is the black substance that accrues lifetime after lifetime from doing bad things and thinking bad or negative thoughts. It comes from past misconduct in this life and past lives (H. Li, 2001d). In the Western Christian context, karma is akin to the concept of committing sins or wrongdoings. When one harbors negative thoughts, and/or does bad things and actions, one accrues karma, or commits a sin, to use the Christian expression. Due to the accumulation of karma from different lifetimes, the human spirit has to go through samsara—the cycle of birth, life, death, and rebirth or reincarnation.

The concept of karma helps to explain the predestined or karmic connections in human existence. In other words, what people experience in their current life, such as an illness or any misfortune is a manifestation of previous wrongdoings either in their past, or present life. This implies that we are partly responsible for our human condition, which is tough for many to accept. Karma—described as an accumulated black substance—can determine one's state of health and wellness, or the lack of it. Falun Gong teaches that every illness condition has a corresponding dark or black energy field (H. Li, 2001b, 2001d). Illness is considered a manifestation of karma; and suffering in this present life is interpreted as repaying our karmic debts (H. Li, 2001b, 2001d).

Hence, all illnesses have a reason and are not accidental. In order to practice cultivation to high levels, Falun Gong practitioners need to improve and refine their moral character and eliminate their karma, which is, the accrued black karmic substance (H. Li, 2001d). Through enduring suffering, tribulations, ordeals, and undergoing a purification process, practitioners are able to transform the black karmic energy into a white substance called virtue, or *de* in Chinese. Virtue is not just an abstract concept; it is "a type of matter" (H. Li, 2001d, p. 28) that is produced by good deeds and enduring difficulties. When this happens, a physically ill body can transform into a healthy body.

Body Purification

Body purification and the elimination of karma are intrinsically connected (H. Li, 2001b, 2001d). Body purification helps to eliminate karma and opens the pathways for true healing. In his written response, Lucas or Respondent 196 had stated that body purification contributed to his improved health and wellness. It is mentioned in *Zhuan Falun* that "we should constantly purify our bodies and constantly progress toward high levels" (H. Li, 2001d, p. 280). This body purification will be done for genuine cultivators, those who truly want to cultivate because a practitioner "cannot practice cultivation with an ill body" (H. Li, 2001d, p. 3). In order for one to cultivate, it is stated that, "All the bad things on your mind, the karmic field surrounding your body, and the elements that make your body unhealthy will be cleaned out" (H. Li, 2001d, p. 6).

Body purification is somewhat akin to the detoxification process in naturopathy (Wilson, 2008), in which 'healing reactions' are considered manifestations of a healing process, rather than side effects, negative or adverse effects, or contraindications. Wilson (2008) described these reactions as "welcome signs of healing" (p. 1), necessary for healing to take place, and not to mistaken it as illness symptoms or a worsening of a health condition. Along with body purification, it is equally important that Falun Gong practitioners get rid of undesirable lifestyle habits, such as drinking alcohol and smoking. Giving up these addictions is part of the purifying process.

Other researchers who focused on the link between psycho-neuroimmunology (PNI), spirituality and/or religion and health, maintained that the absence of or lower alcohol consumption and smoking are reliable predictors of a better health-wellness outcome (Koenig, 2004b; Koenig & Cohen, 2002). Religious/spiritual beliefs and practices were shown to foster positive and healthy behaviors, such as reducing alcohol consumption and cigarette smoking, discouraging unhealthy behaviors like drug use, risky sexual practices, and other unsafe activities (Koenig, 2004b; Koenig & Cohen, 2002).

After starting Falun Gong, a good number of individuals will experience different body purification reactions that include vomiting, diarrhea, copious phlegm, flu-like symptoms, and pus or blood in their excrements. Some people will feel cold, dizzy, uncomfortable, or their bones may ache as if they have a cold. Others like Barbara did not have any of these flu-like symptoms. Her most memorable healing experience happened when she started reading *Zhuan Falun*. She reported feeling a strong tingling sensation going up her hands and forearms, so strong that it woke her up in the middle of the night. "It lasted for a few minutes and it was amazing because that was the first night I slept right through without waking up for pain killers." After that occurrence, "everything was good," said Barbara.

Many practitioners will also notice that the symptoms of their previously cured or treated illnesses may reappear, causing pain and discomfort, as it is necessary to remove the cause of an illness from its origin. When body purification happens, "you may feel that your illnesses have recurred" (H. Li, 2001d, p. 89). Besides Fa-study, it is important to continue doing the exercises and to endure the discomfort. Body purification is a one-time process in some instances. For others, the purifying process can recur, like peeling layer after layer of an onionskin before everything normalizes. Novice practitioners need to understand that body purification and illness-like reactions are normal and that they are not sick per se. They need to realize that the cleansing process is a positive occurrence, that once they recover from the symptoms' manifestation, they will truly feel better. Hence, it is helpful to have veteran practitioners share their body purification experiences with newer practitioners.

Once practitioners have undergone this body purification process, their health and well-being improve. Many experience full recovery from their medical conditions. Seen from this perspective, an illness manifestation is *not* really an illness, but rather, a manifestation of karma from past wrongdoing. To eliminate the karma, practitioners endure some discomfort or suffering. This synergy of karma elimination and body purification is a way to explain why Falun Gong respondents seldom take medication, or herbal supplements or consult a medical practitioner. This is because after undergoing body purification, practitioners will experience better health-wellness than non-Falun Gong people. Hence, there will be no need for them to consult medical doctors, take prescription, or over-the-counter drugs.

According to Falun Gong teachings, the balance of karma and virtue or the black and white substances determines a person's health and wellness. During body purification and depending on the individual's cultivation state, the black karmic substance will be transformed into a white matter or positive energy field (H. Li, 2001d). The more white substance one has, the better one's health and wellness will be. The more black substance a person has, the more likely this person will have illness manifestations and other tribulations. With more black substance, it means a person's karmic field is denser than one who has more white substance (H. Li, 2001d). Whereas, the more white substance a person has, the clearer the karmic field and hence the more this person can be in a state without illness (H. Li, 2001d). This implies that as one cultivates, one can change the ratio of the black and white substances. To increase the white matter or virtue, one has to improve one's *xinxing* (or moral character) and become a virtuous person. In other words, through becoming a virtuous person, the white substance or virtue increases, while the black or karmic stuff is correspondingly reduced.

The white substance, virtue, or *de* in Chinese, translates into having a positive energy field (H. Li, 2001d). Through suffering, doing good deeds, enduring hardships and tribulations in everyday life, one can accumulate virtue, which is linked with *xinxing*, or moral character improvement, and spiritual elevation. During karma elimination or body purification through sickness karma or enduring hardships, a cultivator transforms the black substance into the white substance (H. Li, 2001d). Hence, a cultivator's positive or negative thoughts, words, and actions can determine his or her health-wellness state. Genuine Falun Gong practitioners understand this. They understand that the teachings do not stop or prevent them from taking medicine or seeking medical treatment, and that it is their choice and decision should they wish to consult medical practitioners when an illness manifestation occurs. As they study *Zhuan Falun*, they realize that the practice is not just for healing or treating illnesses or to keep fit physically, mentally, and emotionally. However, it may be difficult for a non-Falun Gong person to comprehend and accept these views.

Righteous Thoughts

On the superficial level, one could say that the practice of righteous thoughts is comparable to the concept of positive thinking. The latter refers to being positive in outlook or having a positive attitude, which motivational speakers, coaches, and writers emphasize in self-help positive-thinking books, tapes, and talks. Also known as mind-power philosophy, positive thinking is the pivotal concept behind positive psychology, mind-body medicine, mind-body practices, business motivation strategies, placebo effects studies, and various self-help approaches.

Righteous thoughts in Falun Gong, however, have a deeper and more encompassing connotation. In a general sense, the practice of having and sending righteous thoughts can be described as cleansing or purging negative factors from our minds, energy field, and the environment. In Falun Gong practice, righteous thoughts are specifically linked with "Sending Forth Righteous Thoughts" (H. Li, 2001c; Minghui.org Editors, 2001b, p. 1, 2005, p. 1) or *Fa*

Zheng Nian (FZN) in Chinese as practitioners—Chinese, Westerners, and English-speaking practitioners—generally call it. Minghui.org editorials specified that the purpose of FZN is to eliminate karma, bad or negative thoughts and notions, interference in the minds of practitioners (Minghui.org Editors, 2001a), and all negative influences (Minghui.org Editors, 2005).

Sending righteous thoughts or FZN is an important component of the practice taught to practitioners after first gaining a basic understanding of the teachings. In his teachings, Mr. Li emphasized the importance of having righteous thoughts. "As you go about cultivation, you must cultivate your mind, get rid of human attachments, and view things with righteous thoughts" (H. Li, 2008, p. 4). Righteous thoughts are explained to be powerful: "One righteous mind can subdue one hundred evils" (H. Li, 2001d, p. 124). Practitioners learn that righteous thoughts will lead to righteous deeds and actions. They experience the strong effect of having and sending righteous thoughts. Hence, they often do FZN for extended periods when they encounter challenging circumstances. Unlike the fifth exercise (or sitting meditation) that requires no mind intent, the 15-minute FZN or righteous thoughts meditation requires active visualization and strong mind intent. During the first five minutes, one mentally focuses on purifying one's mind and eliminating all traces of negative thoughts. Then during the next ten minutes, one evokes positive or righteous thoughts to eliminate all negative forces (Minghui.org Editors, 2001b).

Since the purpose of doing righteous thoughts is to eliminate negative factors, it is important to stay calm and focused, in order to produce a strong effect. "Your mind has to be absolutely clear and rational, the force of your thoughts needs to be focused and strong, with an air of supremacy and of destroying all evil in the cosmos" (H. Li, 2002b, p. 1). Done this way, FZN will help practitioners to maintain a pure and positive state of mind. "It strengthens my thoughts and when I really do it well, I can feel immediate effects," said Barbara.

Performing righteous thoughts meditation is beneficial for others, the environment, and oneself. It enhances resilience and can have a powerful effect on oneself, others, and any given situation by promoting optimism and strong positive thoughts. Although righteous thoughts carry a more profound and encompassing meaning than positive thinking or a positive attitude, current mind-body philosophies validate the benefits of having righteous thoughts. As mentioned earlier, positive psychology emphasizes positive states of mind, such as happiness and optimism, as healthy states. Countless authors, coaches, and motivational speakers often use positive affirmations and the power of positive thinking and attitude to help others create happiness and success in all aspects of their life. They teach and train people to create and maintain positive states of mind and emotions, such as hope, joy, tranquility, optimism, positive thinking, and righteous thoughts can enhance health and wellness. This is not a new and modern idea.

Those familiar with China's 5,000 years of civilization know that all the great Chinese physicians in ancient times knew that emotions and the human state of mind have a deep and lasting influence on health and well being. According to the Yellow Emperor's book on internal medicine or *Huangdi Neijing*, the oldest text on traditional Chinese medicine and a major ancient classic on Taoist theory and lifestyle, emotions play a vital role in one's health and well-being. Good health is connected with our states of mind and human emotions. Emotions, such as anger, anxiety, fear, grief, over-thinking, sadness, and worry can detrimentally affect our internal organs, the immune, nervous, and endocrine systems, as well as other bodily functions—causing imbalances and various illnesses. Traditional Chinese medicine thus considers emotions as the root of all illnesses. Likewise, Hippocrates, the father of Western medicine, also alluded to the mind-body connection and taught that good health depends on a harmonious balance of mind, body, and environment.

It is explicitly stated that negative emotions, such as sadness and disappointment, could make one "feel very bitter and tired, always finding things unfair," and always competing and fighting "with a deeply wounded heart" (H. Li, 2001d, pp. 284-285). These negative feelings can cause different kinds of health problems, whereas positive feelings of joy and happiness help to foster optimism, resilience, better health, and wellness. Through cultivation, Falun Gong practitioners learn to live harmoniously in today's hectic society, following the path of non-action, non-intention, or *wuwei* (H. Li, 2001d, pp. 359, 397) in Chinese. This is because "genuine cultivation toward higher levels is in a state of *wuwei* and free of any mind activities" (H. Li, 2001d, p. 333). In other words, one simply goes with the flow of things, like water from a stream flowing down and eventually ending in the ocean. As one relinquishes pursuit for everything—the material things in life and even spiritual enlightenment—one's mind becomes free. One is able to live moment-by-moment, in the here and now. The results from the Australian survey suggested that those who embarked on the Falun Gong path were indeed transformed. Health and wellness seemed to permeate their mind and body; many Falun Gong respondents found themselves achieving and maintaining better mind-body and spiritual health and wellness.

A Respondent's Experience with Righteous Thoughts

Barbara's narrative emerged from the Australian survey as respondent 289. Later she became one of the participants for the follow-up longitudinal study. Snippets of her narratives here touch upon looking within and having righteous thoughts. In one of the follow-up interviews, she spoke about her way of coping with daily life issues—how she mindfully focused on the strengths, the positive, and enlightened side of a person instead of looking at his or her shortcomings or negative traits. She noted that whenever she did this with strong righteous thoughts, "the negative aspects [of that person] would melt away, and miracles happen" (sic) and that situations would often change with strong righteous thoughts. "When more people have positive righteous thoughts, more good things will happen," stated Barbara. Then she added, "When I first moved into our neighborhood, there were many people fighting, arguing, and things being damaged or stolen from houses." She noticed that after doing righteous thoughts meditation and talking to the neighbors about Falun Gong, the situation seemed to improve. "Everyone is happier and I live in a more peaceful environment," said Barbara.

During a follow-up interview in late 2012, when asked again the same question about how she handled daily challenges, Barbara said, "All the answers are inside myself. Falun Gong has provided me with a tool to look within for answers to solve my problems." The practice has helped her to handle difficult moments in her life, she said. She spoke about the power of righteous thoughts and how this has made a difference in her life. "This positive energy is so powerful that we can reverse a negative situation," as she recalled an incident that happened during her first trip to New York. "I thought to myself: 'Oh, it's going to be a very long flight.' I should wear special elastic stockings to improve the circulation in my legs." Later she realized that harboring the negative thought—that something not good would happen to her—was not right. Upon arriving in New York, she found a big lump on her leg. "It looked like a big bruise and it was very painful." When she realized what was happening, she quickly rectified her thinking. "I decided not to acknowledge it and didn't tell anybody about the lump. I just went ahead to do my exercises and sat in full-lotus meditation for an hour in sheer agony," said Barbara. After the meditation, the pain stopped and she was able to sleep soundly that night.

The next morning she found the bruise was gone. The lump had also disappeared as mysteriously as it had manifested after she negated what she described as unrighteous thinking and declined to acknowledge the physical manifestation. This occurrence may be difficult for non-Falun Gong practitioners to understand. However, this phenomenon of having a physical ailment or pain disappearing soon after one rectifies one's thinking and emphasizes strong positive righteous thoughts is not unusual amongst Falun Gong practitioners. To explain it simply, it is a situation of mind over matter—the concept that mind and matter are one and the same (H. Li, 2001d). Hence, what does not exist in your mind will not exist in your body.

At a subsequent face-to-face interview in New York in May 2013, Barbara again mentioned that mishaps would happen to make her realize how often her unrighteous or negative thoughts created or intensified her tribulations. She recounted two personal incidents that reinforced the importance of always having righteous thoughts. Both of these incidents related to her thoughts about her fall that happened on November 11, 2003 (11/11). Ever since the fall, Barbara said she harbored negative thoughts about the 11/11 combinations. "Once I said to my friends that the number 11/11 is not good for me. The next day I got a speeding ticket and the time of the offense was 11

Photo by Oliver Trey

Barbara and the author in deep conversation during a face-to-face meeting. New York, NY, US. May 2013.

past 11." She laughingly said she incurred a traffic fine for harboring unrighteous thoughts. She saw the incident as a hint for her to look within and eliminate her fear of the 11/11 combinations.

However, the traffic fine incident was merely peeling off one layer of her deep attachment of fear of 11/11. Another incident happened. This time, she found herself unable to move for more than 12 hours, after she slipped and fell on the concrete steps, outside her home on November 11, 2011. It was raining and the steps were slippery, she said. "I fell and hurt my back. Nevertheless, I jumped up immediately, ran up the steps, and sat in meditation for an hour. Then I read one chapter of *Zhuan Falun*." Feeling happy with herself, she thought, "I've done well. Now I can lie down." As soon as she lay down on the floor, Barbara found herself paralyzed from her chest down. "I could move my arms but I couldn't feel the rest of my body," she said. It was about five o'clock in the afternoon and her husband was out of town that day. She spent about seven hours on the floor before he returned around midnight. Alarmed, he wanted to call an ambulance but Barbara said, "No." She assured her husband that everything would be fine and to just let her lie on the carpet—with a glass of water, her Falun Gong books, and her cell phone.

When asked if she was afraid, Barbara shook her head: "No, I understood immediately that I set it up for myself." She realized her predicament was due to her not having righteous thoughts and for harboring negative thoughts about 11/11—even though eight years had passed since her fall. "I should never have said or even thought that the number 11/11 was not good for me," said Barbara emphatically. When asked about how she had spent her 12 hours lying paralyzed on the floor, Barbara said: "The first thing I did was to look within—examine what and why this had happened to me. I started looking for my attachments and then I eliminated them one by one from my mind. I spent the time reciting from memory, "Lunyu" [in *Zhuan Falun*] and some of Master's poems."

She did not panic, she said: "I was positive and knew in my heart and mind that I was going to be fine." Throughout the ordeal, Barbara remained calm. "As Falun Gong practitioners, we are taught to always look within for the causes of any tribulations we encounter." She continued, "I also realize that I have very strong attachments to pride and that I seldom ask for help. To get rid of my pride, I called fellow practitioners to ask for their help to send righteous thoughts for me." She paused, and with a smile of one who has gained an 'Aha!' insight, she said, "it definitely helped."

Asked what else did she do, Barbara said, "I was doing the [Falun Gong] exercises in my mind. Early the next morning, my bodily sensations gradually returned. I was able to move and get up" (sic). She regained full mobility with no after effects. "On the third day of the incident, I was standing up all day in a shopping center, promoting Shen Yun Performing Arts.[2] Towards the end of the day, I checked and found out that I had helped to sell *11* Shen Yun tickets."

Cultivating the Heart

This expression 'cultivating the heart' implies tempering one's moral character and disposition. It is a fundamental aspect of the practice. According to the teachings of Falun Gong, "true cultivation practice depends fully upon the heart" (H. Li, 2001d, p. 92). "Without cultivating the heart, no one can make it" (H. Li, 2001d, p. 102); hence, "you must truly cultivate your heart to make it work" (p. 102). In fact, "whether one succeeds in cultivation all depends on cultivating the heart. The same is true for everyone, and one cannot fall short even a bit" (H. Li, 2001d, p. 287). Cultivating the heart is so important that it is frequently reiterated: "In genuine cultivation practice one must cultivate one's

2   Shen Yun Performing Arts is a premier non-profit classical Chinese dance group based in New York, with the mission to revive 5,000 years of traditional Chinese culture.

own heart and inner self... You must cultivate your heart if you want to succeed in cultivation" (H. Li, 2001d, p. 358).

The heart is the cradle for compassion. It epitomizes the center of a person's deepest and most authentic sense of wisdom embodied in compassion. In counseling, it is crucial that the client looks within and responds from the heart to make life-transforming changes. Similarly, when a Falun Gong practitioner has the heart for cultivation, the heart to improve his or her moral character, or elevate his or her *xinxing*, great transformations will occur. Improving *xinxing* refers to cultivating the heart and becoming a virtuous person with high moral values. The term *xinxing* is translated as "heart or mind nature" or "moral character" (H. Li, 2001d, p. 397). It embodies "virtue (a type of matter), tolerance, forbearance, enlightenment quality, sacrifice, giving up ordinary people's desires and attachments, being able to endure hardships..." (H. Li, 2001d, p. 28). During cultivation, "every aspect of *xinxing* must be improved for you to make real progress" (H. Li, 2001d, p. 28), before a cultivator can reach enlightenment (or consummation in Falun Gong language).

Then, what is *xinxing* cultivation? It encompasses many aspects and involves improving one's moral character and behavior. It calls for being truthful, kind, and being able to endure and practice self-restraint during tribulations. Falun Gong practitioners endeavor to cultivate the heart and mind. During the cultivation process, amidst trials and tribulations, practitioners need to remain calm and compassionate, caring less about personal feelings and desires, and not vying for personal gain or self-validation when in a conflict with others. The purpose of cultivating *xinxing* is to attain a higher standard of moral conduct in everyday life. In other words, a Falun Gong practitioner must have "a heart of compassion and kindness" (H. Li, 2001d, p. 162)—be kind to others and to always consider others first. *Xinxing* cultivation and the process of cultivating the heart are likened to removing dirty stuff from a sealed bottle that has been thrown into the water (H. Li, 2001d). The bottle will sink to the bottom. When one empties the bottle bit by bit, the bottle will begin to rise to the surface. Likewise, during "cultivation practice, you must clean out various bad things in your body so that you can move up" (H. Li, 2001d, p. 29). Often a tempering of the heart will trigger the transformation of one's character and behavior. Hence, without a change of heart, it would not be possible to raise one's *xinxing*. And "If you do not cultivate your *xinxing* or elevate your moral standard, or if your ill thoughts and bad substances have not been removed, it will not let you ascend" (H. Li, 2001d, p. 29).

Falun Gong practitioners improve *xinxing* by assimilating to the highest qualities of the universe that are expressed as truthfulness, benevolence, and forbearance, or "*Zhen-Shan-Ren*" (H. Li, 2001d, pp. 14-17, 398) in Chinese. In essence, cultivation requires following these universal principles that are taught by all major religious, philosophical, and ancient spiritual teachings. Having virtue, being good, and doing good have their roots in both ancient Eastern traditions, such as Buddhism, Taoism, Confucianism, and in the Western traditions of Christianity and classical philosophy. The Greek philosopher, Aristotle defined two types of virtue: intellectual virtue, or wisdom attained through teaching; and moral virtue, or moral excellence of character arising from good habits or high moral conduct (Kemerling, 2011). Aristotle elucidated that achieving happiness involved having virtue or having good moral behavior and sound reasoning based on wisdom (Easton, 2005; Kemerling, 2011).

Seligman, the modern guru of happiness, stated that having a meaningful and purposeful life is a loftier kind of happiness. There are three types of 'happy' life—the pleasant, the good, and the meaningful life (Seligman, 2008). According to Seligman, a pleasant life does not ensure a high level of happiness or a lofty level of life satisfaction; whereas a meaningful life offers the highest life satisfaction. Likewise, in classical philosophy the quest for meaning in life is considered the most esteemed of eudemonia—the Greek word for happiness—which is often translated as virtue or highest human good in Aristotle's writings (Kemerling, 2011).

Contrary to ancient Eastern and Western classical teachings, there is little emphasis in the education and development of the individual toward excelling in virtue and high moral conduct in our contemporary society. In contrast, Falun Gong offers meaning and purpose in life for practitioners. The practice stresses the importance of being a morally good and virtuous person. It teaches that the only way to increase gong or cultivation energy and to become a truly enlightened being is to be a morally good person. When *xinxing* improves, mind-body and spiritual health and wellness prevail. Hence, it was not surprising that findings from the Australian survey reflected this understanding. Over 91 percent of Falun Gong respondents (n=328) reported that the reason for their health and wellness was related to "improving *xinxing* or moral character based on the principles of truthfulness, compassion, and forbearance."

Along with cultivating the heart and *xinxing* or moral character development, looking within to examine oneself or one's behavior is another important aspect of the practice. When practitioners are able to look within honestly to identify their issues and let go of their attachments, they can often resolve any presenting issues or situations. This constant looking within in Falun Gong cultivation is similar to the healing process in counseling and psychotherapy culture. It is akin to undergoing therapy or self-therapy. The counselor helps the client to look within, explore issues, and gain that 'Aha!' insight before healing can take place. Seen from this perspective, looking within and constant self-examination during cultivation practice are similar to the healing process in counseling and psychotherapy culture.

Since Falun Gong teaches that "genuine cultivation depends entirely upon a person him or herself" (H. Li, 2001d, p. 171), every Falun

Gong practitioner needs to look within. Each step of the process is like peeling off a layer of the onionskin of attachments. Attachments can refer to negative emotions, desires, and various mental states, such as anger, fear, insecurities, pride, lust, past hurts and traumas, a competitive mentality, worry, and other undesirable states. Regardless of how long practitioners have been cultivating, looking within and relinquishing attachments is an on-going process. But, letting go of attachments can be challenging. In the Fa teaching on "True Cultivation," Mr. Li (2001a) stated: "Cultivation itself is not painful—the key lies in your inability to let go of ordinary human attachments," (p. 6). When a practitioner succeeds in relinquishing these undesirable states or emotions layer by layer, like peeling the onionskin, true health and wellness prevail.

Transcending Boundaries

The results from the Australian survey showed that many Falun Gong respondents achieved significant improvements in all health-wellness domains. There are many complex reasons for this healing phenomenon. Certainly, cultivating diligently and integrating the principles of truthfulness, compassion, and forbearance into their daily life play a significant role in the health and well-being of Falun Gong practitioners. Yet, there is something indiscernible and imperceptible to human logic about Falun Gong that defies explanation. Barbara (R289), Sebastian (R182), and numerous other practitioners have their own unique crossings with Falun Gong. To glean greater insights, experience mind-body and spiritual wellness, and transcend boundaries, we will need to make the crossing ourselves—like the millions of Falun Gong practitioners around the world have done.

From 1992 to 1999, Falun Gong spread rapidly by word of mouth across China. The practice was so popular that by 1999, almost one in thirteen Chinese people were practicing Falun Gong. There would be even more people experiencing health and wellness, if Jiang Zemin, the former leader of the Chinese Communist Party (CCP), had not embarked on the persecution campaign against Falun Gong. Although the practice is deeply rooted in ancient Chinese traditions that have existed since time immemorial, Falun Gong offers a revolutionary paradigm change for our modern society. The practice teaches people to consider others first and to always look within rather than outside when encountering difficulties in everyday life. While this can be challenging to do, a practitioner must cultivate and maintain a compassionate heart. "Then, when you run into a problem, you will be able to do well because it gives you room to buffer the confrontation. You should always be benevolent and kind to others, and consider others when doing anything" (H. Li, 2001d, p. 162).

The practice emphasizes heart-mind cultivation and having righteous thought that reinforces the concept of mind over matter. It teaches that often the true cause of illness or the lack of health and wellness is not external but rather something within our responsibility and control. We can therefore transform our life and destiny through *xinxing* or moral character improvement. When Falun Gong practitioners practice diligently, truly cultivate their *xinxing*, gain insight, and apply the concept of mind over matter, they experience inner peace, harmony, and overall mind, body, and spiritual health and wellness.

Based on the self-reports from Barbara and other respondents from the follow-up study, this self-transformational process can transform people, our environment, and community. In the main text, *Zhuan Falun*, Mr. Li Hongzhi mentions how, after a practitioner from a clothing factory in Shandong province taught his colleagues the practice, everyone's moral character improved, and nobody would pilfer things from the factory (H. Li, 2001d). In another example, a factory manager commended that Falun Gong contributed to

Canadian Falun Gong practitioners gather in Queen's Park to do the exercises before having a rally and a parade to celebrate the benefits of Falun Gong to millions of people around the world and to raise awareness about the persecution of the practice in China. Toronto, Canada. May 2010.

the success of his business as he had noticed the workers' attitude improved and they "no longer compete for personal gain" (H. Li, 2001d, p. 164).

Although Falun Gong "does not intend to do such a thing, it can nonetheless assume a great constructive role by promoting spiritual civilization in society" (H. Li, 2001d, p. 164). Mr. Li (2001d) emphasized, "If every one of us cultivates his inner self, examines his own *xinxing* to look for the causes of wrongdoing so as to do better next time, and considers others first when taking any action, human society would become better and ethical standards would again rise" (p. 382). Man-made laws cannot control people's hearts: "When they are not seen, they will still do bad deeds" (H. Li, 2001d, p. 383). Whereas when a Falun Gong practitioner cultivates his *xinxing* and moral character, transformation comes from within. "No one would need to be governed, as everyone would discipline him or herself and search their inner self" (H. Li, 2001d, p. 382) and become a better person and citizen.

Local Falun Gong practitioners participate in the State Christmas Parade, showcasing the Falun Gong exercises. Perth, Western Australia. December 4, 2011.

Peruvian practitioners convey birthday greetings to Master Li on World Falun Dafa Day with beautiful handmade lotus flowers. Peru, South America. May 13, 2006.

CHAPTER 13

Integrating Falun Gong with Counseling

"Whenever something unexpected happens, I'd [sic] step back and try to look inside myself for the causes. Falun Gong has taught me to constantly look inside for answers to solve my problems," said Barbara. This constant inward reflection that Falun Gong teaches is an empowering way to manage stress, conflicts, and handle tribulations in our life. "Sometimes when I don't feel so good, the teachings of the practice help me to stay calm and rational, and I would often find the right solutions to the problem," she continued. Seen from this perspective, one could say that it is like a form of therapy.

Indeed, Falun Gong can be like a 'self-therapy.' This is a great practice for self-regulation, self-awareness, mindfulness training, and overall mind-body and spiritual development. Falun Gong teaches people to examine themselves for the causes of their problems whenever something happens. Upon gaining insight, they endeavor to change by relinquishing their unrighteous thoughts, conduct, or habits and become a better person. One can say this process is almost akin to the 'Aha!' realization and subsequent healing process that counseling clients often have to go through during the course of therapy. As a professional counselor and prior to embarking on the Australian survey, the author-researcher has introduced and successfully integrated Falun Gong exercises and elements of the teachings of the practice with counseling. This fruitful outcome from the integrated approach triggered the wish to research the health-wellness effects of Falun Gong and hence initiated the Australian survey.

Integration can take place in two ways. Of course, the ideal way is to begin our own journey with the practice. Learn the exercises and study the teachings of the practice. Often clients can intuit whether the counselor is coming from the heart with their integrative practice. Once the practice resonates with us and as we experience enhanced health and wellness in different aspects of our life, it will be more authentic—coming from the heart—to integrate Falun Gong into your professional practice. In addition, we can share our knowledge and first-hand experience with those clients who show an interest in Falun Gong and assist them in their journey toward wholeness and wellness.

The second way is to learn about Falun Gong without actually taking up the practice ourselves. However, it is still important to be familiar with the practice so that we can comfortably talk about it and recommend interested clients to learn the meditative exercises at a Falun Gong practice site. This approach can be useful when working with clients who are already familiar with the practice and who have friends, relatives, or family members already practicing Falun Gong. This way requires minimal, real hands-on integration. However, in this scenario, we might still need to be ready to answer the clients' query about our reasons for recommending the practice, just as the author had been asked before why she did not continue with Vipassana meditation or yoga practice, and instead chose to practice Falun Gong. The only way is to be honest with the client about our stance. Inform them of the benefits of the practice and our personal choice in a way that is helpful to them. Keep some written literature—booklets or fliers with the practice sites' addresses in the counseling or waiting room. Also, consider visiting a Falun Gong practice site to speak with the volunteer teaching assistant. Let him or her know of your plans to recommend interested individuals to the practice site. Alternatively, collect the assistant's contact details in case you need to reach him or her or to pass it to any interested individuals.

For those interested in integrative practices, this chapter unfolds three scenarios from the author's own experience of integrating Falun Gong with counseling. Then points to consider when embracing integrative practices follow the brief narratives. Plus the six-step approach as a resource guide on how to integrate Falun Gong with counseling and health care. All real names and distinguishing information about the clients have been removed for privacy and confidentiality issues.

Oskar the Wild

It was a sultry April evening in the fruit-growing region of Australia. The warm autumn air was laden with humidity. The setting sun threw fiery orange and crimson shimmers across the lake. Everything was still and serene, like out of a picture book. I stood by the lakeshore, holding up my arms in the first position of Falun Gong Exercise Two. There was a faint movement in front of my face. Slowly I opened my eyes and recognized him immediately. We had built a positive connection before his counseling sessions were over. There he stood with his face six inches away from mine, grinning broadly. "Nice music," he said happily and chuckling softly. The Falun Gong meditation practice was something he had grown familiar with during therapy. I smiled, nodded, and asked if he would like to join in. He shook his head, smiling before sauntering away as silently as he had appeared.

Oskar (not his real name), a mentally challenged client in his thirties, had a history of aggressive behaviors to boast of. Yet, he was a kind and gentle soul at heart who could be like an unruly child as his mental age was that of a young teenager. Like all the other clients, his doctor at the medical center had referred him for counseling support. During the first meeting, the first thing Oskar asked was, "Have you ever been attacked [by a client] during a counseling session?" It was obvious that he did not want to come. Oskar sat in his chair, clenching his fists until the knuckles turned white against his pale skin. I shook my head, managed to smile congenially, and said, "No." He then described one after the other his socially unacceptable behaviors. With a child-like pride, Oskar informed me of his physical strength and that he had received several police restraining orders. I endeavored to stay calm and relaxed. However, while I sat calmly in my chair, amiably engaging with my 'reluctant client,' I did cast a quick eye on the exit door, mentally measuring the distance between the door and myself—in case I needed to sprint for the exit. However, I did not need to. Oskar's persona quickly changed like a child who felt safe, after I engaged with him using the integrative approach.

This approach involved integrating Falun Gong principles of truthfulness, compassion, and forbearance with Carl Rogers' (1951) three principles—accurate empathy, congruence, and unconditional positive regard (Elliott & Freire, 2007; Mearns & Thorne, 2007; Merry, 2002; C. R. Rogers, 1951). It worked beautifully and encouraged Oskar to talk about himself. As I listened to his story with compassion and positive righteous thoughts, Oskar gradually relaxed and became less intimidating. It soon became clear that he was under duress to receive counseling in order to secure his release from detention. By the end of the counseling session, Oskar was smiling and chatty. He agreed to return for on-going sessions.

Oskar responded well to art therapy and disclosed traumatic childhood events that provided a deeper insight about his presenting issues. However, it was challenging to engage Oskar with any consistent form of therapy as he was like a child and would lose interest quickly once his presenting issue, whether be it anger or sadness abated. Often he would chuckle and tell me that I did not know what to do with him, or ran out of things to do with him—"like all the others," he added smiling smugly. However, I noted Oskar frequently mentioning with warmth a former caregiver who would always remind him to be good and he would mimic this caregiver in a playful manner. It sounded like he had a positive connection with this caregiver. I therefore tapped into his fond memories to improve our rapport and described in simple terms Falun Gong's three universal principles of truthfulness, compassion, and tolerance, considering others first and to be "True, Good, and Endure" (H. Li, 2003, pp. 12, 13). This turned out to be an anchor for Oskar that helped him connect the present with his positive memories of this caregiver.

One day Oskar came looking dejected and told me that he had had a quarrel with his girlfriend. She wanted to leave him, he said. I asked if the police were involved. He shook his head. I was relieved and encouraged him to tell his story, to which Oskar said that he had picked up a kitchen knife. Then he added, "I remember you said that I must show compassion and consider the other person first. So I did," he paused. "And I didn't hurt her. I put the knife down instead." I smiled and nodded, to let him know that he was doing the right thing to put away the knife. Another pause. "I showed compassion but, she still left me," he added with sadness in his voice. Since I had shown Oskar the *Zhuan Falun* book during previous sessions, I asked him if he would like me read a few sentences from the 'blue book' (how he described it). He nodded and I picked the second last paragraph from the book: "When it's difficult to endure, you can endure it. When it's impossible to do, you can do it ... After passing the shady willow trees, there will be bright flowers and another village ahead!" (H. Li, 2001d, p. 385). When I stopped reading, Oskar's countenance had visibly relaxed.

There was a long moment of silence, more soothing than uncomfortable. It was late summer. Outside the window, a symphony of birds was chirping merrily in a Waratah bush. Inside the counseling room, Oskar must have experienced a light shining on his 'dark night of the soul' ordeal. He brushed the corner of his eye with his index finger. I offered him a box of tissues and we made friends with silence again. After a couple of minutes, he asked if I would write those sentences on a piece of paper for him. Gently, I said, "How about you copy the sentences?" to which he replied, "I'm dyslexic... But I want to put it on my fridge," he said in a subdued voice. This was one of those moments when I too wished for the tissue box.

Our talking sessions, as Oskar liked to call it, were ending and Oskar intuitively knew that too. Something shifted in me that no words could describe. That was the final time I saw him in my counseling room, before he showed up smiling into my face for that fleeting moment by the lakefront. I was glad to see him then and to know that he was all right. This fleeting encounter was our last. Somewhere, some time, Oskar might be telling another caregiver, with his child-like chuckle, about the counselor who reminded him to be "True, Good, and Endure" (H. Li, 2003, pp. 12, 13).

With Wings, Will Fly

"When I first started learning the Falun Gong exercises, I felt really good physically and mentally. It was something to focus on and it gave me a sense of purpose in my life," said April (not her real name), during a telephone interview in 2014. When asked about how Falun Gong had affected her life, April stated that the practice had helped her to soar to new heights. "Falun Gong calms my mind and body. I no longer need counseling sessions. Whenever emotional stuff resurfaces, it [Falun Gong] helps me to stay calm," stated April.

More than a decade ago, April and her husband moved to the country to look after her ailing father-in-law. The transition from city to country life took some time for her to adjust. Her life suddenly revolved around cooking, cleaning, and taking her father-in-law for frequent medical appointments. Consequently, she did not have time to socialize and make friends with whom she could chat over cups of tea and home-baked scones, she said in a shy and self-conscious voice.

The first time April came for counseling, she sat upright on the edge of the seat and spoke timidly. "My doctor suggested that I come to talk to you." When asked about her reason for coming, April said, "I feel anxious easily." This mild anxiety and constant vigilance had become part of her personality for a long time, she said. However, she found it difficult to pinpoint the cause of her needling anxiety. An integrated approach, blending truthfulness, compassion, and forbearance (H. Li, 2001d) with Rogers' principles of accurate empathy, congruence, and unconditional positive regard (Elliott & Freire, 2007; Mearns & Thorne, 2007; Merry, 2002; C. R. Rogers, 1951) soon helped April to externalize her feelings and thoughts. "Caring for my father-in-law is not the issue, although it takes much of my time," she said. As we built better rapport, April opened up even more. She talked about "the 'demons' that haunt me all the time... they are never far away. They go wherever I go." April said she grew up with these words—"that I was no good"—ringing in her ears. Hence, all her life, she strove to be good, constantly seeking approval from others.

Open as she was to different approaches, April was not keen about using behavioral self-observation charts. She preferred the more intuitive and spontaneous approach and responded more readily to the person-centered approach, art therapy, visualization techniques, and eventually meditation exercises. During the first month, April came every week, tapering off to once every two weeks. Then it was once every three weeks, and later to whenever she needed to bounce things off someone she trusted. When the therapeutic effects with the above-mentioned intervention strategies reached a plateau, April was ready to engage more readily with the integrated approach and began first to learn the Falun Gong exercises.

She tried the sitting meditation and sat for 20 minutes during her first endeavor. In the beginning, she found the hand gestures a little daunting to follow. Nonetheless, she found the exercise music soothing and stated that the meditation had a calming effect on her busy mind. It benefited her tremendously. "I feel more relaxed, less anxious, and less stuff buzzing in my head," said April. This encouraged her to persevere to learn the hand movements. Then she could meditate for 30 minutes and use the remaining time for sharing and expressing her thoughts and feelings. Her anxiety level dipped. Soon it was a non-issue. Falun Gong meditation helped to ease her anxieties and to come out of her cloistered shell.

April began to talk and smile more, as she felt more secure within herself. Slowly her confidence returned. Negative thoughts about demons troubling her disappeared. She could handle the suppressed memories of her childhood when they surfaced. Her father was a drunk, she said. "He'd rather spend his pay on drinks, cigarettes, and gambling." Soon she disclosed reasons for her constant need to stay vigilant and her fears around taking showers with her eyes closed or having water sprayed into her face with a garden hose. "Mom used to chase us kids around the yard with a strap. She threw boiling water at me a few times. Once, it scalded the back of my neck," she said as the tsunami of memories came upon her. One by one, she cleared the cobwebs of her past. One day April talked about how someone had pulled her out from under a pier and saved her from drowning. Through practicing Falun Gong, April was able to let go of these unpleasant childhood memories.

As April wrestled and defeated her inner demons one by one through counseling integrated with Falun Gong, her confidence and self-esteem grew. She spread her wings to explore new horizons. Falun Gong helped her to cross the threshold of painful memories from her childhood and overcome her timidity. The practice became her crossing. She was eager to learn the four standing exercises. In the beginning, she took small steps and preferred to do the exercises during counseling sessions instead of going to the community center. It was still "too scary," said April, to be in a large group. Eventually she overcame her anxieties and attended the local Falun Gong group practice.

From conversations during therapy and from the Falun Gong fliers, April learned about the principles of the practice, the importance of having a strong conscious mind, and studying the teachings of the practice for overall mind-body improvement. When the demons in her mind popped up, April remembered that those thoughts were not her true self. She realized that her consciousness must stay strong to reject the negative thoughts that were dragging her down. When she was ready, she started reading *Zhuan Falun* by herself at home and later joined the local small Fa-study group.

Fifteen years had passed since her crossing with Falun Gong in 2001. Falun Gong is still part of her life. In a recent letter to the author-counselor, she wrote, "Falun Gong is never far from my mind. I have read *Zhuan Falun* many times. Every time I read it, I would come across something new that I didn't remember reading the last time. It's quite amazing."

Apollo Crossing

When Apollo (not his real name) first stepped into my office, the room seemed to shrink. Standing at over six foot, he looked every inch a hunk. Yet, his voice was gentle, like a soft gurgling brook meandering through a grove of golden wattle trees that are native to Southeastern Australia. When asked what had brought him to the session, he stated in a quiet monotone, "anxiety." I looked at the hunk that dwarfed the armchair and asked if he could talk more about it. As our first 50-minute session progressed, Apollo recounted his tale of anxieties that had prevented him from living a normal life for some years.

"I'm anxious around strangers," he said with a tight smile. "What happens when you're anxious?" I asked quietly. He paused, fixed his eyes on the carpet in front of us, as if he could find the answers there. My eyes shifted from him to the carpet. Together we studied the carpet patterns. The seconds fleeted by. You could hear a pin drop. I heard myself asking softly, "How do you know you are anxious?" The tick-tock of the clock suddenly sounded deafening. He murmured, "My palms become clammy. I perspire. My throat feels dry." He paused. I smiled, nodding congruently and empathically. He felt encouraged and gave an example. For instance, he would feel anxious to step into the gas-station office to make the payment himself after he refueled the car. Someone else would have to make the payment. Consequently, Apollo seldom left the house alone.

Apollo was a man of few words. With incredible effort, he hurdled over an avalanche of words during his first visit. When asked if there was any information he needed to tell me, Apollo disclosed that he was diagnosed with a mental illness and that he was on medication for this condition. He explained that he had come to seek help only for his anxiety issues and mentioned that he was familiar with cognitive behavioral therapy and behavioral techniques taught by the Flinders University in Adelaide, South Australia. He had tried them and most other techniques but he could not completely overcome his anxiety.

Apollo was open and consented to the integrative approach, although he had never heard of Falun Gong. He was keen to give it a try and began learning the sitting meditation during the counseling session. After the first 20-minute sitting meditation, he reported feeling calmer. Like April, he found the exercise music soothing. Thereupon we agreed to dedicate a portion of the counseling session for meditation. In the beginning, he sat cross-legged for about 15 to 20 minutes, then 30 minutes. Each time he reported feeling less anxious. Apollo began to smile more and look more relaxed. This greatly encouraged him to continue coming for the integrative therapy. His curiosity about Falun Gong grew and he asked to learn the standing exercises.

Due to his clinically diagnosed mental health condition and the fact that he was on medication, it was necessary to inform Apollo right at the onset of therapy about the contraindication for individuals with mental health illness and the practice's stance on mental health illness. I carefully explained to Apollo that Falun Gong cultivates the conscious mind and that it would be challenging for individuals with mental health issues to practice Falun Gong. I let Apollo know that it was not expected of him to practice Falun Gong in public settings, or to study the teachings of the practice. This information, however, did not deter Apollo from wanting to learn the exercises during counseling sessions or to practice them at home. One day, Apollo came for his appointment with the blue *Zhuan Falun* book in his hand. Wearing a quiet and happy smile, he said that as he had the occasion to travel to the nearest city, he bought the book and started reading it at home.

As the time between sessions stretched to once every two to three weeks, I gave him an exercise music CD and self-observation papers to record and monitor his changes and improvement. One day, Apollo returned for a session after an interval of several weeks. He looked subtly different—relaxed, happier, and more confident about himself. I asked him what had been happening. With a soft smile, he quietly announced that he had gone to pay for the gas himself when he refueled the car. It was a huge step for Apollo, a major crossing over the threshold in his journey to wellness. As his anxiety disorder had abated, it was no longer necessary for him to seek further counseling and thus his crossing with Falun Gong and integrative counseling ended on a positive and uplifting note.

Points to Consider when Embracing Integration

The three scenarios described here concerned working with non-Falun Gong clients who had no initial knowledge about Falun Gong. But they were open and trusted the integrated approach. Thus they benefited from the experience. Besides these three scenarios, there were numerous other cases, some involving only a one-time encounter with the Falun Gong sitting meditation. The integrated counseling practice touched the hearts of the majority of clients who consented to give Falun Gong a try; so much so that it inspired the author-counselor to embark on the Australian survey to study the health-wellness effects of the practice, and to explore its application in counseling.

There are several points to consider when embracing an integrative approach with Falun Gong meditation practice. The first is to consider the clients first, whether this approach is the most appropriate and the most beneficial for their desired outcomes. It also pertains to whether they are receptive to a mind-body integrative approach that involves an eastern meditative spiritual practice. For best practice, speak to the clients and make sure to seek their consent before starting any integrative work. It is likely that most clients would not be Falun Gong practitioners. As findings from the Australian health and wellness survey indicated, Falun Gong respondents rarely visited health and medical professionals or counselors. While the chances of counseling experienced Falun Gong practitioners will be slim, there will be circumstances where novice practitioners and those who practice on and off may seek counseling and healthcare services. However, future integrative approaches using Falun Gong may be different with non-Falun Gong people as more people learn about this meditative practice. Many people in the West are familiar with other Eastern meditative practices, such as mindfulness meditation, yoga, or tai chi. This seems likely the case with Falun Gong in the future.

The second point to consider is how to explain to the clients what integration will entail. Many will ask questions about the practice. Due to their different religious and/or spiritual orientation, some clients may want to know more about the practice before they agree with integration work. Therefore, be mindful and be prepared to introduce the practice in a rational and objective manner. It is often useful to mention the various studies done on the health-wellness effects of the practice. While some clients may have heard about Falun Gong, not many will have in-depth knowledge about the practice. Hence, it is important to briefly introduce Falun Gong to them and to answer all their questions. It also helps to keep some fliers in the counseling or waiting room. For Internet savvy clients, furnish them with Falun Gong website addresses so that they can do their own reading on the Internet, if you do not have a flier handy. Due to the Chinese Communist Party's persecution of the practice, it is necessary to briefly explain these issues so that clients are aware of what is happening, while learning that the practice is good and beneficial for their health and well-being.

The third consideration is to be aware that not everyone shares an affinity for meditation and for others integrative work may not be possible or suitable due to contraindications, such as Apollo's case. Falun Gong is unsuitable for individuals clinically diagnosed with severe mental health disorders. Therefore, it is best not to adopt an integrative approach with clients who suffer from severe schizophrenia, bipolar illness, or other serious mental disorders. Apollo's case is really one of the few exceptions. He was clear that the aim of the integrative work was to help him relax and overcome his anxiety issues. And when meditation helped to reduce his anxiety, Apollo's curiosity for the practice naturally grew. Although the author-counselor had explained about the contraindications, Apollo wanted to read about the teachings of the practice and took the initiative to buy the *Zhuan Falun* book so that he could read it at home. The integrative counseling sessions ended soon after his anxiety abated.

An important consideration when blending Falun Gong practice with professional counseling is that integrationists need a competent working knowledge of Falun Gong. Sound knowledge about the practice helps to demystify, minimize misconceptions, and help integrationist counselors to better explain the practice to clients. It will infuse counselors with confidence and help them to apply integration competently. So, familiarize yourself with the practice, even if you do not wish to become a Falun Gong practitioner. It will be easier to answer questions, exchange views, or engage with clients who already have some knowledge of Falun Gong. Consider doing your own reading to find out more about the practice. A quick and easy way is to visit the official Falun Gong websites, http:// en.minghui.org/ or www.falundafa.org. Another way is to seek out Falun Gong practitioners. They usually organize various activities to raise awareness about the benefits of the practice, the Chinese regime's on-going persecution of Falun Gong, and the issue of forced organ transplantation. Collect a few fliers and information booklets, or speak with a practitioner to get a first-hand experience of the practice. Similarly, integrationists of other meditative practices would have received training in Vipassana or mindfulness meditation or yogic practices before they feel competent to adopt an integrated approach. Hence, it is beneficial to learn the Falun Gong exercises and read the teachings of the practice, even if you do not wish to be a Falun Gong practitioner. How far you wish to walk down this path is your own choice. However, the more knowledge, insight, and personal experience you have of the practice, the easier it is to adopt the integrative approach with Falun Gong.

The fifth consideration is the benefits of the practice and the knowledge that many Falun Gong practitioners actually first embrace the practice because of their health problems. Falun Gong can be a form of 'self-help strategy.' It is free of charge and has no formal registrations or any fees to pay for learning the practice. As per the author's experience, most counseling clients are open to learning a self-help strategy. Take April's case, Falun Gong was something she learned and took away from her counseling experience that has benefited her all these years. Moreover, having a self-help strategy for our clients is encouraging them to be self-sufficient and resilient, like showing them how to fish, instead of encouraging them to keep buying fish.

A huge part of the author-counselor's integrative approach involves helping clients to become independent from therapy. After successive integrative sessions and seeing positive outcomes, it may be time to gradually wean clients off from on-going integrative work, especially if they are fee-paying clients. This is because practicing Falun Gong is free and no one is allowed to charge fees for teaching the practice. As counselors, we charge for our professional counseling service, not for teaching or integrating Falun Gong into our counseling work. One way of weaning clients off from on-going integrative work with Falun Gong practice is to encourage them to take up the practice as a self-help intervention strategy and suggest that they practice the exercises at a local practice site organized by Falun Gong teaching volunteers. However, different clients will have different needs and it is best to discuss this with them. Some clients like April for instance, choose to continue with integrative counseling for a much longer period, until they feel confident to attend group practice. Others responded whole-heartedly to the integrative approach, resolved their issues, then terminated the counseling relationship and their connection with the practice.

The sixth consideration highlights the quality of client-counselor interactions—an important facet of the therapeutic relationship. Integrationist counselors are encouraged to embody the Falun Gong principles of truthfulness, compassion, and forbearance (or tolerance) in the therapeutic relationship. Embodying these three universal principles helps to build a better rapport and therapeutic outcome. In the example with Oskar, the author was able to blend these universal principles successfully. When conventional techniques failed to touch his heart, the author-counselor demonstrated these principles and engaged Oskar with simple conversations about them: being true, good, and enduring, and putting others first. Later, when an altercation with his girlfriend occurred, Oskar remembered these conversations and was able to break his pattern of resorting to physical violence.

Another worthy consideration is having Falun Gong classes in community settings. In many Australian cities and other parts of the world, this is already happening. Although the ultimate goal of practicing Falun Gong is not its health and wellness benefits, the results from the Australian survey indicate that many respondents began practicing Falun Gong because of its healing potential. Most communities are open to having such wellness activities for their residents. As an ancient Chinese spiritual practice for the modern age, there is no system of membership, no rituals, no obligations, and no tuition fees for learning Falun Gong. The moral teachings, gentle standing exercises, and sitting meditation offer a unique and enjoyable way to improve one's health and well-being. The practice can be readily integrated into daily life as a self-help intervention system for people from all walks of life. Due to its powerful healing benefits and the fact that it is freely available, Falun Gong can offer a significant health and medical cost-saving potential for any individual and for the ageing society. And of course, having practice sites in local community settings will make the practice more accessible and convenient not only for interested individuals but also integrationist counselors who wish to make referrals for clients to attend a local group meditation practice class.

Finally, whatever the integration scenario may involve, it is imperative to consider existing competency guidelines; for instance those outlined by The Association for Spiritual, Ethical, and Religious Values in Counseling (ASERVIC) (2009). Likewise, Canda and Furman (2009) advocate a spiritually sensitive social work model when working with clients in a holistic and culturally appropriate manner.

A Six-Step Approach

The author-counselor's endeavors with integration and findings from the Australian survey elicited this six-step approach. The six-steps embody basic counseling skills, Carl Rogers' person-centered approach (Egan, 1990; Howatt, 2000; Merry, 2002; C. R. Rogers, 1951, 1961), the crisis intervention model (James & Gilliland, 2008), and the mindful application of Falun Gong principles of truthfulness, compassion, and forbearance within the counseling context. The approach comprises six stages of support. It involves defining the problem (or tribulation as Falun Gong practitioners call it), externalizing feelings and thoughts, identifying issues (or attachments), looking within and cultivating the heart, formulating strategies, and committing to change.

The six-step approach to wellness outlines an integrated approach that integrative counselors are already familiar with. In no way is the six-step approach a part of Falun Gong teaching. Nor should it be considered or used as a replacement for Fa-study by Falun Gong practitioners. In short, the six-steps simply map the spontaneous and sequential flow during the counseling process. Nevertheless, for some people, the six-steps could serve as a self-help guide or resource—stepping-stones for identifying and letting go of issues in a systematic way towards health and wellness. See Table 5 for the Six-Step Approach to Wellness.

Table 5

The Six-Step Approach to Wellness

Step One: Defining the problem
Tell your story. Explore and describe the problem, scenario, or tribulation. Talk, write, draw, display symbols, or use a sand tray.

Step Two: Externalizing feelings and thoughts
Describe feelings and thoughts. Write down all positive and negative words, phrases, and sentences that describe how you feel and think. e.g. "I feel sick in my tummy," "I feel fearful, upset, angry, worried, etc."

Step Three: Identifying presenting issues (or attachments)
Identify and highlight main issues from written statements in Step Two. Be honest. Look within; examine your thoughts and behavior.

Step Four: Supporting change of heart
Facilitating and supporting change of heart; cultivating the heart and mind for health and wellness. Replace negative thoughts with positive/wellness states. Take every crisis and tribulation as opportunity for self-improvement. Reassure, support, or seek help.

Step Five: Examining strategies and making plans
Assess and brainstorm strategies for action. Apply the principles of truthfulness, compassion, and forbearance. Mindfully maintain positive states and cancel negativity. Make short and medium-term plans.

Step Six: Committing to change and setting goal
Review, summarize, and set goals to make it happen. Commit to a definite action plan. Make it happen. Ask what you need to achieve your goal. How and when will you know your plan is realized? (*Helpful questions to ask: "Now that you've gone through these steps, what is your goal? What specific actions will you take to carry out your plan? How will you handle this issue if it reoccurs?"*)

(Egan, 1990; Howatt, 2000; James & Gilliland, 2008; Lau, 2010a; Merry, 2002)
NOTE: The six-steps is merely an integrated counseling approach outlining a process that occurs during a therapeutic interaction. It is not part of Falun Gong practice.

CONCLUSION

Journey to Wellness

New York City: It was 2013, a warm sunny spring Friday afternoon in Manhattan on May 17th. Barbara and hundreds of Falun Gong practitioners from all over the world gathered at the Dag Hammarskjold Park in front of the United Nations building to support the 'Stop the Persecution of Falun Gong' rally. Ten years had passed since she started her journey to health and wellness—walking the Falun Gong path. As we sat on a bench along First Ave, Barbara said, "I want to help more people to have a better understanding of Falun Gong." This wish has brought her and thousands of other Falun Gong practitioners who have benefited from the practice to New York every year in May for their annual activities and experience-sharing conference.

Falun Gong is "profound, something supernatural, and mystical," said Barbara as we were sitting on the park bench. At 60, her health has never been better, she said during the face-to-face interview. "I have a lot of energy and a positive attitude. I'm finding joy in life that more people know about the beneficial effects of the practice." Back in Australia, she continues to tell the story of Falun Gong and of her journey to health and wellness. With other Australian practitioners, she visits different country towns telling the story of Falun Gong—its healing benefits, the Chinese Communist Party's (CCP) persecution of Falun Gong, and the issue of forced live organ harvesting of Falun Gong practitioners in China.

Naturally, Falun Gong has greatly influenced the way Barbara navigates through life and how she handles daily challenges. "It involves constantly looking within and changing the way I look at and do things in any given situation. I try my best to use the opportunity to improve my moral character," said Barbara. Life is good. Her health is the least of her problems. "I have a healthy body, a clear and peaceful mind," she continued. Despite her serious head injuries from the 23 feet (seven meters) fall back in 2003, Barbara affirmed that she had not had a headache since she started practicing Falun Gong.

From 2013 to December 2015, Barbara's self-reports of her health and wellness status have remained the same. She has been well in mind, body, and spirit. Asked about what had stood out in her current journey, she mentioned that she realized that cultivation is not about giving up everything in her everyday life. "I have my family. They don't practice Falun Gong and I need to consider their needs and to care for them." Her words reflected the conclusions from the Australian survey, which indicated that Falun Gong practitioners live a normal life in society. They are like anyone else—single or married, with or without families, and with occupations in society. The fundamental difference between Falun Gong practitioners and non-Falun Gong practitioners lies in their belief in a practice that offers overall mind, body, spiritual health, and wellness—and beyond.

When asked about how her health and well-being again during one of the telephone interviews in 2014, Barbara cheerfully responded with, "Doing the exercises every day, I have lots of energy. Studying the Fa every day, I gain insights on how to be compassionate and considerate of others." She continued, "I not only have my life back. My life has become more meaningful and fulfilling." The artist-cum-wife, mother-grandmother takes everyday and every moment of her life as a gift. "Often, the toughest test is enduring a psychological conflict, while remaining compassionate and considerate of others," said Barbara. "Daily Fa-study helps to give me peace of mind and a bigger heart to endure." It has helped her to overcome bottlenecks in conflicts.

During the last phone interview in 2015, twelve years after she began practicing Falun Gong, Barbara was asked to review her journey to wellness and how she had walked her path. Her response mirrored the written responses of other Falun Gong respondents from the Australian survey. She reported that Fa-study, righteous thoughts meditation, daily exercise, and clarifying the truth about Falun Gong hold the key to her on-going health, wellness, and resilience. During the long-distance telephone conversation, she was full of gratitude. Her words reaffirmed the resilience of Falun Gong practitioners: "The practice has helped me to have a calm and open mind, stay positive, and have a strong will." One could say that her path to wellness reflects that of many other Falun Gong practitioners—the millions in China and around the world.

Conclusion

Like all research studies, the Australian survey was not without its limitations. Having said that, it still served as a worthy stepping-stone for the follow-up longitudinal study or the *Hearts Uplifted* project. The survey's international flavor and diversity was a noteworthy strength, while the online administration of the questionnaire helped to foster honesty and candor in the participants' written responses. It encouraged both positive and adverse self-reports of the health-wellness effects of Falun Gong. Several respondents expressed concerns about having non-Falun Gong friends and family members as a comparison group.

One respondent wrote to the researcher expressing her concern that the health-wellness reports from her non-Falun Gong spouse were not that different from hers. This respondent alluded to Falun Gong teachings that mentioned how the strong energy fields of Falun Gong practitioners could positively affect the health and wellness of those around them; she wondered if this phenomenon would distort data and interfere with what the researcher was aiming to establish in her study—that Falun Gong respondents have better health-wellness than non-Falun Gong respondents. However, this phenomenon did not impact the overall findings of the Australian survey, which showed that the health-wellness statuses of Falun Gong respondents were still better than the non-Falun Gong.

Another notable finding from the Australian survey worth reiterating is that while Falun Gong respondents were not unlike the non-Falun Gong respondents in their demographic profiles, when it came to their health-wellness reports, the Falun Gong respondents were more likely to report excellent health than non-Falun Gong respondents. Falun Gong respondents reported little or no use of medication, and incurred less medical and health expenses compared to non-Falun Gong respondents. They had a more positive perception of their health. What a positive message to convey—that practicing Falun Gong offers mind-body health-wellness benefits and spiritual improvement.

This pioneering Australian survey indicated a link between practicing Falun Gong and having better health and wellness. Snippets of interview data from the *Hearts Uplifted* project also highlighted this positive connection. Preliminary findings from this on-going project suggested that Falun Gong people, especially veteran or experienced practitioners are resilient and well equipped to navigate through the trials and tribulations in our fast-paced modern society. The narratives from the *Hearts Uplifted* project also confirmed that Falun Gong practitioners are more likely to enjoy a healthier lifestyle than those who do not practice Falun Gong.

Finally, it is hoped that *The Mindful Practice of Falun Gong* helps to clarify the misconceptions about Falun Gong and that Barbara's story and the written responses from other Falun Gong respondents will continue to inspire us to embark or continue our journey to ultimate health and wellness.

Perchance more people will gain a greater insight into the health-wellness effects of Falun Gong and be interested to try out the practice. With ever-increasing health costs and stressful lifestyles in our modern society, this mind-body-spiritual cultivation practice offers a free self-intervention system for the present and future society. Those interested in integrating religion/spirituality with their work may find it worthwhile to immerse in the practice just to find out more about it and be able to point interested individuals in the right direction. Perchance the aim of this book is to introduce those with a pre-destined relationship to the mindful practice of Falun Gong. If you have come this far, be inspired by these words from the 18th Century British poet Lord Byron. In his long poem, *Don Juan*, Lord Byron reminds us:

> *But words are things, and a small drop of ink,*
> *Falling like dew, upon a thought, produces*
> *That which makes thousands, perhaps millions, think*
> – Canto III, Stanza LXXXVIII

Acknowledgements

A myriad of individuals, whose names are too many to list here, have contributed toward this pioneering research and dissertation-to-book writing. I am grateful to my supervisors, Dr. John Court and Dr. Heather Mattner. Without them, I would not have been able to begin and finish my doctoral research on the health and wellness effects of Falun Gong. Their guidance in the theoretical, methodology, and research design greatly shaped the development of my research project, called the Australian survey from here on. I thank Professor Kurt Lushington and Associate Professor Margaret Peters from The University of South Australia (UniSA) for seeing me through to the completion of my doctoral studies, and members of the Human Research Ethics Committee for their recommendations and for stipulating the mandatory involvement of the Australian Falun Dafa Associations.

My appreciation extends to key members of the Australian and European Falun Dafa Associations—John Andress, John Deller, Peter Jauhal, Dr. Michael Pearson-Smith, and Simon Vereshaka, president of the Victorian Falun Dafa Association at the time. I am grateful for the valued input from pilot study members, including Dr. J. Y. Luo, Dr. Y. Luo, and Michael Tsang.

I'm thankful for the help of the Adelaide Falun Dafa practitioners: Sheaumay Chang, Dr. J. J. Lu, Barbara and Brian Thompson, Wendy Tiong, Wang Ping, and especially Peter Tiong of the Pagoda Restaurant for his positivity and unwavering support. Sincere thanks go to Professor David Ownby, Professor Deborah Dysart-Gale, Leigh Smith, April Sun, and former colleagues—Steve Denholm, Jean Bacon and Craig Roissetter—at Transitional Accommodation, the Government of South Australia.

I thank all Falun Gong and non-Falun Gong respondents who participated in the Australian survey; the adolescent and adult clients who benefited from the integrated approach with Falun Gong and counseling; and participants of the City of Unley Falun Gong Total Health and Wellness project. I am grateful to my brother Stephen for introducing me to Falun Gong, my brother and sister-in-law in Adelaide for their support during my doctoral journey. To my sister Cathy in London, I am deeply appreciative of your unfailing encouragement during my doctoral days. Your regular phone calls were glowing lights in a dark tunnel during those solitary nights of dissertation writing. Heart-felt appreciation goes to my brothers Mike and John, who cared for our mother whom I could not visit as often as I wished due to work and study commitments.

Indeed, many individuals have helped to shepherd this book from inception to what you see before you. My heart-felt appreciation goes to Barbara Schafer for letting me weave her story through this first book that explores the health and wellness effects of Falun Gong, based on the results from the Australian survey and subsequent research on the lived experiences of Falun Gong practitioners. Thank you for meeting me regularly via Skype chats during the final phase of this book journey.

My heart-felt thanks go to the editorial team: Damian Robin, Liam Hutchison, Dr. Ted L'Estrange, and Oliver Trey for their meticulous efforts and support. Sincere thank you to Angel Maurizzio for reading a portion of the manuscript and offering insightful feedback. I thank Kate Vereshaka for the book cover design, Liam Hutchinson for the interior design and formatting, Daniel Ulrich and James Smith for photography, and Oliver Trey for image collection.

I am indebted to the following individuals, whose generosity and compassionate spirit have touched my heart: Associate Professor Maria Cheung for her practical recommendations and Kay and David Rubacek for furnishing the right information and advice just when I needed them. These special individuals—Sterling Campbell, Fabio Emma, Esther Hack, Sarah Hack, Jane Lau, Penelope Mantyk, Kaye Petty, Grace Rubacek, Michelle Smith, Vivian Song, Lia Onely-Tompkins, Yuensuo Yang, Flynn Vereshka, Nick Vereshka, and Jillian Ye—have made a positive difference and vital contribution to the book.

Through the joys and pains of writing, I remain grateful to my 97-year-old mother whose wise words during this decade-long journey have touched my heart and honed my endurance. Finally, to my husband Oliver, I thank you for filming the parade and the face-to-face interviews with Barbara, finding time to read the manuscript, offering insightful comments, and sharing the house chores so that I have more time for this book. Above all, I thank you for riding the waves with me.

Yet, most significantly, I dedicate this book to all of you—readers—seeking to make a crossing that would profoundly touch your life. I am deeply grateful to be part of your journey to health, wellness, and beyond.

Glossary

Buddha	Sanskrit (ancient Indian language) word for a great enlightened person
Cultivation	An Eastern concept for mind, body, and spiritual improvement
Dafa	Great Law, and short term for Falun Dafa
De	Virtue or merit; a precious white energy that is acquired through enduring hardships and tribulations. It is required for *xinxing* improvement and spiritual progress.
Ding	A meditative state of tranquility in which the mind is empty, yet conscious.
Fa	Law or principles
Falun	Law Wheel
Gong	Cultivation energy or a practice cultivating such energy
Karma	A Sanskrit word meaning action or deed referring to bad or negative actions. In Falun Gong teachings, it is described as a black substance or energy field that is the opposite of *de*.
Qi	Life force or vital energy that is present in all beings. In Falun Gong teachings, it is considered different from *gong*.
Qigong	A general term referring to a form of ancient Chinese cultivation practice that involves physical exercises, meditation, and in the case of Falun Gong, it includes *xinxing* cultivation.

Ren	Forbearance, tolerance, endurance, patience, self-control, restraint, and/or perseverance. It is one three principles of Falun Gong.
Shan	Benevolence, compassion, or kindness, one of the three principles of Falun Gong and is traditionally stressed in Buddhist practice.
Shifu	Master or Teacher, a respectful way to address a teacher in traditional Chinese culture.
Tai chi	A form of traditional Chinese exercises involving slow, gentle, rhythmic movements that improve *qi*, or vital energy.
Wuwei	Non-action, inaction, or without intention
Xinxing	Heart-mind nature or moral character. In Falun Gong, it involves letting go of attachments; enduring hardships; cultivating compassion and forbearance; gaining insight; and elevating our moral character.
Xiulian	A Chinese term for cultivation: *Xiu* means repair, restore, or fix, while *lian* means to improve or refine.
Yuanfen	Predestined relationship
Zhen	Truthfulness, one of the three principles of Falun Gong and is traditionally stressed in Taoist practice.
Zhen-Shan-Ren	Truthfulness-compassion-forbearance, the three principles of Falun Gong teachings.

Bibliography

Ackerman, S. E. (2005). Falun Dafa and the new age movement in Malaysia: Signs of health, symbols of salvation. *Social Compass*, 52(4), 495-511.

Ader, R. (1980). Psychosomatic and psychoimmunologic research. *Psychosomatic Medicine*, 42(3), 307-321.

Adler, J. A. (2005). Chinese religion: An overview–a revised and expanded version of Daniel L. Overmyer's article in the 1st ed. (1986) [Electronic Version]. In *Lindsay Jones, ed., Encyclopedia of Religion*, 2nd ed. Retrieved November 11, 2015, from http://www2.kenyon.edu/Depts/Religion/Fac/Adler/Writings/Chinese%20Religions%20-%20Overview.htm

Ai, A. L. (2003). Assessing mental health in clinical study on qigong: Between scientific investigation and holistic perspectives. *Seminars in Integrative Medicine*, 1(2), 112-121. Retrieved June 30, 2004, from http://www.sciencedirect.com/science/article/pii/S154311500300022X

ASERVIC. (2009). Competencies for addressing spiritual and religious issues in counseling. Retrieved November 30, 2013, from http://www.aservic.org/resources/spiritual-competencies/

ASERVIC. (2015). A White Paper of the Association for Spiritual, Ethical, and Religious Values in Counseling. Retrieved February 11, 2016, from http://www.aservic.org/resources/aservic-white-paper-2/

Astin, J. A. (1998). Why patients use alternative medicine: Results of a national study. *Journal of American Medical Association*, 279(19), 1548-1553. doi:10.1001/jama.279.19.1548.

Atkinson, N. L., & Permuth-Levine, R. (2009). Benefits, barriers, and cues to action of yoga practice: A focus group approach. *American Journal of Health Behavior*, 33(1), 3-14.

Atwood, J. D., & Maltin, L. (1991). Putting Eastern philosophies into Western psychotherapies. *American Journal of Psychotherapy*, 45(3), 368-382.

Australian Bureau of Statistics & Statistics New Zealand. (2006). ANZSCO: Australian and New Zealand standard classification of occupations. Retrieved April 23, 2008, from http://www.abs.gov.au/ausstats/abs@.nsf/Previousproducts/E3031B89999B4582CA2575DF002DA702?opendocument.

Author Unknown. (1998). Falun Dafa has great effects on improving health status: Survey of over 6,000 cultivators. Retrieved March 3, 2004, from http://www. clearwisdom.net/eng/science_eng/healthsurvey_dalian.html

Author Unknown. (2003). Russia: Report on the healing effects of Falun Gong from the Moscow business committee. Retrieved April 1, 2003, from http:// clearharmony.net/articles/200302/10494.html

Author Unknown. (2009). Yoga for anxiety and depression [Electronic Version]. *Harvard Mental Health Letter*, 25, 4-5. Retrieved April 22, 2009, from http://www. health.harvard.edu/mind-and-mood/yoga-for-anxiety-and-depression

Authors Unknown. (1999). Summary of results from the 1999 health survey of Falun Gong practitioners in North America. Retrieved March 3, 2004, from http://www.pureinsight.org/node/15333

Authors Unknown. (2002). Summary of health surveys conducted in mainland China to assess Falun Gong's effects on healing illness and maintaining fitness. Retrieved March 13, 2002, from http://www.pureinsight.org/node/841

Authors Unknown. (2003a). Report on 235 cases of a Falun Gong health survey in North America. Retrieved March 3, 2004, from http://www.clearwisdom.net/ emh/articles/2003/3/31/33996.html

Authors Unknown. (2003b). Research report from Taiwan illustrates the power of Falun Gong in improving physical and emotional health while reducing health care expenses. Retrieved March 8, 2003, from http://www.clearwisdom.net/emh/ articles/2003/1/1/30401.html

Authors Unknown. (2003c). Summary of results from the 1999 health survey of Falun Gong practitioners in North America. Retrieved March 3, 2004, from http:// www.pureinsight.org/node/1533

Balasubramaniam, M., Telles, S., & Doraiswamy, P. M. (2013). Yoga on our minds: A systematic review of yoga for neuropsychiatric disorders. *Frontiers in Psychiatry*, 3(117).

Barker, C., Pistrang, N., & Elliot, R. (2005). Chapter 6: Self-Report Methods. In *Research Methods in Clinical Psychology: An Introduction for Students and Practitioners*, 2nd ed. *(pp. 94-118).* doi:10.1002/0470013435.ch6): John Wiley & Sons, Inc.

Barnes, P. M., Powell-Griner, E., McFann, K., & Nahin, R. L. (2004). Complementary and alternative medicine use among adults: United States, 2002. *Seminars in Integrative Medicine*, 2(2), 54-71. doi:10.1016/j.sigm.2004.07.003.

Bendig, B. W. (2013). *Cognitive and Physiological Effects of Falun Gong Qigong.* Unpublished Dissertation, University of California, Los Angeles, US.

Bishop, F. L., & Lewith, G. T. (2010). Who uses CAM? A narrative review of demographic characteristics and health factors associated with CAM use. *Evidence-based Complementary and Alternative Medicine*, 7(1), 11-28. doi:10.1093/ecam/nen023.

Bogart, G. (1991). The use of meditation in psychotherapy: A review of the literature. *American Journal of Psychotherapy*, 45(3), 383-412.

Bruseker, G. (2000). *Falun Gong: A modern Chinese folk Buddhist movement in crisis.* Unpublished Honors History thesis, The University of Alberta, Edmonton, Canada.

Burgdoff, C. A. (2003). How Falun Gong undermines Li Hongzhi's total rhetoric. Nova Religio: The Journal of Alternative and Emergent Religions, 6(2), 332-347. doi:10.1525/nr.2003.6.2.332.

Canda, E. R. (2009). *Spiritually sensitive social work: An overview of American and international trends.* Paper presented at the International Conference on Social Work and Counseling Practice, City University of Hong Kong. Hong Kong. Retrieved January 3, 2015, from https://spiritualdiversity.ku.edu/sites/spiritualitydiversity. drupal.ku.edu/files/docs/Practice/Spirituality%20and%20SW%20Hong%20Kong%20 plenary%20paper.pdf

Canda, E. R., & Furman, L. D. (2009). *Spiritual diversity in social work practice: The heart of helping.* New York: Oxford University Press.

Carpenter, J. T. (1977). Meditation, esoteric traditions: Contributions to psychotherapy. *American Journal of Psychotherapy*, 31(3), 394-404.

Carson, J. W., Carson, K. M., Porter, L. S., Keefe, F. J., Shaw, H., & Miller, J. M. (2007). Yoga for women with metastatic breast cancer: Results from a pilot study. *Journal of Pain and Symptom Management*, 33(3), 331-341. doi 10.1016/j.jpainsymman.2006.08.009.

Cashwell, C. S., & Watts, R. E. (2010). The new ASERVIC competencies for addressing spiritual and religious issues in counseling. *Counseling and Values*, 55(1), 2-5.

Cashwell, C. S., & Young, J. S. (Eds.). (2011). *Integrating spirituality and religion into counseling: A guide to competent practice* (2nd ed.). Alexandria, VA: American Counseling Association.

Chai, D., & Pan, B. (Producer/Writer) (2002). Zhang Cuiying, an exceptional Contemporary Chinese Painter [broadcast]. In *Journey to the East*, Australia: New Tang Dynasty Television Production.

Chen, K., Chen, M., Chao, H., Hung, H., Lin, H., & Li, C. (2009). Sleep quality, depression state, and health status of older adults after silver yoga exercises: Cluster randomized trial. *International Journal of Nursing Studies*, 46(2), 154-163. doi:10.1016/j. ijnurstu.2008.09.005.

Chen, K. W., Berger, C. C., Manheimer, E., Forde, D., Magidson, J., Dachman, L., et al. (2012). Meditative therapies for reducing anxiety: A systematic review and meta-analysis of randomized controlled trials. *Depression and Anxiety*, 29(7), 545–562. doi:10.1002/da.21964.

Cheung, M. (2016). The intersection between mindfulness and human rights: The case of Falun Gong and its implications for social work. *Journal of Spirituality and Religion in Social Work: Social Thought*, 25(1-2), 57-75. doi:10.1080/15426432.2015.1067586.

Cormier, S., Nurius, P., & Osborn, C. (2009). *Interviewing and change strategies for helpers: Fundamental skills and cognitive behavioral interventions* (6th ed.). Boston, MA: Cengage Learning, Inc.

Coruh, B., Ayele, H., Pugh, M., & Mulligan, T. (2005). Does religious activity improve health outcomes? A critical review of the recent literature. *The Journal of Science and Healing*, 1(3), 186-191. doi:10.1016/j.explore.2005.02.001.

Coulter, I. D., & Willis, E. M. (2004). The rise and rise of complementary and alternative medicine: A sociological perspective. *The Medical Journal of Australia*, 180(11), 587-589.

Court, J. H., & Court, P. C. (2001). Spirituality and health from forgotten factor to reconciliation. *Lukes Journal*, 6(3), 8-11.

Crombie, W. J. (2002, April 18). Meditation changes temperatures: Mind control body in extreme experiments. *Harvard University Gazette*, 1-4.

D'Souza, R. (2007). The importance of spirituality in medicine and its application to clinical practice. *The Medical Journal of Australia*, 186(10), S57-S59.

Dan, L., Pu, R., Li, F., Li, N., Wang, Q., Lu, Y., et al. (1998). Falun Gong health effect survey of ten thousand cases in Beijing. Retrieved January 12, 2001, from http://www.clearwisdom.net/eng/science_eng/survey98_1eng.htm

Danhauer, S. C., Mihalko, S. L., Russell, G. B., Campbell, C. R., Felder, L., Daley, K., et al. (2009). Restorative yoga for women with breast cancer: Findings from a randomized pilot study. *Psycho-Oncology*, 18, 360-368. doi:10.1002/pon.1503.

Davidson, R. J., Kabat-Zinn, J., Schmumacher, J., Rosenkranz, M., Muller, D., Santorelli, S. F., et al. (2003). Alterations in brain and immune function produced by Mindfulness Meditation. *Psychosomatic Medicine*, 65(4), 564-570. doi:10.1097/01.PSY.0000077505.67574.E3.

Delmonte, M. M. (1985). Meditation and anxiety reduction: A literature review. Clinical Psychology Review, 5(2), 91-102. doi:10.1016/0272-7358(85)90016-9.

Easton, M. (2005, Spring). What makes us happy? *University of Toronto Magazine,* 32, 20-26. Toronto, Canada.

Egan, G. (1990). *The skilled helper: A systematic approach to effective helping* (4th ed.). Pacific Grove, CA: Brooks/Cole Publishing Company.

Eisenberg, D. M., Davis, R. B., Ettner, S. L., Appel, S., Wilkey, S., Van Rompay, M., et al. (1998). Trends in alternative medicine use in the United States, 1990-1997: Results of a follow-up national survey. *Journal of American Medical Association,* 280(18), 1569-1575. doi:10.1001/jama.280.18.1569.

Elliott, R., & Freire, E. (2007). Classical person-centered and experiential perspectives on Rogers (1957). *Psychotherapy: Theory, Research, Practice, Training,* 44(3), 285-288. doi:10.1037/0033-3204.44.3.285.

Fadiman, J., & Frager, R. (1994). *Personality and personal growth* (3rd ed.). New York: HarperCollins College Publishers.

Falun Dafa Information Center. (2008). Falun Gong: Timeline. Retrieved January 3, 2013, from http://www.faluninfo.net/topic/24/

Falun Dafa Information Center. (2015a). Falun Gong: An ancient tradition for mind, body, and spirit. Retrieved January 3, 2015, from http://www.faluninfo. net/topic/22/

Falun Dafa Information Center. (2015b). Why is Falun Gong persecuted in China? Retrieved June 30, 2015, from http://www.faluninfo.net/topic/5/

Fernandez, M. (Producer/Writer) (2012). US Congress Holds Hearing on Forced Organ Harvesting [Broadcast]. In *Forced Organ Harvesting.* US: New Tang Dynasty Television Production. http://www.ntd.tv/en/news/china/20120919/74650-us-congress-holds-hearing-on-forced-organ-harvesting.html

Fernandez, M., Magnason, M., & Gnaizda, M. (Writers) (2012). Killed for Organs: China's secret state transplant business [Broadcast]. In M. Fernandez (Producer), *Forced Organ Harvesting.* US: New Tang Dynasty Television Production. http://www.ntd.tv/en/news/china/20121021/75221-killed-for-organs-chinas-secret-state-transplant-business.html

Frass, M., Strassl, R. P., Friehs, H., Müllner, M., Kundi, M., & Kaye, A. D. (2012). Use and acceptance of Complementary and Alternative Medicine among the general population and medical personnel: A systematic review. *Ochsner Journal,* 12(1), 45-56.

Fredrickson, B. L. (2000). Cultivating positive emotion to optimize health and well-being. *Prevention and Treatment,* 3, 1-24.

Frick, K. D., Kung, J., Parrish, J. M., & Narrett, M. J. (2010). Evaluating the cost-effectiveness of fall prevention programs that reduce fall-related hip fractures in older adults. *Journal of the American Geriatrics Society*, 58(1), 136–141. doi: 10.1111/j.1532-5415.2009.02575.x.

Gale, D. D., & Gorman-Yao, W. M. (2003). Falungong: Recent developments in Chinese notions of healing. *Journal of Cultural Diversity*, 10(4), 124 -127.

Gallup Jr., G. H. (2002). Why are women more religious? Retrieved August 16, 2009, from http://www.gallup.com/poll/7432/Why-Women-More-Religious.aspx

Garzon, F. L. (2011). Spirituality in Counseling [Electronic Version]. *Faculty Publications and Presentations*, Paper 62. Retrieved October 8, 2014, from http://digitalcommons.liberty.edu/ccfs_fac_pubs/62

Girodo, M. (1974). Yoga meditation and flooding in the treatment of anxiety neurosis. *Journal of Behavior Therapy and Experimental Psychiatry*, 5(2), 157-160.

Goldberg, R. J. (1982). Anxiety reduction by self-regulation: Theory, practice, and evaluation. *Annals of Internal Medicine*, 96(4), 483-487.

Goleman, D. (1976). Meditation and consciousness: An Asian approach to mental health. *American Journal of Psychotherapy*, 30(1), 41-54.

Goleman, D., & Gurin, J. (1993). Mind/body medicine - at last. *Psychology Today*, 26(2), 16-18.

Gordon, J. S., & Edwards, D. M. (2005). Mind body spirit medicine. *Seminars in Oncology Nursing*, 21(3), 154-158. doi:10.1016/j.soncn.2005.04.002.

Graneheim, U. H., & Lundman, B. (2004). Qualitative content analysis in nursing research: concepts, procedures and measures to achieve trustworthiness. *Nurse Education Today*, 24, 105-112. doi:10.1016/j.nedt.2003.10.001.

Gutmann, E. (2009, July 20th). An Occurrence on Fuyou Street. *National Review*, 71.

Gutmann, E. (2014). *The Slaughter: Mass Killings, Organ Harvesting, and China's Secret Solution to its Dissident Problem*. Amherst, New York: Prometheus Books.

Hanson, W. E., Creswell, J. W., Clark, V. L. P., Petska, K. S., & Creswell, J. D. (2005). Mixed methods research designs in counseling psychology. *Journal of Counseling Psychology*, 52(2), 224-235. doi:10.1037/0022-0167.52.2.224.

Hattie, J. A., Myers, J. E., & Sweeney, T. J. (2004). A factor structure of wellness: Theory, assessment, analysis, and practice. *Journal of Counseling & Development*, 82(3), 354-364.

Haynes, A., Hilbers, J., Kivikko, J., & Ratnavuyha, D. (2007). *Spirituality and religion in health care practice: A person-centred resource for staff at the Prince of Wales Hospital* (Research report). SESIAHS, Sydney, Australia.

He, M. (2011). Falun Gong and health benefits – Part I.   Retrieved September 25 2012, from http://en.minghui.org/html/articles/2011/3/5/123614.html#. UMASqYU7zwM

Hedges, B., (Producer) & Trey, M. (Writer) (2012). 7000 attend Falun Dafa conference in Taipei. In *Discovering China*. US: New Tang Dynasty Production. http://www.ntd.tv/en/news/china/20121122/75828-7000-attend-falun-dafa-conference-in-taipei.html

Heerwegh, D. (2009). Mode differences between face-to-face and web surveys: An experimental investigation of data quality and social desirability effects. *International Journal of Public Opinion Research*, 21(1), 111-121. doi:10.1093/ijpor/edn054.

Heppner, P. P., Kivlighan, J., Dennis M., & Wampold, B. E. (1999). *Research design in counselling* (2nd ed.). Belmont, CA, US: Wadsworth Publishing Company.

Hilbers, J., Haynes, A., Kivikko, J., & Ratnavuyha, D. (2007). *Spirituality/Religion and health: (Phase two)*. (Research report). SESIAHS, Sydney.

Hogan, M. (2005). Physical and cognitive activity and exercise for older adults: A review. *International Journal of Aging & Human Development*, 60(2), 95-126. doi:10.2190/PTG9-XDVM-YETA-MKXA.

Holzel, B. K., Carmody, J., Evans, K. C., Hoge, E. A., Dusek, J. A., Morgan, L., et al. (2010). Stress reduction correlates with structural changes in the amygdala [Electronic Version]. Scan.oxfordjournals.org, 5, 11-17. doi:10.1093/scan/nsp034.

Holzel, B. K., Carmody, J., Vangela, M., Congletona, C., Yerramsettia, S. M., Garda, T., et al. (2011). Mindfulness practice leads to increases in regional brain gray matter density. Psychiatry Research: *Neuroimaging*, 191, 36-43. doi:10.1016/j.pscychresns.2010.08.006.

Howatt, W. A. (2000). *The human services counseling toolbox*. Belmont, CA: Brooks/Cole Thomson Learning.

Irons, E. (2003). Falun Gong and the sectarian religion paradigm Nova Religio: *The Journal of Alternative and Emergent Religions*, 6(2), 244-262. doi:10.1525/nr.2003.6.2.244.

Jacobs, G. D. (2001). The physiology of mind–body interactions: The stress response and the relaxation response. *Journal of Alternative and Complementary Medicine*, 7 (Supplement 1), S-83-S-92. doi:10.1089/107555301753393841.

James, R. K., & Gilliland, R. K. (2008). *Crisis intervention strategies* (6th ed.). Array Belmont, CA: Thomson Brooks/Cole.

Johnson, S. S., & Kushner, R. F. (2001). Mindbody medicine: An introduction for the generalist physician and nutritionist. *Nutrition in Clinical Care*, 4(5), 256-264.

Kemerling, G. (2011). Aristotle: Ethics and the virtues. *Philosophy Pages*. Retrieved April 30, 2013, from http://www.philosophypages.com/hy/2s.htm

Kessler, R. C., Davis, R. B., Foster, D. F., Van Rompay, M. I., Walters, E. E., Wilkey, S. A., et al. (2001). Long-term trends in the use of complementary and alternative medical therapies in the United States. *Annals of Internal Medicine*, 135(4), 262-268.

Khalsa, H. K. (2003). Yoga: an adjunct to infertility treatment. *Sexuality, Reproduction and Menopause*, 1(1), 46-51. doi:10.1016/j.sram.2004.02.024.

Khalsa, H. K. (2004). How Yoga, meditation, and a yogic lifestyle can help women meet the challenges of perimenopause and menopause. *Sexuality, Reproduction and Menopause*, 2(3), 169-175. doi:10.1016/j.sram.2004.07.011.

Kilgour, D. (2013). International efforts to stop forced organ harvesting from Falun Gong in China. Retrieved January 8, 2014, from http://www.stoporganharvesting. org/news/latest-news/80-international-efforts-to-stop-forced-organ-harvesting-from-falun-gong-in-china

Kjaer, T. W., Bertelsen, C., Piccini, P., Brooks, D., Alving, J., & Lou, H. C. (2002). Increased dopamine tone during meditation-induced change of consciousness. *Cognitive Brain Research*, 13(2), 255-259. doi:10.1016/S0926-6410(01)00106-9.

Koenig, H. G. (1999). *The healing power of faith: Science explores medicine's last great frontier*. New York: Simon & Schuster.

Koenig, H. G. (2004a). Religion, spirituality, and medicine: Research findings and implications for clinical practice. *Southern Medical Association*, 97(12), 1194-1200.

Koenig, H. G. (2004b). Spirituality, wellness, and quality of life. *Sexuality, Reproduction & Menopause*, 2(2), 76-82. doi:10.1016/j.sram.2004.04.004.

Koenig, H. G. (2007). Religion, spirituality and medicine in Australia: Research and clinical practice [Electronic Version]. *The Medical Journal of Australia (eMJA)*, 186, S45-S46. Retrieved May 1, 2008, from http://www.mja.com.au/public/issues/186_10_210507/koe10330_fm.html

Koenig, H. G. (2012). Religion, spirituality and health: The research and clinical implications. *International Scholarly Research Network*, 2012. doi:10.5402/2012/278730.

Koenig, H. G., & Cohen, H. J. (Eds.). (2002). *The link between religion and health: Psychoneuroimmunology and the faith factor.* New York: Oxford University Press.

Koenig, H. G., McCullough, M. E., & Larson, D. B. (2001). *Handbook of religion and health.* New York: Oxford University Press.

Kutolowski, M. (2007). Transcending the mundane. Retrieved June 8, 2008, from http://www.faluninfo.net/article/503/Transcending-the-Mundane/

Lau, M. M. (2001). *Exploring counselors' burnout and alternative coping strategies: Falun Dafa as an alternative coping strategy.* Unpublished case study submitted in partial fulfillment for the Master of Social Science (Counseling), The University of South Australia, Adelaide, Australia.

Lau, M. M. (2010a). *The effect of Falun Gong on health and wellness as perceived by Falun Gong practitioners.* Unpublished doctoral dissertation, The University South Australia, Adelaide, Australia.

Lau, M. M. (2010b). *The effect of Falun Gong on health and wellness: Executive summary of research findings.* Unpublished report, The University of South Australia, Adelaide, Australia.

Lazar, S. W., Kerr, C. E., Wasserman, R. H., Gray, J. R., Greve, D. N., Treadway, M. T., et al. (2005). Meditation experience is associated with increased cortical thickness. *NeuroReport, 16*(17), 1893-1897.

Lee, L., Director (Producer) (2014). Human Harvest: China's illegal organ trade [Documentary film]. Vancouver, Canada: Flying Cloud Productions, Inc.

Lemonick, M. D. (2005, January 17). The biology of joy. *Time Magazine, 165,* 50-53.

Leung, Y., & Singhal, A. (2004). An examination of the relationship between qigong meditation and personality. *Social Behavior & Personality, 32*(4), 313-320.

Li, F., McAuley, E., Harmer, P., Duncan, T. E., & Chaumeton, N. R. (2001). Tai Chi enhances self-efficacy and exercise behavior in older adults. *Journal of Aging and Physical Activity, 9*(2), 161-171.

Li, H. (2000). *Zhuan Falun* (3rd translation ed.). New York: Universal Publishing Company.

Li, H. (2001a). *Essentials for further advancement. Gloucester,* MA, US: Fair Winds Press.

Li, H. (2001b). *Falun Gong.* Gloucester, MA, US: Fair Winds Press.

Li, H. (2001c). The Effect of Righteous Thoughts. Retrieved October 1, 2008, from http://en.minghui.org/html/articles/2001/7/18/12385.html

Li, H. (2001d). *Zhuan Falun*. Gloucester, MA, US: Fair Winds Press.

Li, H. (2002a). *Explaining the content of Falun Dafa*. Gillette, NJ: Yih Chyun Corp.

Li, H. (2002b). Righteous Thoughts. Retrieved May 30, 2008, from http://en.minghui. org/html/articles/2002/10/14/27578.html

Li, H. (2003). *Zhuan Falun: Turning the Law Wheel* (February 2003 translation, North America ed.) Gillette, NJ: Yih Chyun Corp.

Li, H. (2008). Fa teaching at the 2008 New York conference, *Falun Dafa Experience Sharing Conference*. New York, US: http://www.clearwisdom.net/emh/articles/2008/6/22/98383.html

Li, H. (2011). Dafa Disciples Must Study the Fa: *Fa teaching given at the 2011 Washington DC Fa Conference*. Washington DC, US: http://en.minghui.org/html/articles/2011/7/30/127111.html

Li, H. (2014). Fa teaching given at the 2014 San Francisco Fa Conference, *Falun Dafa Experience Sharing Conference*. San Francisco, US: http://en.minghui.org/html/articles/2014/11/3/146687.html

Li, Q., Li, P., Garcia, G. E., Johnson, R. J., & Feng, L. (2005). Genomic profiling of neutrophil transcripts in Asian Qigong practitioners: A pilot study in gene regulation by mind-body interaction. *Journal of Alternative and Complementary Medicine*, 11(1), 29-39. doi:10.1089/acm.2005.11.29.

Life and Hope Renewed. (2005). *The healing power of Falun Dafa*. Gillette, NJ: Yih Chyun Corp.

Lindberg, D. A. (2005). Integrative review of research related to meditation, spirituality, and the elderly. *Geriatric Nursing*, 26(6), 372-377. doi:10.1016/j.gerinurse.2005.09.013.

Lio, M., Hu, Y., He, M., Huang, L., Chen, L., & Cheng, S. (2003). The effect of practicing qigong on health status: A case study of Falun Dafa practitioners in Taiwan. Unpublished research article.

Lord Byron, G. G. (1819). The Works of Lord Byron [Electronic Version], *Poetry Volume 6*. Retrieved February 16, 2016, from http://www.gutenberg.org/files/18762/18762-h/18762-h.htm#Page_143.

Lowe, S. (2003). Chinese and international contexts for the rise of Falun Gong Nova Religio: *The Journal of Alternative and Emergent Religions*, 6(2), 263-276. doi:10.1525/nr.2003.6.2.263.

Maciocia, G. (1989). *The foundations of Chinese medicine.* Edinburgh: Churchill Livingston.

MacLennan, A. H., P Myers, S., & Taylor, A. W. (2006). The continuing use of complementary and alternative medicine in South Australia: costs and beliefs in 2004. *The Medical Journal of Australia,* 184(1), 27–31.

Madsen, R. (2000). Understanding Falun Gong. *Current History: A Journal of Contemporary World Affairs,* 99(638), 243-247.

Mamtani, R., & Cimino, A. (2002). A primer of complementary and alternative medicine and its relevance in the treatment of mental health problems. *Psychiatric Quarterly,* 73(4), 367-381. doi:10.1023/A:1020472218839.

Mao, J. J., Farrar, J. T., Xie, S. X., Bowman, M. A., & Armstrong, K. (2007). Use of complementary and alternative medicine and prayer among a national sample of cancer survivors compared to other populations without cancer. *Complementary Therapies in Medicine,* 15(1), 21-29. doi:10.1016/j.ctim.2006.07.006.

Marlatt, G. A., & Kristeller, J. L. (1999). Mindfulness and meditation. In W. R. Miller (Ed.), *Integrating spirituality into treatment: Resources for practitioners.* (pp. 67-84): American Psychological Association.

Matas, D. (2009). Why Chinese communists repress Falun Gong. *Remarks delivered to an International Conference on Religious Freedom in China, European Parliament.* Brussels. Retrieved April 28, 2009, from http://www.david-kilgour.com/2009/Apr_14_2009_01.php

Matas, D., & Cheung, M. (2012). Concepts and precepts: Canadian tribunals, human rights and Falun Gong. *Canadian Journal of Human Rights,* 1(1), 61-91.

Matas, D., & Kilgour, D. (2006). *Report into allegations of organ harvesting of Falun Gong practitioners in China.* Ottawa, Canada.

Matas, D., & Kilgour, D. (2007). *Bloody harvest: Revised report into allegations of organ harvesting of Falun Gong practitioners in China.* Ottawa, Canada.

Matas, D., & Kilgour, D. (2009). *Bloody harvest: The killing of Falun Gong for their organs* (5th ed.). Woodstock, ON, Canada: Seraphim Editions.

Matas, D., & Trey, T. (Eds.). (2012). *State organs: Transplant abuse in China.* Woodstock, ON, Canada: Seraphim Editions.

McCown, D. (2004). Cognitive and perceptual benefits of meditation. *Seminars in Integrative Medicine,* 2(4), 148-151. doi:10.1016/j.sigm.2004.12.001.

McCoy, W. F., & Zhang, L. (Eds.). (n.d.). *Falun Gong stories: A journey to ultimate health* (1st ed.): Golden Lotus Press.

McGreevey, S. (2012). Meditation's positive residual effects: Imaging finds different forms of meditation may affect brain structure. *Harvard Gazette.* Retrieved May 1, 2013, from http://news.harvard.edu/gazette/story/2012/11/meditations-positive-residual-effects/

McHorney, C. A., Ware, J. E., Lu, R. J. F., & Sherbourne, C. D. (1994). The MOS 36-Item Short-Form Health Survey (SF-36): III. Tests of data quality, scaling assumptions, and reliability across diverse patient groups. *Medical Care, 32*(1), 40-66. doi:10.1097/00005650-199401000-00004.

Mearns, D., & Thorne, B. (2007). *Person-centred counselling in action* (3rd ed.). Los Angeles: Sage Publications.

Mehta, D. H., Phillips, R. S., Davis, R. B., & McCarthy, E. P. (2007). Use of complementary and alternative therapies by Asian Americans: Results from the National Health Interview Survey. *Journal of General Internal Medicine, 22*(6), 762-767. doi:10.1007/s11606-007-0166-8.

Melville, G. W., Chang, D. C., Colagiuri, B., Marshall, P. W., & Cheema, B. S. (2012). Fifteen minutes of chair-based yoga postures or guided meditation performed in the office can elicit a relaxation response [Electronic Version]. *Hindawi Publishing Corporation, Evidence-Based Complementary and Alternative Medicine,* doi:10.1155/2012/501986.

Merry, T. (2002). *Learning and being in person-centred counselling* (2nd ed.). Llangarron: Bath Press, Bath, UK.

Miles, M. B., & Huberman, A. M. (1994). *Qualitative data analysis: An expanded sourcebook* (2nd ed.). Thousand Oaks, CA, US: Sage Publications, Inc.

Minghui.org Editors. (2001a). Editorial: Send Forth Righteous Thoughts Again. Retrieved January 30, 2015, from http://en.minghui.org/html/articles/2001/5/28/10449.html

Minghui.org Editors. (2001b). The two hand positions for Sending Forth Righteous Thoughts. Retrieved January 30, 2015, from http://en.minghui.org/emh/articles/2001/6/12/11429.html

Minghui.org Editors. (2005). Editorial: The essentials to Sending Forth Righteous Thoughts (Update 2). Retrieved September 30, 2010, from http://en.minghui.org/html/articles/2005/3/12/58362.html

Myers, J. E., & Sweeney, T. J. (Eds.). (2005). *Counseling for wellness: theory, research, and practice.* Alexandria, VA, US: American Counseling Association.

Myers, J. E., Sweeney, T. J., & Witmer, J. M. (2000). The Wheel of Wellness counseling for wellness: A holistic model for treatment planning. *Journal of Counseling & Development,* 78, 251-266.

Nania, J. (2013, July 20, 2014). Falun Gong, Popular and Serene. Retrieved November 15, 2014, from http://www.theepochtimes.com/n3/21898-falun-gong-popular-and-serene/

NCCIH. (2008). Complementary, alternative, or integrative health: What's in a name? Retrieved May 28, 2008, from https://nccih.nih.gov/health/integrative-health

NCCIH. (2009a). Tai chi and qigong. Retrieved April 25, 2009, from https://nccih.nih.gov/health/taichi

NCCIH. (2009b). The use of Complementary and Alternative Medicine in the United States: Cost data. Retrieved December 06, 2012, from https://nccih.nih.gov/news/camstats/costs/costdatafs.htm

NCCIH. (2015). National survey reveals widespread use of mind and body practices, shifts in use of natural products. Retrieved March 10, 2015, from https://nccih.nih.gov/research/results/spotlight/0021015

Newport, F. (2011). More Than 9 in 10 Americans continue to believe in God. Retrieved February 12, 2015, from http://www.gallup.com/poll/147887/Americans-Continue-Believe-God.aspxx

NHMRC. (2007). *National statement on ethical conduct in human research.* Retrieved May 5, 2008, from http://www.nhmrc.gov.au/publications/synopses/e72syn.htm

Ospina, M. B., Bond, K., Karkhaneh, M., Buscemi, N., Dryden, D. M., Barnes, V., et al. (2008). Clinical trials of meditation practices in health care: Characteristics and quality. *Journal of Alternative & Complementary Medicine,* 14(10), 1199-1213. doi:1089/acm.2008.0307.

Ownby, D. (2000, December). Falungong as a cultural revitalization movement: An historian looks at contemporary China. *Transnational China Project Commentary.* Retrieved November 27, 2005, from http://www.ruf.rice.edu/~tnchina/commentary/ownby1000.html

Ownby, D. (2001). Falungong and Canada's China policy. *International Journal,* 56(2), 183-204.

Ownby, D. (2003a). A history for Falun Gong: Popular religion and the Chinese state since the Ming Dynasty. *Nova Religio: The Journal of Alternative and Emergent Religions,* 6(2), 223-243. doi:10.1525/nr.2003.6.2.223.

Ownby, D. (2003b). The Falun Gong in the new world. *European Journal of East Asian Studies*, 2(2), 303-320.

Ownby, D. (2005). Unofficial religions in China: Beyond the Party's rules - Statement of Professor David Ownby. Retrieved November 27, 2005, from http://www.cecc.gov/pages/roundtables/052305/Ownby.php

Ownby, D. (2008). *Falun Gong and the future of China*. New York: Oxford University Press.

Oxford Dictionary. (2005). *Oxford Dictionary of English*, revised (2nd ed.). In C. Soanes & A. Stevenson (Eds.), Oxford: Oxford University Press.

Oz, M. C. (2003, January 20). Medical Meditation: Say "Om" before surgery. *Time Magazine, US ed., Special Issue: How your mind can heal your body*, 161, 1-2.

Palmer, D. (2007). *Qigong fever*. New York: Columbia University Press.

Palmer, S. J. (2003). From healing to protest: Conversion patterns among the practitioners of Falun Gong. *Nova Religio: The Journal of Alternative and Emergent Religions*, 6(2), 348-364. doi:10.1525/nr.2003.6.2.348.

Parker, N. (2004). What is Falun Gong? An introduction to the practice and how it developed in China and around the world. *Compassion Magazine*, 5, 40-43.

Peach, H. G. (2003). Religion, spirituality and health: How should Australia's medical professionals respond? *The Medical Journal of Australia (eMJA)*, 178(2), 86-88 PMID: 12526730.

Pelletier, K. R. (2002). Mind as healer, mind as slayer: MindBody medicine comes of age. *Advances in Mind-Body Medicine*, 18(1), 4-15.

Penny, B. (2003). The life and times of Li Hongzhi: Falun Gong and religious biography. *The China Quarterly*, 175, 643-661. doi:10.1017/S0305741003000389.

Penny, B. (2005). The Falun Gong, Buddhism and "Buddhist qigong." *Asian Studies Review*, 29(1), 35-46. doi:10.1080/10357820500139513.

Penny, B. (2012). The religion of Falun Gong. Chicago: The University of Press.

Perez-De-Albeniz, A., & Holmes, J. (2000). Meditation: Concepts, effects and uses in therapy. *International Journal of Psychotherapy*, 5(1), 49-58. doi:10.1080/13569080050020263.

Philips, J. (2013). Facing discrimination in New York, Chinese stand for persecuted faith. *The Epoch Times*. http://www.theepochtimes.com/n3/710012-facing-discrimination-in-ny-chinese-stand-for-persecuted-faith/?photo=2

Porter, N. (2003). *Falun Gong in the United States: An ethnographic study.* Parkland, Florida: Dissertation.com.

Porter, N. (2005). Professional practitioners and contact persons: Explicating special types of Falun Gong practitioners. *Nova Religio: The Journal of Alternative and Emergent Religion,* 9(2), 62-83. doi:10.1525/nr.2005.9.2.062.

Pullen, L. C. (2000). CBS health watch: Three part series on Falun Dafa. Retrieved June 16, 2006, from http://www.clearwisdom.net/emh/articles/2000/4/17/8467p.html

Qi, X. (2012). How the Chinese Communist Party first split on Falun Gong. *The Epoch Times.* Retrieved May 1, 2013, from http://www.theepochtimes.com/n3/1485561-how-the-chinese-communist-party-first-split-on-falun-gong/3/

Rankin, L. (2013). *Mind over medicine: Scientific proof that you can heal yourself* (1st ed.). New York Hay House, Inc.

Reynolds, E. (2015). China's other big business: Harvesting organs from prisoners when they're still alive. Retrieved April 8, 2015, from http://www.news.com.au/entertainment/tv/chinas-other-big-business-harvesting-organs-from-prisoners-when-theyre-still-alive/story-e6frfmyi-1227294577229

Ricard, M., Lutz, A., & Davidson, R. J. (2014). Neuroscience reveals the secrets of meditation's benefits [Electronic Version]. *Scientific American,* 311, 13. Retrieved December 22, 2014, from http://www.scientificamerican.com/article/neuroscience-reveals-the-secrets-of-meditation-s-benefits/

Robertson, L. A. (2008). *The spiritual competency scale: A comparison to the ASERVIC spiritual competencies.* Unpublished dissertation submitted in partial fulfillment of the requirements for the degree of Doctor of Philosophy in the Department of Child, Family, and Community Sciences in the College of Education. University of Central Florida, Orlando, Florida.

Rogers, C. E., Larkey, L. K., & Keller, C. (2009). A review of clinical trials of Tai Chi and qigong in older adults. *Research Western Journal of Nursing,* 31(2), 245-279. doi:10.1177/0193945908327529.

Rogers, C. R. (1951). *Client-centered therapy: Its current practice, implications, and theory* (1965 paperback ed.). Boston: Houghton Mifflin Company.

Rogers, C. R. (1961). *On becoming a person: A therapist's view of psychotherapy* (1st ed.). London: Constable & Company Ltd.

Sancier, K. M. (1996). Medical applications of qigong. *Alternative Therapies in Health and Medicine,* 2(1), 40-46.

Sancier, K. M. (1999). Therapeutic benefits of qigong exercises in combination with drugs. *Journal of Alternative and Complementary Medicine,* 5(4), 383-389. doi:10.1089/acm.1999.5.383.

Sandelowski, M. (2000). Combining qualitative and quantitative sampling, data collection, and analysis techniques in mixed-method studies. *Research in Nursing and Health,* 23(3), 246-255.

Sandlund, E. S., & Norlander, T. (2000). The effects of Tai Chi Chuan relaxation and exercise on stress responses and well-being: An overview of research. *International Journal of Stress Management,* 7(2), 139-149. doi:10.1023/A:1009536319034.

Schopen, A., & Freeman, B. (1992). Meditation: The forgotten Western tradition. *Counseling and Values,* 36(2), 123-134.

Selhub, E. (2007). Mind-Body Medicine for treating depression: Using the mind to alter the body's response to stress. *Alternative and Complementary Therapies,* 13(1), 4-9. doi:10.1089/act.2007.13107.

Seligman, M. (2008). Martin Seligman: The new era of positive psychology. Retrieved January 31, 2013, 2013, from http://www.ted.com/speakers/martin_seligman.html

Shallcross, L. (2012). Where East meets West. *Counseling Today,* 55(4), 28-37.

Shapiro, S. L., Schwartz, G. E., & Bonner, G. (1998). Effects of Mindfulness-Based Stress Reduction on medical and premedical students. *Journal of Behavioural Medicine,* 21(6), 681-599. doi:10.1023/A:1018700829825.

Sharif, F., & Masoumi, S. (2005). A qualitative study of nursing student experiences of clinical practice [Electronic Version]. *BMC Nursing,* 4, doi:10.1186/1472-6955-4-6. Retrieved September 8, 2008 from http://www.biomedcentral.com/1472-6955/4/6

Shorofi, S. A., & Arbon, P. (2009). Complementary and alternative medicine (CAM) among hospitalised patients: An Australian study. *Complementary Therapies in Clinical Practice.* doi:10.1016/j.ctcp.2009.09.009.

Singer, R. (2006). Mindfulness meditation in Western society. Retrieved February 16, 2009, from http://ezinearticles.com/?Mindfulness-Meditation-in-Western-Society&id=228788

Singh, A. N. (2006, April). *Role of yoga therapies in psychosomatic disorders.* Paper presented at the International Congress Series, Proceedings of the 18th World Congress on Psychosomatic Medicine, 21-26 August 2005, Kobe, Japan.

Skoro-Kondza, L., Tai, S. S., Gadelrab, R., Drincevic, D., & Greenhalgh, T. (2009). Community based yoga classes for type 2 diabetes: An exploratory randomised controlled trial [Electronic Version]. *BMC Health Services Research,* 9. doi:10.1186/1472-

6963-9-33. Retrieved April 22, 2009, from http://www.biomedcentral.com/1472-6963/9/33

Smith, B. J., Tang, K., & Nutbeam, D. (2006). WHO health promotion glossary: new terms. Health Promotion International, 340-345. doi:10.1093/heapro/dal033.

Smith, C., Hancock (Mattner), H., Blake-Mortimer, J., & Eckert, K. (2007). A randomised comparative trial of yoga and relaxation to reduce stress and anxiety. Complementary Therapies in Medicine, 15(2), 77-83. doi:10.1016/j.ctim.2006.05.001.

Smith, L. (2009). Tragedy Heralds New Beginning. New Tang Dynasty Television production. Retrieved November 28, 2012, from http://www.ntd.tv/en/news/life/20090514/45411-tragedy-heralds-new-beginning.html

Spiegel, M. (2002). Dangerous Meditation: China's campaign against Falungong. New York: Human Rights Watch.

Standard, R., Sandhu, D., & Painter, L. (2000). Assessment of spirituality in counseling. Journal of Counseling and Development, 78(2), 204-210.

Stone, K. (Director), Silber, I., (Writer) (2015). Hard to believe [Documentary film]. In K. Rubacek (Producer). New York, US: Swoop Films.

The Epoch Times. (2004a). Nine Commentaries on the Communist Party. Gillette, NJ, US: Yih Chyun Corp.

The Epoch Times. (2004b). On the collusion of Jiang Zemin and the communist party to persecute Falun Gong. In Nine Commentaries on the Communist Party (pp. 115-147). Gillette, NJ, US: Yih Chyun Corp.

Tourangeau, R., Couper, M. P., & Steiger, D. M. (2003). Humanizing self-administered surveys: Experiments on social presence in web and IVR surveys. Computers in Human Behavior, 19(1), 1-24. doi:10.1016/S0747-5632(02)00032-8.

Turnbull, K. (2010, Spring). An inside job. Bendigo Magazine, Australia.

Upchurch, D. M., Chyu, L., Greendale, G. A., Utts, J., Bair, Y. A., Zhang, G., et al. (2007). Complementary and alternative medicine use among American women: Findings from the National Health Interview Survey, 2002. Journal of Women's Health, 16(1), 102-113. doi:10.1089/jwh.2006.M074.

VandenBos, G. R. (2007). APA Dictionary of Psychology. In G. R. VandenBos (Ed.), (1st ed.). Washington, D.C.: American Psychological Association.

Voukelatos, A., Cumming, R. G., Lord, S. R., & Rissel, C. (2007). A randomized, controlled trial of Tai Chi for the prevention of falls: The Central Sydney Tai Chi trial. *Journal of the American Geriatrics Society,* 55(8), 1185-1191. doi:10.1111/j.1532-5415.2007.01244.x.

Wallis, C. (2005, January 17). The new science of happiness. *Time Magazine,* 43-49.

Walsh, R. (1989). Asian psychotherapies. In *R. J. Corsini & D. Wedding* (Eds.), *Current Psychotherapies* (4th ed., pp. 547-559). Itasca, Illinois: F. E. Peacock Publishers, Inc.

Walsh, R., & Bugental, J. (2005). Long-term benefits from psychotherapy: A 30-year retrospective by client and therapist. *Journal of Humanistic Psychology,* 45(4), 531-542. doi:10.1177/0022167805280266.

Walsh, R., & Vaughan, F. (Eds.). (1993). *Paths beyond ego: The transpersonal vision.* New York: Jeremy P. Tarcher/Perigee.

Wang, Q., Li, N., Zheng, L., Qu, e., Tian, X., & Jing, L. (1998). The effect of Falun Gong on healing illnesses and keeping fit: A sampling survey of practitioners from Beijing Zizhuyuan Assistance Center [Electronic Version]. Retrieved January 12, 2001 from http://www.clearwisdom.net/eng/science_eng/survey98_2eng.htm

Ware Jr., J. E. (2008). SF-36® Health Survey update. Retrieved January 25, 2008, from http://www.sf-36.org/tools/SF36.shtml

Ware Jr., J. E., & Sherbourne, C. D. (1992). The MOS 36-Item Short-Form Health Survey (SF-36): I. Conceptual Framework and Item Selection. *Medical Care,* 30(6), 473-483.

Wessinger, C. (2003). Nova religio symposium: Falun Gong - introduction and glossary. *Nova Religio: The Journal of Alternative and Emergent Religions,* 6(2), 215-222. doi:10.1525/nr.2003.6.2.215.

Williams, D. R., & Sternthal, M. J. (2007). Spirituality, religion and health: evidence and research directions [Electronic Version]. *The Medical Journal of Australia (eMJA),* 186, S47-S50. Retrieved May 2008 from https://www.mja.com.au/journal/2007/186/10/spirituality-religion-and-health-evidence-and-research-directions

Wilson, L. (2008). Retracing, healing reactions and flare-ups. Retrieved September 19, 2009, from http://www.drlwilson.com/Articles/retracing.htm

Winseman, A. L. (2002a). Religion and gender: A congregation divided. *Religion and gender.* Retrieved August 17, 2009, from http://www.gallup.com/poll/7336/Religion-Gender-Congregation-Divided.aspx

Winseman, A. L. (2002b). Religion and gender: A congregation divided, Part II. *Religion and gender.* Retrieved August 17, 2009, from http://www.gallup.com/poll/7390/Religion-Gender-Congregation-Divided-Part.aspx

Winseman, A. L. (2003). Spiritual commitment by age and gender. Retrieved August 17, 2009, from http://www.gallup.com/poll/7963/Spiritual-Commitment-Age-Gender.aspx

World Health Organization. (2003). WHO definition of health. Retrieved October 28, 2006, from http://www.who.int/about/definition/en/print.html

World Health Organization. (2007). Mental health: Strengthening mental health promotion. Retrieved July 16, 2008, from http://www.who.int/mediacentre/factsheets/fs220/en/

World Organization to Investigate the Persecution of Falun Gong (WOIPFG). (2004). *Investigation report on the persecution of Falun Gong: Volume one* (2nd ed.). Hyde Park, MA: WOIPFG.

World Organization to Investigate the Persecution of Falun Gong (WOIPFG). (2014). *WOIPFG Releases the First List of Medical Personnel Suspected of Extracting Organs from Living Falun Gong Practitioners* (Report): WOIPFG.

World Organization to Investigate the Persecution of Falun Gong (WOIPFG). (2015). Chapter Five: A comprehensive data analysis indicates the number of liver and kidney transplants performed by Chinese hospitals is significantly larger than previously understood. Retrieved November 23, 2015, from http://www.upholdjustice.org/print/291

Wu, P., Fuller, C., Liu, X., Lee, H.-C., Fan, B., Hoven, C. W., et al. (2007). Use of complementary and alternative medicine among women with depression: Results of a national survey. *Psychiatric Services, 58*(3), 349-356. doi:10.1176/appi.ps.58.3.349.

Xia, C. (2014). Artist experiences miracles of Falun Dafa. Retrieved December 5, 2014, from http://en.minghui.org/html/articles/2014/11/23/147009.html

Xie, F. T., & Zhu, T. (2004). *Ancient wisdom for modern predicaments: The truth, deceit, and issues surrounding Falun Gong.* Paper presented at the American Family Foundation Conference in October 17-18, 2003, published in Cultic Studies Review. Retrieved June 17, 2007, from http://franktianxie.blog.epochtimes.com/article/show?articleid=4511

Xu, J. (1999). Body, discourse, and the cultural politics of contemporary Chinese Qigong. *The Journal of Asian Studies, 58*(4), 961-991. doi:http://dx.doi.org/10.2307/2658492.

Xue, C. C., Zhang, A. L., Lin, V., Da Costa, C., & Story, D. F. (2007). Complementary and Alternative Medicine use in Australia: A national population-based survey. *The Journal of Alternative and Complementary Medicine, 13*(6), 643-650. doi:10.1089/acm.2006.6355.

Yahiya, A. P. D. H. N. (2010). Effectiveness of the Falun Dafa exercises on some psychological skills, and the level of performance in the sport of judo. *Procedia Social and Behavioral Sciences*, 5, 2394–2397. doi:10.1016/j.sbspro.2010.07.469.

Yang, J., & Nania, J. (2002). A meditation for health, and beyond. Retrieved March 3, 2007, from http://www.asianresearch.org/articles/928.html

Yeager, D. M., Glei, D. A., Au, M., Lin, H., Sloan, R. P., & Weinstein, M. (2006). Religious involvement and health outcomes among older persons in Taiwan. *Social Science & Medicine*, 63(8), 2228–2241. doi:10.1016/j.socscimed.2006.05.007.

Young, M. (2012, May 24th). Chinese Leader's Fear Turned Country Inside Out. *The Epoch Times.* Retrieved March 1, 2013, from http://www.theepochtimes. com/n2/opinion/chinese-leaders-fear-turned-country-inside-out-241854.html

Young, M. (2013, February 20th). Political Campaign in China Threatens to Undo Its Makers. *The Epoch Times.* Retrieved March 1, 2013, from http://printarchive. epochtimes.com/a1/en/us/was/2013/02-Feb/21/A6_EET20130221-DCUS.pdf

Zhang, R., & Xiao, J. (1996). A report on the effect of Falun Gong in curing diseases and keeping fit based on a survey of 355 cultivators of Falun Gong at certain sites in Beijing, China [Electronic Version], 11. Retrieved December 17, 2003.

Index

About the Author

Photo by Daniel Ulrich

Sarawak-born Australian, M. M. Trey lives in upstate New York, with her hilarious Italian-speaking German-born husband who plays the French horn. Besides writing, she navigates DIY adventures tackling never-ending repairs in their half-renovated home. Inspired by her late granduncle, book author N. I. Low, she majored in English at The University of Toronto (Canada) and later received her counselor training from The University of South Australia in Adelaide, Australia. Curiosity and passion for antiquated wisdom enthused M. M. Trey to train in traditional Chinese medicine, Indian and Okido yoga, shiatsu, the yin-yang macrobiotic way of life, and Vipassana meditation—before practicing Falun Gong. Personal lineage (her Chinese grandfather being a 19th Century Taoist cultivator) plus belief in mind-body-spirit connection inspire M. M. Trey's integrated approach toward helping others.

Follow her on Facebook, Twitter @deitywellness, and her blog at <u>deitywellness.com</u> for anecdotes and reflections on nurturing a mindful, healthful lifestyle.

Made in the USA
Las Vegas, NV
21 February 2022

44318268R00146